Palgrave Shakespeare Studies

General Editors: **Michael Dobson** and **Dympna Callaghan**
Co-founding Editor: **Gail Kern Paster**

Editorial Advisory Board: **Michael Neill**, University of Auckland; **David Schalkwyk**, Folger Shakespeare Library; **Lois D. Potter**, University of Delaware; **Margreta de Grazia**, University of Pennsylvania; **Peter Holland**, University of Notre Dame

Palgrave Shakespeare Studies takes Shakespeare as its focus but strives to understand the significance of his oeuvre in relation to his contemporaries, subsequent writers and historical and political contexts. By extending the scope of Shakespeare and English Renaissance Studies the series will open up the field to examinations of previously neglected aspects or sources in the period's art and thought. Titles in the *Palgrave Shakespeare Studies* series seek to understand anew both where the literary achievements of the English Renaissance came from and where they have brought us.

Titles include:

Pascale Aebischer, Edward J. Esche and Nigel Wheale (*editors*)
REMAKING SHAKESPEARE
Performance across Media, Genres and Cultures

James P. Bednarz
SHAKESPEARE AND THE TRUTH OF LOVE
The Mystery of 'The Phoenix and Turtle'

Silvia Bigliazzi and Lisanna Calvi (*editors*)
REVISITING THE TEMPEST
The Capacity to Signify

Mark Thornton Burnett
FILMING SHAKESPEARE IN THE GLOBAL MARKETPLACE

Carla Dente and Sara Soncini (*editors*)
SHAKESPEARE AND CONFLICT
A European Perspective

Cary DiPietro and Hugh Grady (*editors*)
SHAKESPEARE AND THE URGENCY OF NOW
Criticism and Theory in the 21st Century

Darlene Farabee
SHAKESPEARE'S STAGED SPACES AND PLAYGOERS' PERCEPTIONS

Kate Flaherty, Penny Gay and L. E. Semler (*editors*)
TEACHING SHAKESPEARE BEYOND THE CENTRE
Australasian Perspectives

Lowell Gallagher and Shankar Raman (*editors*)
KNOWING SHAKESPEARE
Senses, Embodiment and Cognition

Daniel Juan Gil
SHAKESPEARE'S ANTI-POLITICS
Sovereign Power and the Life of the Flesh

Adam Hansen and Kevin J. Wetmore, Jr. (*editors*)
SHAKESPEAREAN ECHOES

Julián Jiménez Heffernan
SHAKESPEARE'S EXTREMES
Wild Man, Monster, Beast

Stefan Herbrechter and Ivan Callus (*editors*)
POSTHUMANIST SHAKESPEARES

David Hillman
SHAKESPEARE'S ENTRAILS
Belief, Scepticism and the Interior of the Body

Anna Kamaralli
SHAKESPEARE AND THE SHREW
Performing the Defiant Female Voice

Jane Kingsley-Smith
SHAKESPEARE'S DRAMA OF EXILE

Katie Knowles
SHAKESPEARE'S BOYS
A Cultural History

Akiko Kusunoki
GENDER AND REPRESENTATIONS OF THE FEMALE SUBJECT IN EARLY MODERN ENGLAND
Creating Their Own Meanings

Lori Leigh
SHAKESPEARE AND THE EMBODIED HEROINE
Staging Female Characters in the Late Plays and Early Adaptations

Rory Loughnane and Edel Semple (*editors*)
STAGED TRANSGRESSION IN SHAKESPEARE'S ENGLAND

Rob Pensalfini
PRISON SHAKESPEARE

Stephen Purcell
POPULAR SHAKESPEARE
Simulation and Subversion on the Modern Stage

Erica Sheen
SHAKESPEARE AND THE INSTITUTION OF THEATRE

Kay Stanton
SHAKESPEARE'S 'WHORES'
Erotics, Politics and Poetics

Alfred Thomas
SHAKESPEARE, DISSENT AND THE COLD WAR

R.S. White, Mark Houlahan and Katrina O'Loughlin (*editors*)
SHAKESPEARE AND EMOTIONS
Inheritances, Enactments, Legacies

Deanne Williams
SHAKESPEARE AND THE PERFORMANCE OF GIRLHOOD

Paul Yachnin and Jessica Slights
SHAKESPEARE AND CHARACTER
Theory, History, Performance, and Theatrical Persons

Palgrave Shakespeare Studies
Series Standing Order ISBN 978-1-403-91164-3 (hardback)
978-1-403-91165-0 (paperback)
(*outside North America only*)

You can receive future titles in this series as they are published by placing a standing order. Please contact your bookseller or, in case of difficulty, write to us at the address below with your name and address, the title of the series and the ISBN quoted above.

Customer Services Department, Macmillan Distribution Ltd, Houndmills, Basingstoke, Hampshire RG21 6XS, England

---

Gender and Representations of the Female Subject in Early Modern England

Creating Their Own Meanings

Akiko Kusunoki
Emeritus Professor, Tokyo Woman's Christian University, Japan

© Akiko Kusunoki 2015

All rights reserved. No reproduction, copy or transmission of this publication may be made without written permission.

No portion of this publication may be reproduced, copied or transmitted save with written permission or in accordance with the provisions of the Copyright, Designs and Patents Act 1988, or under the terms of any licence permitting limited copying issued by the Copyright Licensing Agency, Saffron House, 6–10 Kirby Street, London EC1N 8TS.

Any person who does any unauthorized act in relation to this publication may be liable to criminal prosecution and civil claims for damages.

The author has asserted her right to be identified as the author of this work in accordance with the Copyright, Designs and Patents Act 1988.

First published 2015 by
PALGRAVE MACMILLAN

Palgrave Macmillan in the UK is an imprint of Macmillan Publishers Limited, registered in England, company number 785998, of Houndmills, Basingstoke, Hampshire RG21 6XS.

Palgrave Macmillan in the US is a division of St Martin's Press LLC, 175 Fifth Avenue, New York, NY 10010.

Palgrave Macmillan is the global academic imprint of the above companies and has companies and representatives throughout the world.

Palgrave® and Macmillan® are registered trademarks in the United States, the United Kingdom, Europe and other countries.

ISBN 978–1–403–93574–8

This book is printed on paper suitable for recycling and made from fully managed and sustained forest sources. Logging, pulping and manufacturing processes are expected to conform to the environmental regulations of the country of origin.

A catalogue record for this book is available from the British Library.

Library of Congress Cataloging-in-Publication Data
Kusunoki, Akiko, 1943–
Gender and representations of the female subject in early modern England: creating their own meanings / Akiko Kusunoki, Emeritus Professor, Tokyo Women's Christian University, Japan.
  pages cm. — (Palgrave Shakespeare studies)
Includes bibliographical references and index.
ISBN 978–1–4039–3574–8 (hardback)
1. English literature—Early modern, 1500–1700—History and criticism.
2. English literature—Women authors—History and criticism.
3. Women and literature—England—History—16th century.
4. Women and literature—England—History—17th century.
5. Women in literature. 6. Identity (Psychology) in literature.   I. Title.
PR428.W63K88 2015
820.9'352209032—dc23   2015018580

Typeset by MPS Limited, Chennai, India.

To Tatsushi

Contents

List of Figures viii

Acknowledgements ix

Introduction: Concepts of Womanhood in
Early Modern England 1

1 Emerging New Attitudes towards Women in
  Early Jacobean England 15

2 Female Selfhood and Ideologies of Marriage in Early Jacobean
  Drama: *The Duchess of Malfi* and *The Tragedy of Mariam* 49

3 Lady Mary Wroth and Ideologies of Marriage in
  Late Jacobean England 87

4 Representing Elizabeth I in Jacobean England 132

5 Women and Publishing Their Works in the
  Late Jacobean Years 145

Conclusion 164

Notes 169

Bibliography 189

Index 207

List of Figures

3.1	The cover of the Penshurst manuscript of *Love's Victory*	88
3.2	A seventeenth-century English cabinet covered with stump work	120
3.3	A double portrait of two ladies, (probably) Lady Mary Wroth and Lady Barbara Sidney. With the inscription 'Lady Wroth and Lady Gamage', dated 1612. By Marcus Gheeraerts II.	127
4.1	The portrait of Charles Louis Stuart with his black page	134

Acknowledgements

In writing and preparing this book, I am greatly indebted to the generosity and kindness extended to me by a number of distinguished people. First I would like to express my deepest gratitude to Viscount De L'Isle for providing me with the precious images in his private collection and permission to use them in my book. With his permission I had the privilege of reading the Penshurst manuscript of *Love's Victory*. My visits to Penshurst Place always inspired me a great deal, not only about Lady Mary Wroth but also about the cultural and political significance of the Sidney family in the English Renaissance.

I owe very much to those who have taken the time to read this work at the manuscript stage. Dr Juliet Dusinberre of Girton College, Cambridge and Dr Trudi Darby of King's College London read through the whole manuscript and gave me sharp and insightful comments and suggestions. Professor Mary Ellen Lamb of Southern Illinois University read the manuscript of the chapters related to Lady Mary Wroth, offering me extremely helpful comments. I am also very grateful to Dr Martin Ingram of Brasenose College, Oxford for reading the whole manuscript and giving me acute and invaluable comments and advice from the historian's points of view. Dr Stephen Miller and Mr Baron Millard read through the whole manuscript at the first stage and amended my English expressions. Professor Reiko Oya of Keio University extended help to me whenever I had problems in finding references. Without these people's overwhelmingly kind help, this book would never have been born. However, if mistakes still remain in the book, the responsibility is solely mine.

I thank King's College London and the Senate House Library of the University of London for enabling me to access their online sources. The librarians of the British Library and of the Library of Tokyo Woman's Christian University helped me a great deal when I was desperately looking for some source materials.

I am grateful to my Shakespearean friends for their long-standing friendship despite the geographical distance separating the places where we live. The vivacious and positive attitude of Professor Marion Wynne-Davies of the University of Surrey has always excited me, encouraging me to explore new fields in relation to English Renaissance women. Professor Alison Findlay of Lancaster University taught me various facts and views on household performances of English Renaissance plays.

Particular thanks go to her for organising the splendid academic conference on Mary Wroth held at Penshurst Place in June 2014, and for including in the programme the public performance of *Love's Victory* by Shakespeare's Globe's Read Not Dead. This world-premiere of the play given at the Baron's Hall of Penshurst Place illuminated various new aspects of not only Lady Mary's works, but also of works of women writers in the English Renaissance in general. I also had the pleasure of going to the Newberry Library to see Mary Wroth's holograph manuscript of *Urania* II with Professor Margaret P. Hannay of Siena College in 2008. It was really a memorable experience for me to share with this authority on Mary Wroth the excitement of reading this extraordinary manuscript. Emeritus Professor Linda Woodbridge of Pennsylvania State University encouraged me to pursue this project from its earliest stages. Professor Mihoko Suzuki of Miami University helped me to find suitable reference books, particularly on female Christians in early modern Japan. Emeritus Professor Ann Thompson of King's College London has always stimulated me through her pioneering and admirable works. Emeritus Professor Richard Proudfoot of King's College London has encouraged me ever since I was a PhD student at King's College. Professor Sandra Clark of Birkbeck College London and her husband Michael kindly took me to many historical places related to the English Renaissance, particularly to places such as Wilton House or Hardwick Hall, which are difficult to reach except by car. Whenever I went back to London, a group of my fellow students at King's College London, Dr Trudi Darby, Dr Stephen Miller, Dr Jo Udall and Dr Fleur Rothschild, with Mr Baron Millard, welcomed me by arranging our reunion dinner. I thank Dr Mary Hamer, now an eminent novelist and biographer, and her husband Nick for invigorating me on each of my return visits to London by hosting a jolly dinner with cheerful conversation and excellent wine.

I owe a great deal to the fine scholarship of numerous brilliant scholars of the English Renaissance; I would like to thank in particular two Japanese scholars, Professor Yasuo Tamaizumi of the Japan Academy and the late Professor Jiro Ozu, who was my supervisor at the Graduate School of the University of Tokyo. My journey to my studies in this field started with their great scholarship.

I extend my appreciation to Paula Kennedy, Ben Doyle and Tom Rene at Palgrave Macmillan for their patience and help.

In the final stage of completing the book, I had to be extremely self-centred. My husband Tatsushi Kusunoki helped me in every possible way. I am dedicating this book to him.

Introduction: Concepts of Womanhood in Early Modern England

We often hear nowadays that feminism is a thing of the past and is no longer relevant. The limitations of this typically Western view become obvious once we turn our attention to the current situations of women in the rest of the world: in some countries they must risk their lives to demand even the basic human right to education.

Although Japan is regarded as one of the most advanced countries in Asia in terms of the latest technology and popular culture, it was only after World War II that the concept of gender equality was generally accepted by Japanese society. When Japan's imperialistic social system collapsed in 1945, the principle of democracy was introduced by Western countries, particularly the United States, which occupied Japan for nearly seven years after the end of the war. For the first time in Japan's history women, as well as men of lower social standing, were able to enjoy the same rights as men from the privileged class, that is, they were now entitled to receive an education, to vote and to own property. Thus, democracy in Japan was not like that in Britain or in France, where people won it through fierce conflict, such as the English Civil War or the French Revolution; instead it was imported from and by Western countries. After World War II, in principle women were able to do whatever they thought was right. However, in practice it was difficult for them to do so because the restrictions of residual traditional values continued to be applied, particularly to women. For a long time, even after the end of World War II, most Japanese women found it hard to recognise their selfhood independent of their national or religious identity, their position in the family (e.g. as wife, mother or sister) or the prevailing conservative notions of womanhood in society (e.g. women were supposed to get married before they reached a certain age). However, in the past twenty years, because of the influence of globalisation, Japanese people have been exposed to many attitudes and ideas from different countries and cultures, especially in relation to women. As a result, in late twentieth- and early twenty-first-century Japan, female desire for self-assertion or for self-actualisation became widely recognised, and society in general began to adopt a much more understanding attitude towards women.

Nevertheless, many Japanese women are still not sure about their sense of self or about how to relate what they feel or think about themselves to what society assumes they are like. Unlike European or North American people, who have had a long cultural history of confronting the diverse definitions of the modern or post-modern self in the light of individualism and democracy, most Japanese people, with their democracy transferred from the West and a long cultural heritage of mutual cooperation, have rarely needed to face the issue of the self or to define their selfhood—in other words, to make their own choices instead of following society's norms. Naturally, women's attitudes towards themselves and their concepts of womanhood have been in a state of constant flux. It is interesting to note that these aspects of Japanese culture today, especially with regard to women's sense of themselves, have much in common with those belonging to the culture of Jacobean England.

Looked at from our post-modern perspective, much of the writing in early modern England may fall short in defining womanhood and appear ambiguous in its treatment of an emerging female sense of self. Catherine Belsey examined representations of subjectivity in English Renaissance drama (*The Subject of Tragedy*, 1985), reaching the conclusion that concepts of subjectivity had not yet been established in most of the plays from that period. It can be said, therefore, that representations of women in plays and other writing in Jacobean England are particularly relevant to Japanese women today: like women in Jacobean England, they are exposed to various ideas and realities concerning womanhood and are conscious of what they feel or want, but are not yet fully sure about how to relate their inner thoughts to society. Probably because of the similarities of the cultures, studies of English Renaissance drama, particularly Shakespeare, are very popular among Japanese female students. However, the curriculums of most Japanese universities do not include female writers from the English Renaissance period. Naturally, even such a prolific writer as Lady Mary Wroth, whose works have been widely studied in England and the United States, is hardly known except to some scholars specialising in English Renaissance literature.[1]

Mary Wroth frequently dealt with societal concerns that had already been raised in Shakespeare's plays, transforming the representations of these issues in significant ways in her pastoral comedy *Love's Victory*, the two parts of her prose romance *Urania* I and II and her Sonnets Sequences. They are the first extant works written by an Englishwoman in these genres. When she published the first part of the *Countess of Montgomery's Urania* in 1621 against the gender propriety of the time, she encountered the fierce criticism of Jacobean courtiers. Nevertheless, as will be discussed below, she continued with her writing. Although Lady Mary's concepts of female selfhood were at times ambiguous and contradictory and thus in a state of flux, her passion for self-expression and her creative energy make her a very important figure not only in the history of English culture but also in the history of women. In order not to misunderstand history, it is necessary to explore how writings by both genders represent the construction of female selfhood and how women were trying to create their own meanings in early modern England. However, unlike the post-Enlightenment periods, the definitions of the concepts of the self, selfhood or autonomy had not yet been established. As Jonathan Sawday explains, 'Selfhood' in the mid-seventeenth century did not suggest the modern idea of the quality of having or possessing a self (1997 29–38),[2] and yet 'a voyage into the interior' (1997, 31) had already started both for men and women; as Stephen Greenblatt illustrated in his book (*Renaissance Self-Fashioning*, 1980), some men both in reality and fiction were self-fashioning according to their positions in society, whereas some women became conscious of the split between their inward thoughts and the outward appearance they tried to adopt. The terms 'self', 'selfhood' and 'autonomy' are used in this book to mean those qualities that people think or feel make them what they themselves are or what they can do by themselves; these can sometimes be at variance with each other, and do not always lead to the construction of 'the unified self', a concept that emerged after the Enlightenment.

It is true that, at any time in history, theory runs at odds with practice. Yet the tension arising from the disparity between society's image of womanhood and what women in actuality thought they were was particularly intense in the Jacobean period, especially in the second decade of the seventeenth century. It is during this period that Thomas Overbury's *A Wife* was published and John Webster's two independent tragedies, which both feature intractable women with an independent will, were written. This tension can be observed in many plays written by male writers of the period, especially in those by Webster, John

Marston, William Shakespeare and Thomas Middleton. Seeing the problems faced by their female contemporaries as related to the problems of their time, these writers portrayed their own dramatic visions of what it meant to be a woman in such circumstances. Indeed, this tension constituted one of the major factors that enriched drama and other genres of literature in the Jacobean period, adding vitality and complexity.

Sir Thomas Overbury's *A Wife* in Jacobean England

Sir Thomas Overbury's poem, *A Wife*, was licensed for the press on 13 December 1613 and published in 1614, after his death in the Tower of London on 15 September 1613. The poem became exceptionally popular, going through five editions in 1614. The second impression appeared with the addition of the *Characters*. The sixth edition of 1615 was greatly expanded; the majority, if not all, of its thirty-two New Characters are generally attributed to John Webster.[3] As will be discussed later, the popularity of the poem was undoubtedly increased by news of the untimely death of the author, who had for some years held a prominent political position as a secretary and close adviser to Robert Carr, King James's favourite, although no suspicion concerning the cause of his death had yet been raised.

Overbury's *A Wife* envisions the prescriptions that Jacobean women were supposed to obey and that Jacobean dramatists had to take into account when presenting their own visions of the nature of woman. In the prose introduction Overbury lists 'Goodnesse, Knowledge, Discretion' (sig. B1r) as absolute qualities that constitute '*a Perfect Woman*' (sig. C2v), and, as an additional requirement, 'Fitnesse' (sig. B1r).[4]

'Goodnesse'

By 'Goodnesse' Overbury means obedience to Christian morality in general, but special emphasis is placed on a wife's obedience to her husband, in particular marital chastity. As Juliet Dusinberre remarked, virtue in women had nearly always been seen in terms of sexual virtue, that is, chastity (2003 32). For women both in Elizabethan and Jacobean England, chastity was an absolute moral norm. Homiletic condemnation of fornication and whoredom, especially of 'the outrageous seas of adultery' (*Certain Sermons*, 1850 118), pervaded Jacobean moral writings with no less vigour than in earlier times. Since Humanists and Protestants (especially Puritans) promoted the ideal of chaste marriage, condemning the courtly love tradition of the Middle Ages, chastity in women underwent a change in concept from virginity to chastity within marriage—that is, from a physical condition to the purity of the soul.[5] Concomitantly, adultery took on even more serious implications than before; the Homily tells us 'we should find the sin of whoredom to be that most filthy lake, foul puddle' (*Certain Sermons*, 1850 125). Especially, murder was considered to be the natural consequence of adultery; many adulteresses in Elizabethan and Jacobean drama, such as Alice in *Arden of Feversham* (Unknown, 1591),[6] Webster's Vittoria, and Middleton's Bianca and Beatrice-Joanna are, directly or indirectly, involved in murder. The concept of chaste marriage also greatly affected attitudes towards men's sexual life. The moral double standard was criticised, and, as a condition of the wife's chastity, the chastity of the husband was also demanded.[7] Adriana in *The Comedy of Errors* (Strange, 1592) rebukes her husband's infidelity by saying, 'How dearly would it touch thee to the quick,/Shouldst thou but hear I were licentious' (2. 2. 121–2).[8]

In view of the goodness of women defined by Christian morality in Renaissance England, as observed in these writings, it is interesting to note that not so great an importance is placed upon a wife's fidelity in *The Tale of Genji*, written by Lady Murasaki Shikibu in the strictly patriarchal society of early eleventh-century Japan. Lady Murasaki was probably the first writer in the world to write a long novel, and *The Tale* was written from around 1005 to 1012. The period when Lady Murasaki was actively writing has generally been called the 'Golden Age of Courtly Culture' in Japan. It was the period when literary activities flourished among courtiers at the Emperor's Court. Particularly remarkable were the literary activities of female writers who dominated the courtly culture by writing original works including poetry, essays, diaries and romances.[9] Lady Murasaki was from a highly educated family and she herself was well educated. She seems to have been well known in society as a lady who could read classical Chinese, an ability that was very rare for a woman at the time. Chinese characters were the official language in eleventh-century Japan, and it was assumed that only men engaged with politics were able to understand the language; educated women were supposed to be able to read and write only Kana, Japanese characters. *The Tale of Genji*, divided into two parts, consists of fifty-four chapters. Most of the stories in the first part deal with the love affairs of Hikaru Genji, an illegitimate son of the Emperor Kiritsubo; the second part deals with the next generation—the descendants of those in the first part—focusing on the love affair of Hikaru's (illegitimate) son Kaoru with Ukifune, a lady whose name signifies a floating boat. In the chapter called 'The Broom Tree' (Seidesticker tr. 1980, Vol. 1. 21–41), the second story of the first part, there is a scene in which several male courtiers, including Hikaru, discuss good and attractive female qualities. This section is generally called 'the assessment of women in the rainy evening'. These courtiers happened to spend one evening in the same place in order to avoid a bad omen foretold about the location in which their residences were situated at the Court. It was a rainy evening, and finding nothing exciting to do, they started to assess women, discussing their characteristics. Obedience, modesty and reticence were the female qualities most highly admired by these courtiers, as they were by men in early modern England. However, because of the non-Christian concept of marriage, chastity or wifely fidelity is not referred to as an absolute quality of 'good' women. In eleventh-century Japan, men of high social rank could have as many as wives as they wanted. Marriage at the time was not the social institution in which a man and wife lived together; instead, husbands visited their wives. When husbands stopped their visits, the marriage was regarded as dissolved.

In *The Tale of Genji*, men made passionate approaches to, or sometimes even raped, other courtiers' wives. In particular, Hikaru, the hero whose appearance and behaviour were irresistibly attractive to women, had love affairs even with the second wife of his father, Lady Fujitsubo, who gave birth to Hikaru's illegitimate son. This affair was kept a strict secret, unknown to the Emperor himself, who loved the newborn prince, thinking he was his own son. Nevertheless, neither Lady Fujitsubo's infidelity to her husband nor Hikaru's betrayal of his own father was critically dealt with in moral terms; instead, the reason why Hikaru and Fujitsubo were so strongly attracted to each other is explained in detail in purely romantic terms in *The Tale* (Vol. 1. 132–40).

'Knowledge'

Although intelligence in women was regarded as necessary, Jacobean attitudes towards women's learning were, generally speaking, unfavourable. Humanists, such as More, Vives and Erasmus, refuted medieval illusions about women, which were reflected both in idolatry and satire, asserting instead the individuality of women and their rational capacity (Camden 1975, 37–58). Under the influence of the Humanist enthusiasm for learning, there emerged in Tudor times a number of admirably learned ladies, such as Katherine of Aragon, Lady Jane Grey, Catherine Parr, the five daughters of Sir Anthony Cooke, and, most important of all, Queen Elizabeth I. However familiar they were with the satirical portrayals of women produced ever since the Middle Ages (Utley, 1944), the Elizabethans saw a brilliant living example of female intelligence in their Queen. Even though their attitudes towards their female monarch were fundamentally different from those towards females in general, the Queen's much admired accomplishments in learning must have encouraged her subjects to appreciate intelligent women and to accept learning in women as a good thing. While some Elizabethan learned ladies, such as Mary, Countess of Pembroke, Lady Ann Bacon, and Lady Anne Clifford, survived well into Jacobean times, King James's Court gathered, around Queen Anne, more Jacobean types of learned ladies, such as Lady Elizabeth Hatton, Lady Penelope Rich, Lucy, Countess of Bedford, Aletheia, Countess of Arundel, and Lady Mary Wroth, who participated in shaping a new style of Jacobean culture, encouraged in particular by the Queen's enthusiasm for courtly masques.[10] Yet King James's notable dislike for female intellectuals discouraged learning for women, and there was a reaction against their intellectual development (Rogers, 131). Although learning in women was still admired in some seventeenth-century writings,[11] Jacobean people in general, as with Sir Thomas Overbury in *A Wife*, showed appreciation of 'Knowledge' in women only in its restricted sense of wisdom, regarding learning as unnecessary or dangerous. Thus, John Donne preached that '*wit, learning, eloquence, musick, memory, cunning*' were unnecessary for a woman, and perhaps even undesirable because they would 'make her never fit' for 'a Helper' (*Sermons*, 1955 Vol. II. 346).

The Jacobean antagonism towards educated women was related to the general revulsion to, and fear of, the social changes that were rapidly taking place at the time, overthrowing traditional values and the social order. Ben Jonson caricatured learned women in Lady Would-be in *Volpone* (King's, 1606) and Mistress Otter and the collegiate ladies in *Epicoene* (Queen's Revels, 1609). These women are seen as overreachers who aim to step out of their allotted female sphere by cultivating wit and learning; the collegiate ladies live apart from their husbands, and 'crie downe, or vp, what they like, or dislike in a braine, or a fashion, with most masculine, or rather *hermaphroditicall* authoritie' (Vol. V. I. i. 78–80).[12] They are made counterparts of male social climbers, commonly dealt with in Jacobean drama as subversive elements in society.

Furthermore, in Jonson's plays, female intellectual pretension is associated with unchastity. In *Epicoene* the collegiate ladies are adept in techniques of contraception and abortion (Vol. V, IV. iii. 56–61), and their licentiousness is fully exposed in their aggressive advances to Dauphine. Truewit describes a learned 'states-woman' (II. ii. 114), who censures poets and their styles, comparing 'Daniel with Spenser, Ionson with the tother youth' (117–8) and who is skilful in controversy, being capable of making 'demonstration and answere, in religion to one; in state, to another, in baud'ry to a third' (122–3). The association of learning in women with moral failings had been popular with conservative moralists, who would justify it on the grounds that a woman who defies the mental restrictions proper to her sex discards all other proprieties as well (Rogers, 1966 128). Jacobean drama evinces this tendency in linking women's aspirations for learning to female sexual desire, which was thought to be unrestricted, dangerous and sinful.

Women's learning could have been seen totally differently in a different cultural context. For instance, Lady Murasaki was commissioned to write *The Tale of Genji* by one of the most powerful lords at the time, Michinaga Fujiwara, whose daughter, Shooshi, was one of the wives of the Emperor Ichijo. As has been explained above, marriage in eleventh-century Japan was not co-residential and men of high social rank could choose to take several wives, with each being given status according to the social standing of the families they came from. The married couple did not live together, but instead, men visited their wives. Therefore, the more the Emperor visited Shooshi, the more highly she was regarded at the Court, and naturally the political power of her father, Michinaga, increased. He commissioned Lady Murasaki, who was renowned as an exceedingly educated lady-in-waiting of Shooshi, to write an interesting tale to read to the Emperor and ladies of Shooshi's Court, so that the Emperor would visit Shooshi frequently in order to hear the continuation of the story. It has been said that Michinaga provided Murasaki with paper and ink, which were very expensive at the time.

In other words, male authority was so securely established in elevencentury Japan that women's intellectual ability did not pose any threat to male power. Rather, it was thought of as a resource for men to make use of in order to fulfil their social ambition. It was not only Lady Murasaki but several other women writers at the Court, such as Seisho Nagon and Izumi Shikibu, who were actively writing their original works in the Heian period (from the tenth century into the eleventh century) in Japan. It is ironic that women's lack of social and political power led to the birth of the cultural mores that allowed women to engage in creative writing, resulting in them contributing to the rich literary culture of the mid-Heian period.

'Discretion'

Discretion in women is universally acclaimed as a prime female virtue in Jacobean writings, as in those of earlier times. In most cases, as in

Overbury's poem, it is represented as modesty, or qualities equivalent to it, like bashfulness or shamefastness. Whenever some character, either in Elizabethan or early Jacobean drama, voices admiration for a woman, the admiration almost always includes praise for her modesty. Jacobean moralists also placed great emphasis on modesty in women. For Barnaby Rich, who wrote several pamphlets exclusively about women, 'Sobriety, shamfastedness and modesty' are the indices of female nobility (Rich, 1613 sig. D2z-D3v).

Society's assumption that modesty is an absolute norm for women deters them from initiating action or expressing their true feelings eloquently. Sophonisba's consciousness of eloquence being immodest, for instance, restrains her from rebuking the Carthaginians' betrayal:

> But since affected wisdom in us Women
> Is our sex highest folly: I am silent,
> I cannot speak lesse well, unlesse I were
> More void of goodnesse. (Marston, Vol. II. II. i. 23)[13]

Confronted by extreme difficulties, some female characters in Shakespeare's plays wish that they were men. This is particularly the case when cruelty is inflicted unreasonably upon them or their relatives and they wish to take revenge. When, for instance, Hero in *Much Ado About Nothing* is dishonoured by Claudio's allegations of her infidelity, Beatrice, her cousin, cries out in exasperation:

> O that I were a man! [. . .]
> O God, that I were a man! I
> would eat his heart in the market-place. (4. 1. 298–301)

Isabella in *The White Devil*, while pretending to burst out in jealousy against her husband's mistress in order to place the blame upon herself for her separation from Brachiano, releases her true hatred of Vittoria in saying:

> O that I were a man, or that I had power
> To execute my apprehended wishes,
> I would whip some with scorpions. (II. 1. 242–4)

Although the circumstances in which these female characters are situated vary, they all, when driven by great emotional upheavals, face the limitations of being women and think that, if they were men, there would be more satisfactory ways to cope with their anger, by transforming it into action, that is, by taking revenge upon wrong-doers. The capacity that these women assume men possess, whereas they themselves do not, is for taking action, in particular revenge.

In order to present the heroines' initiation of action or articulate expression of their emotions as virtuous, Shakespeare resorted to various devices in both his Elizabethan and Jacobean plays. The Romantic heroines' disguise as men enables them to leap over the gender barrier without violating conventional views of a good woman. Only disguised as men, can Rosalind and Viola express their passion freely to the men they love. A heroine's male disguise was effective in producing various meanings, particularly because female characters were played by boy actors in the English Renaissance.[14] Women in Shakespeare's plays who speak out assertively to men in their own person, like Tamora in *Titus and Andronicus* (Pembroke's, Sussex's, 1594) and Goneril and Regan in *King Lear* (King's, 1605), are described as most vicious; the eloquence of Goneril and Regan turns out to be a mask for their desire to acquire King Lear's political power and estate, while Cordelia's 'silence' is presented as the symbol of the truth. One remarkable exception to this pattern is Helena, 'a poor physician's daughter', in *All's Well That Ends Well* (King's, 1603–4). Her highly ambitious action to win Bertram, Count of Rossillion, as her husband is presented as virtuous, in spite of her ambition and assertion for self-realisation, because throughout the play she is also made out to be an embodiment of the goodness of a vanishing old order, represented by the Countess of Rossillion, the French King and Lafew. At crucial moments, Shakespeare's tragic heroines, such as Ophelia in the nunnery scene in *Hamlet* (Act 3 Scene 1) or Desdemona in the brothel scene in *Othello* (Act 4 Scene 2), are remarkably inarticulate; only in madness, freed from the psychological constraints imposed by the norm of modesty, does Ophelia release her true feelings for Hamlet by singing indecent songs, such as *'Valentine'* or *'Robin'*, which were popular among common people.[15] Shakespeare's Romance plays do present articulate heroines, like Hermione in the trial scene of *The Winter's Tale* (King's, 1610) or Marina in the brothel scene and in her reunion with her father in *Pericles*. Moreover, their language has power to influence the course of the action of the play. Yet, by investing their language with dignity as well as simplicity, Shakespeare prevents their seeming aggressive or immodest.[16]

In *The Tale of Genji* modesty is also described as one of the most admired female qualities, but the point is that even modest-looking women engage in illicit love affairs with Hikaru. Lady Murasaki's focus is, however, almost always placed on the effects of the love on women that the central character, Hikaru Genji, feels for them. Her narrative primarily considers how these women succumb to Hikaru's approaches or how they feel about him after having been raped. Usually, they come to love him, continuing their affairs until his affections become focused on other women. In *The Tale* modesty in women is depicted as implying a female malleability to male approaches, suggesting that no possibility of threat should be felt by the men.

'Fitnesse'

Modesty in women is also associated with their submission to male authority, 'Fitnesse', in Jacobean England. All women were under the control of some man, such as a husband, father or guardian, because they were supposed to be tied with

> *the shamefac't band*
> *With which wise nature did strongly binde,*
> *T'obey the bests of mans well-ruling hand; [. . .]*
> (*Hic Mulier, Or The Man-Woman*, 1620 sig. C2v)

'Fitnesse', derived from the Pauline doctrine of a wife's obedience to her husband, remained an important female virtue in Jacobean writing as a whole. In the later years of the second decade of the seventeenth century, as will be discussed later in this book, a number of pamphlets appeared (some of them allegedly written by women) in which the authors insisted on the equality or even the superiority of women.

In reality, however, the symbolic meaning attached to a husband's authority held serious moral implications for women, making it difficult to flout this authority in practice. The Biblical comparison of the relation of man and wife to that of Christ and the Church, and of the Prince and the State, upheld the concept of the household as a microcosm of the State (*Certain Sermons*, 1850 506). In this concept of the Great Chain of Being, a wife's obedience to her husband symbolised the duties that maintained social stability. In rebuking the intractable wives, the tamed Kate in *The Taming of the Shrew* (1594, Sussex's (?) Chamberlain's (?)) points out this parallel:

> Such duty as the subject owes the prince
> Even such a woman oweth to her husband.
> And when she is froward, peevish, sullen, sour,
> And not obedient to his honest will,

> What is she but a foul contending rebel
> And graceless traitor to her loving lord? (5. 1. 167–72)

Jacobean moralists and King James repeatedly asserted the analogy between the ideal familial relation and the ideal society, seeing women's deviation from their submissive role as both a cause and a symbol of social disorder.

However, the existence of Overbury's *A Wife* in fact points to a possible disparity between the image and the reality with regard to womanhood. According to Ben Jonson, Overbury seems to have attempted through his poem to make a sexual approach to the Countess of Rutland (*Jonson's Conversation*, 1923, 20–1). If Jonson's account is to be trusted, whatever the Countess's reactions might have been, the author attempted to make her act against the qualities of a good woman, which he praised in his poem. On the other hand, Overbury's father is said to have revealed that, when the prospect of Carr's marriage to Frances Howard, wife of the third Earl of Essex, became imminent, Overbury attempted to direct his master's attention to his poem in order to dissuade him from the marriage.[17] As will be seen below, their marriage involved the political interest of the Howard faction as well as Lady Essex's desire, and the reasons for Overbury's objection to it seem to have been more complicated than the simple moral grounds that his poem could have provided. Nevertheless, this incident is significant in that social assumptions about womanhood were confronted with the reality embodied in the Countess of Essex; her '*Beauty, Birth*', and '*Portion*' (Overbury, Sig. B1r) were notable, but her adulterous passion for Carr was already on peoples' tongues at the Court in 1612 (Chamberlain, Vol. I. 377). The tension between the social norms of womanhood and women's own feelings in Jacobean England led to the appearance of some female writers who articulated their own views on this issue.

This book

This book explores the interaction between social and cultural assumptions about womanhood and women's actual voices represented in works by writers of both genders in early modern England. Special emphasis is placed on Lady Mary Wroth's works, since they are replete with women's views expressed in their dramatic communication with others. Although this book mainly deals with plays and polemical writings in Jacobean England, Wroth's romance, *Urania* Part I and II, are included, because the stories are conducted mostly through dramatic communications between the characters. However, as a result of focusing on women's dramatic communications with others, the exceedingly rich field of poetry produced in this period is regrettably largely excluded from the discussion.

The book consists of five chapters, each of which examines how female self-assertion is represented in drama and other writing in Jacobean England. Chapter 1 discusses the emerging new attitude towards women in early Jacobean drama, an attitude triggered by the introduction of Michael Montaigne's *Essays* through John Florio's translation in 1603. Chapter 2 addresses the Jacobean discourses upon marriage, about which women writers often expressed quite different views from their contemporary male writers. The difference is discussed chiefly through the comparison between John Webster's *The Duchess of Malfi* (King's Men, 1614) and Elizabeth Cary's *The Tragedy of Mariam* (1613), the first extant tragedy written by an Englishwoman. Chapter 3 examines the discourse of marriage presented in Mary Wroth's works, her pastoral comedy, *Love's Victory* and the two parts of *Urania*. As mentioned above, her romance is different from other romances of the period in that the stories unfold mainly through dramatic communication between the characters. This technique enables readers to understand the female characters' views in response to other characters' actions.

Jacobean representations of Queen Elizabeth I by male and female writers are discussed in Chapter 4. The significance of comparing the images of two queens of the same name, the former Queen Elizabeth of England and Queen Elizabeth of Bohemia, the eldest daughter of King James, is examined, mainly in the context of Mary Wroth's *Urania* Parts I and II. Chapter 5 discusses women's entry into the field of authorship and publication in the light of the print culture of the time. In the late Jacobean years, when some women's aggressive actions were drawing public attention, Swetnam's notorious tract against women, *The Araignment of Lewd, Idle, Froward, and unconstant women* (1615) was rebutted in print by three women, two of them using female pseudonyms. On the other hand, two anonymous pamphlets entitled *Hic Mulier* and *Haec-Vir* were published in 1620. Thus there was a series of pamphlets promoting a Jacobean revival of *the querelle des femmes* one year before the publication of Wroth's *The Countess of Montgomery's Urania*. This chapter also considers the significance of the early religious activities of some Puritan women at the time. The examination of these activities and publications makes it clear that by the late Jacobean period many women had come to think that they needed not only to construct their selfhood but also to make their views public by printing them.

The book also has cross-cultural aspects. It compares the ways in which women's desire and frustration are represented in some Jacobean plays with those in two Kabuki plays, which, like English Renaissance plays, were performed by an all-male cast in the seventeenth century (in the case of Kabuki this tradition still continues in the twenty-first century). Further, as has already been demonstrated above, the book presents a comparative study of the representations of female selfhood in women's writings in Jacobean England and those in Lady Murasaki Shikibu's *The Tale of Genji*, a long novel written in eleventh-century Japan.

These comparative studies aim to clarify how female as well as some male writers in Jacobean England engaged in shaping a new culture, a culture predicated on the acknowledgement of the female desire for self-actualisation. This aspect of seventeenth-century English culture seems to me to constitute the very origin of what characterises British culture in general, even that of the twenty-first century, and despite the presence of many national cultures in contemporary British society.

1
Emerging New Attitudes towards Women in Early Jacobean England

Whereas the orthodox concept of a good woman permeated Elizabethan and Jacobean drama, a sceptical tone, which emerged around 1600, marks the playwrights' handling of female characters, mostly in the plays written for private theatres. These plays pose questions about conventional female virtues by considering them in a social context, satirising them or parodying the works intended to promulgate such norms. In the dramatic works, such sceptical viewpoints developed into a new attitude towards women, an attitude that recognised the capacity for the integrity of women who acted against orthodoxy or, at least, in ways not necessarily in accordance with it. In the late Elizabethan and early Jacobean years, this new attitude was explored ardently, though inconclusively, by John Marston. The attempt culminated in Shakespeare's *Antony and Cleopatra* (King's, 1607) and John Webster's *The White Devil*. In the second decade of the seventeenth century, the plays that reflect this attitude increased in number, but no dramatist pursued the issue as thoroughly as Webster did in his two great tragedies, *The White Devil* and *The Duchess of Malfi*. Although various factors—social, economic, political, moral—contributed to the emergence of this new perspective on the nature of woman, one incident that worked as a trigger was the introduction of Montaigne's *Essays* to English readers via John Florio's translation of 1603.[1] Lucy, Countess of Bedford, instigated Florio's venture, and Florio dedicated all three books to the learned ladies of the time: Book I to the Countess of Bedford herself and her mother, Lady Anne Harington; Book II to Elizabeth, Countess of Rutland, and Lady Penelope Rich; and Book III to Lady Elizabeth Grey and Lady Marie Nevill. Florio's translation was extremely popular, not only among intelligent men, but also among educated women; for instance, Lady Anne Clifford, Countess of Dorset, who later became Countess of

Montgomery and Pembroke, wrote in her diary on 9 November 1616: 'I sat at my work and heard *Rivers* and *Marsh* read Montaigne's Essays which book they have read almost this fortnight' (*Diary*, 1923 41).[2] Judging from her borrowings from Florio's Montaigne, Elizabeth Cary, later Countess of Falkland, must have possessed a copy of the volume.[3] The list of books that Lady Would-be boasts of having read in *Volpone* includes Montaigne (III. iiii. 90). As shown below, Marston, Shakespeare and Webster, who contributed greatly to the exploration of these new attitudes towards women, were all greatly indebted to Montaigne, both in terms of ideas and expressions.

The impact of Montaigne's idea of the nature of woman on early Jacobean drama

Montaigne's particular brand of scepticism itself contains various potential qualities for what became a new approach to the perception of womanhood. His anti-rationalism, elaborated in 'An Apologie of *Raymond Sebond*', stemmed from a keen awareness of the limits of man's rational capacity, pointing to the senses as the only possible medium for the search for truth. Such an idea inevitably leads to the repudiation of male superiority, which was asserted by men on the grounds of their excellence in the capacity of reasoning; ever since classical times, there had been an assumption that women were inferior, irrational creatures governed by their senses and emotions. Montaigne, on the other hand, argues for an essential similarity between the sexes: '*both male and female, are cast in one same moulde: instruction and custome excepted, there is not great difference between them*' (1910, Vol. III. 128).[4] Furthermore, his emphasis on the power of the senses might have stimulated interest in the power of female emotions—one of the characteristic features of Jacobean drama is the increasing importance placed on them in the dramatic action.

Montaigne's views greatly contributed to introducing new attitudes towards women in Jacobean England, by insisting on a realistic observation of their natural state and refuting conventional assumptions about womanhood. His naturalistic concept is most explicitly apparent in 'Upon Some Verses of *Virgil*', a chapter on human sexuality. Here he describes sensuality in women as part of their innate nature and as even stronger than men's: 'It is a cunning bred in their vaines and will never out of the flesh' (Vol. III. 81). He therefore thinks it 'ridiculous' for men to impose upon women the norm of chastity: 'It lieth not in them [. . .] to shield themselves from concupiscence and avoid desiring' (Vol. III. 91).

Reminding men of the difficulty with which they fight against their own sexuality, Montaigne criticises the double standard in society and exposes the absurdity of male egotism in demanding chastity in women: 'we on the other side would have them sound, healthy, strong, in good liking, wel-fed, and chaste together, that is to say, both hot and colde' (Vol. III. 79). Such attitudes in society, he argues, force women to dissimulation and hypocrisy:

> It is then folly, to go about to bridle women of a desire so fervent and so naturall in them. And when I heare them bragge to have so virgin-like a will and cold mind, I but laugh and mocke at them. They recoile too farre backward. If it be a toothlesse beldame or decrepit grandame, or a young drie pthisicke starveling; if it be not altogether credible, they have at least some colour or apparence to say it. But those which stirre about, and have a little breath left them, marre but their market with such stuffe. (Vol. III. 92)

Montaigne's criticism is extended to society's arbitrary attitude towards human sexuality itself:

> Oh impious estimation of vices. Both wee and they [women] are capable of a thousand more hurtfull and unnaturall corruptions, then is lust or lasciviousnesse. But we frame vices and waigh sinnes, not according to their nature, but according to our interest; whereby they take so many different unequall formes. (Vol. III. 85)

In his opinion a lie is worse than lechery. Human existence, he argues, consists of both soul and body, and sexuality is fundamental to the human make-up. It is, therefore, wrong that society's moral codes dictate the annihilation of human physicality; such an act is to 'honour their nature, by disnaturing themselves' (Vol. III. 108).

Furthermore, he denounces the social assumption about propriety, which regards reference to sexual intercourse as indecent:

> Why was the acte of generation made so naturall, so necessary and so just, seeing we feare to speake of it without shame, and exclude it from our serious and regular discourses? we prononce boldly, to rob, to murther, to betray; and this we dare not but between our teeth. Are we to gather by it, that the lesse we breath out in words the more we are allowed to furnish our thoughts with? (Vol. III. 70)

'*Vertue is a pleasant buxom qualitie*', says he, quoting Plato: '*Let us not bee ashamed to speake, what we shame not to thinke*' (Vol. III. 67). Although Montaigne's critique on hypocrisy concerns social manners and customs in general, its impact must have been especially strong on women, for whom the adherence to propriety was an absolute condition if they were to be accepted in society.

Montaigne's scepticism strips love and marriage of their conventional meanings. While love is considered as '*nothing else but an insatiate thirst of enjoying a greedily desired subject*' (Vol. III. 105), the object of marriage is defined in equally pragmatic terms as preservation of posterity. A sharp distinction is drawn between marriage and love, and though the benefits of marriage are recognised as 'honour, justice, profit and constancie: a plaine, but more generall delight', it is denied the pleasures of love, which are 'more ticklish; more lively, more quaint, and more sharpe' (Vol. III. 77). He emphasises the rarity of happy marriage, comparing marriage to a 'cage, the birds without dispaire to get in, and those within dispaire to get out' (Vol. III. 75). This is an expression that Webster borrows in *The White Devil*. What gives his detached attitudes toward marriage its particular interest is that he justifies a wife's dissatisfaction with her husband as well as a husband's discontent with his wife, by offering a pragmatic understanding of human nature. The evil of a wife's adultery is extenuated, not through the Christian doctrine of forgiveness, but through a naturalistic acceptance of sexuality inherent in a woman's nature. Sympathy is extended to rebellious wives who defy social norms, because he thinks that

> Women are not altogether in the wrong, when they refuse the rules of life prescribed to the World, forsomuch as onely men have established them without their consent. (Vol. III. 77–8)

Furthermore, Montaigne's concept of human integrity, based on both naturalism and stoicism, provides a new perspective on aberrant women. His vision of life as constant flux undermines Renaissance ideals of honour and glory, as well as conventional values of custom and ceremony; they reside solely in others' judgements which '*change uncessantly*' (Vol. III. 33). For him the only certainty is one's sense of self, and integrity of life exists in absolute honesty to one's selfhood:

> I care not so much what I am with others, as I respect what I am in my selfe. I will bee rich by my selfe, and not by borrowing. [. . .] See how all those judgements, that men make of outward apparances,

are wonderfully uncertaine and doubtfull, and there is no man so sure a testimony, as every man is to himselfe. (Vol. II. 348–9)

Reducing man's reason to 'the chiefest source of all the mischiefs that oppresse him, as sinne, sicknesse, irresolution, trouble and despaire' (Vol. II. 151), he thinks it better to follow the law of nature in one's self than man-made codes:

> it is safer to leave the reignes of our conduct unto nature, than unto ourselves. [. . .] For, I would prize graces, and value gifts, that were altogether mine owne, and naturall unto me, as much as I would those, I had begged, and with a long prentiship, shifted for. *It lyeth not in our power to obtain a greater commendation, than to be fauoured both of God and Nature.* (Vol. II. 152)

With respect to the development of new attitudes towards women, Montaigne's insistence on trust in one's own sense of self is of great importance. It offers a positive viewpoint towards women's assertion of themselves, which unless it had been for the expression of Christian virtues, would have been denied in sixteenth and seventeenth-century England. In other words, it served as a kind of sanction for women's defiance of conventional norms in society, such as those prescribed in Overbury's *A Wife*, and for women following the dictates of their own conscience.

Women in John Marston's plays and Florio's Montaigne

The influence of Montaigne upon Marston is seen not only in his extensive borrowings of phrases and ideas from Florio's translation of the *Essays*, but also in his attitude towards women; those of his plays written after the publication of Florio's translation of Montaigne's *Essays* are marked, as in Montaigne, by an acceptance of female physicality. In this respect, *The Malcontent* (Queen's Revels, 1604) seems to represent a transitional phase. It contains no borrowing from Montaigne, and the date of its original version is unknown, though it has been placed as early as 1600 (Chambers, 1967, Vol. III. 431–2). Even so, Marston's naturalistic understanding of women is already present, though his approach is different from that in his later plays. In his *Satires* and early plays, he portrays women (except for a stereotypically chaste woman like Mellida in *Antonio and Mellida*) as symptoms and causes of the evil and folly of the decadent age. Not only is a woman 'craftie natures paint' and 'Her intellectuall is a fained nicenes/Nothing but clothes, & simpering precisenes' (*The Scourge of Villanie* viii, 1961 153), but she also causes human degradation by corrupting men's reason; women are like 'Glowe wormes bright/That soile our soules, and dampe our reasons light' (*The Scourge of Villanie* vii, 1961 146).

In some parts of *The Malcontent*, however, he modifies such a simple condemnation, by viewing errant women in relation to the state of the society in which they live. The female characters in the play, with the exception of Maria, who appears only in the last act, embody the typical feminine vanity and disorderliness attacked by moralists and satirists since the Middle Ages. They are sexually aberrant, and, as Mendozo cynically remarks, concerned only with their beauty and sex, fearing 'Bad clothes, and old age' (1. 6. 158). The Court itself is represented in the image of a brothel, with Maquerelle, a vigorous and ribald bawd, presiding over this world of sexual vice.

What separates Marston's bawd from other bawds in Elizabethan and Jacobean drama is her pragmatic perception of the situation in which women are placed. Unlike Middleton's bawds, who exploit human sexuality simply for materialistic gains, Maquerelle seduces women into sexual licence not only for profit, but out of her own awareness of the helplessness of women. Act 2 Scene 4 offers the satirical spectacle of her beauty salon, in which she invigorates Emilia and Beancha by means of her posset. Maquerelle tells them of the importance of youth and beauty for women: 'youth and beauty once gone, we are like Beehives without honey: out a fashion, apparell that no man will weare, therefore use me your beauty' (2. 4. 168). She advises them to disregard male criticism of female vanity, saying that they do not understand the position of women:

> Men say, let them say what they will: life a woman, they are ignorant of your wants, the more in yeeres the more in perfection they grow: if they loose youth and beauty, they gaine wisdome and discretion: But when our beauty fades, godnight with us, there cannot be an uglier thing to see then an ould woman, from which ò pruning, pinching, and painting, deliver all sweete beauties. (2. 4. 168)

Some of the phrasing, and much of the sentiment, of Maquerelle's traditional advice is taken from the 1602 translation of Guarini's *Il Pastor Fido*, but Marston constructs the play's world in a way that gives depth to her words.

A little more than a decade later, Mary Wroth describes the issue of ageing for women as a more serious matter in terms of their sense of selfhood. In *Urania* Part 1, she ironically makes Bellamira, one of her alter-egos, explain to Amphilanthus, an embodiment of male changeability, that the reason for her suitor's change of heart is due to her ageing:

> and yet Sir, truly can I not hate this man, but love him stil so wel, as if he could look backe on me with love, all former ills should be forgotten, but that cannot be, such an unfortunate strangnes hath beene betwixt us, as wee never meete, or if we did, what can this wrinckled face, and decayed beauty hope for? (*Urania* I 390)[5]

Towards the end of the published Part I of *Urania*, Pamphilia, another (and the main) alter-ego of the author, expecting the long-awaited visit of Amphilanthus, is worried about his change of affection because of the wrinkles on her face.

> "What Pamphilia?" said shee. "Is it possible that thou hast lived to see Amphilanthus kind againe? Can he smile on these wrincles, and be loving in my decay?" (*Urania* I 568)

Wroth's view on women's ageing may have been based not only on experience of women in general but also on her knowledge of Marston's play.

The Genoese Court in *The Malcontent* under the rule of Pietro, a 'too soft duke', is in an amoral state. The courtiers are indulging in hedonistic extravagances, and the only principles that work are based on Machiavellian statecraft, which not only the villain Mendozo and the foolish Bilioso, but also the deposed good duke Altofronto, disguised as Malevole, employ to gain power. In this male-dominated world, women are tools either for men's sexual gratification or for their political advancement, being utterly unable to control their own lives. The chaste Maria, the former Duchess, is locked up in the citadel, and the lustful and defiant Aurelia is also banished from the Court, after being sexually and politically exploited by Mendozo. Since a sexual relationship with men is the only way in which women can obtain, however briefly, security or self-satisfaction, beauty and youth are, as Maquerelle says, of vital importance. Moreover, the transience of youth and the ugliness of age are made to seem more real through being described by the old Maquerelle.

Whereas Marston satirises feminine weakness, he also ridicules conventional male attitudes towards women. Mendozo's demonstration of

Petrarchan adoration for women (1. 5. 154) is made absurd because of the inappropriateness of its object, the adulteress Aurelia. When he later learns of Aurelia's betrayal, he rails against women in a misogynistic manner: 'these monsters in nature, models of hell, curse of the earth [. . .] rash in asking, desperate in working, impatient in suffering, extreame in desiring, slaves unto appetite, mistresses in dissembling' (1. 7. 157). This conventional invective is also made ridiculous because of the sudden change in Mendozo's attitude and his gullibility, when set against his former confidence in his ability to manipulate women.

In the ironic use of familiar railings against women, Marston is different from Cyril Tourneur, as is made apparent in *The Revenger's Tragedy* (King's, 1606). As L. G. Salingar remarks, 'Tourneur adheres to the Morality mode' in employing railings for a didactic purpose. For instance, when Vindice, with skull in hand, inveighs against 'every proud and self-affecting dame' who consumes milk for her baths when many an infant starves (Salingar, 1961 212), Tourneur's satire is directed simply at the vice of female vanity. Marston's satire, on the other hand, works against the male railer as well as the railed-at women.[6]

Thus, Marston in *The Malcontent* sheds new light on the conventional topic of women's perceived sexual aberrations; but it is traditional female virtues, embodied by Maria, that he emphasises in the play. In *The Dutch Courtesan* (Queen's Revels, 1605), however, he overtly challenges these values in the fashion of Montaigne. While the two plots of the play are based on separate sources,[7] it is saturated with quotations and paraphrases from the *Essays*, approximately half of which are from 'Upon Some Verses of Virgil'. William M. Hamlin says, 'No play composed in early modern England draws more heavily on Montaigne's *Essays* than does *The Dutch Courtesan*' (2013 95).

Marston's most significant addition to the source material is Crispinella. She, like Freevill, claims to speak for naturalism, and voices Montaigne's scepticism about conventional views of woman. In questioning their values, Marston even further develops Montaigne's criticism of social manners in general into an attack on female manners specifically. For instance, in making Crispinella articulate Montaigne's attack upon hypocrisy regarding human sexuality, Marston makes it an attack upon female modesty:

> now bashfulnes seaz you, we pronounce boldly Robbery, Murder, treason, which deedes must needes be far more lothsome then an act which is so naturall, just and necessary, as that of procreation. You shall have an hipocriticall vestall virgin speake that with close

teeth publikely, which she will receive with open mouth privately [. . .] (3. 1. 98-9)

Rebuked for immodesty by Beatrice, Crispinella denounces the virtue of 'Discretion' asserted by Overbury; furthermore, Marston has her express Montaigne's concept of virtue, but with the focus shifted to female virtue:

Fye, Fye, vertue is a free pleasant buxom qualitie: I love a constant countenance well, but this froward ignorant coynes, sower austere lumpish uncivill privatenes, that promises nothing but rough skins, and hard stooles [. . .] (3. 1. 99)

Furthermore, when Crispinella voices Montaigne's scepticism about marriage, it becomes a criticism of the wifely virtue of 'Fitnessee'. She scoffs at the ideal of chaste marriage, saying that there are few men who can satisfy such an ideal: 'husbands are like lotts in the lottery: you may drawe forty blankes before you finde one that has any prise in him' (3. 1. 99-100). Saying that once married, a man grows 'a stiffe crooked knobby inflexible tyrannous creature' (3. 1. 100), she sardonically points out to Tysefew the absurdity of the norm of a wife's subjection:

O I faith, tis a faire thing to be married, and a necessary, To hear this word, *must*; if our husbands be proud, we must bear his contempt, if noysome we must beare with the Gote under his armeholes, if a foole we must beare his bable, and which is worse, If a loose liver, Wee must live uppon unholsome Reversions: Where, on the contraty side, our husbands because they may, and we must. (4. 1. 113)

She therefore vows to live a single life: 'Ile live my owne woman' (3. 1. 100). In a way, she is a predecessor to Moll Cutpurse in *The Roaring Girl* (Prince Henry's Men, 1611). As has often been pointed out, Crispinella seems partly to be modelled on Beatrice in *Much Ado About Nothing*, and her combat of wits with Tysefew does indeed recall the Beatrice–Benedick battle (Wood, 1938, Vol.2. 323; Geckle, 1980 160-6). Yet it is noteworthy that, whereas Shakespeare's heroine employs her wit on a range of subjects, Crispinella's is directed almost exclusively at social assumptions about female virtues and a wife's role in marriage; in the case of Beatrice, her wit is absolutely intrinsic to her and part of who she is, whereas wit for Crispinella seems rather superficial.

Crispinella's naturalistic stance shares the same basis as Maquerelle's: both women reject society's image of a good woman on the grounds of its incongruity with reality. The difference in Marston's handling of them indicates an alteration in his attitude towards female advocates of naturalism, a change which probably owed much to his knowledge of Florio's Montaigne.[8] Whereas Maquerelle's naturalism points to those subversive physical elements women face, Crispinella's naturalistic attitude is presented as complementary to the orthodox morality represented by Beatrice. Its ultimate object is not to invalidate orthodox female virtues, but to establish true virtues by exposing the falsehoods underlying conventional assumptions; for all her satirical comments on marriage, she fully endorses the virtue of Beatrice's marriage with Freevill. In terms of dramatic function, however, Marston's positive approach restricts her action. Although Crispinella is one of the most interesting women in early Jacobean drama, the author, in order to keep her in a subversive position, can make her no more than a satiric commentator espousing Montaigne's ideas. Her unorthodoxy, unlike Maquerelle's, is not transformed into dramatic action, nor does it affect the development of the plot of the play; it has an effect only on Tysefew, who jokingly assures her of financial and spiritual independence after marriage (4. 1. 114). Moreover, unlike Dekker and Middleton's Moll Cutpurse, despite her former avowal, she accepts Tysefew's marriage proposal, thus conforming to the social expectations of a good woman.

Moreover, Marston's approach to the naturalism of women contradicts his treatment of the naturalism of men. In contrast to the rigid, puritanical stance represented by Malheureux, Freevill's Montaignesque naturalism, which accepts physicality as essential in human existence, is presented as an ideal attitude to cope with the complex realities of life.[9] The ideal image of womanhood, however, is represented not by the 'quick and lively' Crispinella, but by the 'modest' (78) and 'Chast' (92) Beatrice, who believes that 'severe modesty is womens vertue' (99). Physicality is utterly absent from her love for Freevill; 'my loves not lust' (103), she says. She assures him of her 'Fitnesse' by saying, 'I am your servant' (81), and through her patience during Francischina's cruel revenge and Freevill's trials, she exhibits Patient Griselda-like passive female virtue. Even the innovative Marston seems to have agreed, fundamentally, with the popular image of 'ideal womanhood'.

In the plays written after the appearance of Florio's Montaigne, one of Marston's continual preoccupations seems to have been the possibility of a woman asserting her physicality without compromising her virtue. *The Fawne* (Queen's Revels, 1605). presents as its heroine Princess

Dulcimel, who is described as a woman of 'equall mixture both of minde and body' (III. 187). She justifies her passion for Prince Tiberio by appropriating Montaigne's concept of the naturalness of sexuality in 'a well-complectioned young' lady (III. 182). And, without endangering her virtue, she wins him for a husband by tricking her father into acting as a mediator, messenger and spokesman for her affection.

In *Sophonisba* (Queen's Revels, 1605), his only sustained tragedy, Marston made another attempt to present a heroine of 'an equall mixture of both minde and body'. On her first appearance, Sophonisba is impatiently waiting for her bridegroom in her bedchamber on her wedding night. Echoing Montaigne, she complains to her chambermaid of the marriage custom that forces women to be dishonest to their natural impulse:

> why the custome is
> To use such *Ceremonie* such strict shape
> About us women: forsooth the Bride must steale
> Before her Lord to bed: and then delaies,
> Long expectations, all against knowne wishes.
> I hate these figures in locution,
> These about phrases forc'd by *ceremonie*;
> We must still seeme to flie what we most seeke
> And hide our selves from that we faine would find us. (I. ii. 11)[10]

Still, her naturalistic acceptance of her own physicality shown here is in no way related to the development of the action in the rest of the play. In respect to its tragic structure, however, the work is significant since it is one of the earliest English plays in which the author attempted to produce a heroic tragedy featuring the spirit of a woman. Although she is heroic and an admirable stoic,[11] in terms of characterisation, Sophonisba belongs to the old type of chaste wife who courageously fights to remain faithful to her husband. As with most of the heroines in Elizabethan and Jacobean dramas, it is only through her reactions, such as her resistance to Syphax's approaches to her and her suicide to avoid being delivered to Scipio, that she is allowed to demonstrate her heroic spirit.

The Insatiate Countesse (Queen's Revels, 1610), Marston's last play and a collaboration with William Barkstead, again centres on a woman who insists on her physicality, but here the heroine's naturalism is reduced to hedonism. In his source, Painter's account of the Countess of Celant in *The Palace of Pleasure*, Marston may have found promising material for the dramatisation of Montaigne's concept of uncontrollable female sexuality. Here, the conventional seduction pattern is completely reversed; it is Isabella, a woman, who ruins men by seducing and discarding them one after another, 'as some rude passenger/Doth plucke the tender Roses in the budde' (4. 1. 70). Men's actions, except for her execution as carried out by the Duke of Medina, are restricted to reactions to her charm or betrayal in such ways as are usually assigned to female roles.

Although the play exhibits little literary merit to save it from T. S. Eliot's label, 'a poor rival of *the White Devil*' (Eliot, 1934 185), Isabella, 'A glorious Divell, and the noble whore' (4. 1. 56), anticipates in many ways, not only Webster's Vittoria, but also the Duchess of Malfi and Middleton's heroines. Like Vittoria, she incites her lover to murder but displays a kind of dignity at her death. Like the Duchess, she is determined to follow her passion, wooing a man (2. 1. 32–3) with a mixture of coyness and boldness (though, in the case of Isabella, it is part of her dissimulation). In giving full rein to her sexual impulse, she also recalls Beatrice-Joanna in *The Changeling* (1622, Lady Elizabeth's), who justifies her 'giddy turning' (1. 1. 159) by thinking that it is dictated by reason. Just as Bianca in *Women Beware Women* (King's, 1621) excuses her elopement with Leantio as a reaction to her overly strict upbringing (4. 1. 30–5), so does Isabella think that her first repressive marriage justifies her claim to self-indulgence once she has become a widow (1. 1. 6).

None of Marston's experiments in providing a new perspective on the nature of woman worked successfully in dramatic terms. Nevertheless, it is highly significant that he explored new fields in female roles in his plays, experimenting with their dramatic possibilities; they were soon to be taken up and developed by his successors. If John Webster, though still a fairly unknown dramatist at the time, wrote the Introduction, as some critics believe, for the revival of *The Malcontent* at the Globe,[12] he must have been especially sensitive to Marston's unique handling of female characters. Webster's characterisation of the heroines in his two great tragedies strongly indicates the influence of Marston's portrayal of women. The characteristics of Webster's women are to be discussed in the final part of this chapter as well as in the first part of Chapter 2.

Shakespeare's *Antony and Cleopatra*

As M. C. Bradbrook points out, the boys' theatres, which tended to experiment with new possibilities in order to satisfy the sophisticated tastes of their audience, prompted the development of female roles. Although the authors' viewpoints may not be as innovative as Marston's, the plays for the boys' companies frequently mark a departure, particularly in their portrayal of bad women, from conventional stereotypes (Bradbrook, 1980 251). Nevertheless, as in the case of Marston, it is mostly in terms of traditional female virtues that they defend the worth of women. In this respect, Shakespeare's *Antony and Cleopatra* is unique among the plays written in the early Jacobean years; it is the only play of the period that dramatises the integrity of a woman who utterly defies orthodox morality. The pagan setting of the play may have allowed Shakespeare an opportunity to extend his exploration of the nature of woman beyond the framework of Christian morality. Cleopatra's 'infinite variety' (2. 2. 272), described by Enobarbus as the essence of her attraction, is a composite of various female characteristics, most of which are attributes of bad women by contemporary standards.

The essence of the unfavourable portrait of Cleopatra, given by Plutarch, is forcefully presented in Philo's opening speech. Each of his three long hyperbolic sentences, describing the heroic Antony of the past, ends with short phrases, 'tawny front' (1. 1. 6), 'gipsy's lust' (1. 1. 10) and 'strumpet's fool' (1. 1. 13), all of which relate Cleopatra to the stereotypes of bad women and effectively convey the soldier's overflowing feelings of disappointment at what he considers his general's dotage (Hibbard, 1980 96–7). Although the following entrance of the lovers reorganises our attitudes towards them because of the grand passion they feel for each other, Cleopatra's discreditable features are further brought out. She is a shrewish, wilful, 'wrangling queen' (1. 1. 53), 'crossing' Antony's feelings in every way. She is also seen deploying all her wiles to detain him in Egypt, harping on his unpleasant ties in Rome with his wife the 'shrill-tongu'd Fulvia' (1. 1. 34) and 'the scarce-bearded Caesar' (1. 1. 22).

In the following scenes, Shakespeare continues to endow his Queen with the characteristics of bad women. Antony's remark that 'She is cunning past man's thought' (1. 2. 138), which recalls the contemporary misogynists' reiterated attack upon female duplicity, is partly justified, since she is constantly play-acting as a way of controlling situations. In her manners and emotions she is extravagant. Worse still, she is a 'triple-turned' adulteress; her sexuality is emphasised both in others' descriptions of her (1. 2. 132–7) and in the witty byplay between her and her attendants during Antony's absence in Act 1 Scene 5. and Act 2 Scene 5. The fatal power of her sexual charm is stressed by the sexual pun on 'dying', which pervades the play, and by the dangerous aspects of the serpents and flies of the Nile, with which she is identified.[13] Cleopatra's Amazonian usurpation of the male role in dominating Antony, presented in the image of Hercules's submission to Omphale (2. 5. 24–6),[14] justifies the moralists' repeated warning of the danger of men subjecting themselves to women's will;[15] here it transforms the 'triple pillar of the world' (1. 1. 12) into the 'noble ruin of her magic' (3. 10. 23). Her 'infinite variety' of temper and mood itself, is, by Jacobean standards, a sign of female irrationality, often associated with a courtesan.[16] The Romans' descriptions of her (including Antony's), as a 'witch' (4. 12. 49), 'whore' (3. 6. 76), 'trull' (3. 6. 107), 'boggler' (3. 13. 134) and 'ribaudred nag of Egypt' (3. 10. 13) characterise her as an antitype of the Jacobean ideal of a woman.[17]

It is, indeed, a remarkable achievement by Shakespeare to present Cleopatra as transcending the stereotypes of bad women while retaining their qualities. In contrast, The Countess of Pembroke's translation, *The Tragedie of Antonie*, and Samuel Daniel's *Tragedie of Cleopatra* both give sympathetic portraits of the Queen by modifying her discreditable features, as given in Plutarch, and by stressing her remorse and the courage displayed at her death. For all the destruction she has inflicted upon Antony and Egypt, one endorses Charmian's last tribute to her mistress, 'a lass unparalleled' (5. 2. 356) and feels, after the death of the lovers, that there remains nothing remarkable in the world.

Essential to this effect is the association of Cleopatra with nature in many ways. Because she is identified with the generative power of nature through various images, such as the Nile, whose slime quickens by fire, its serpents bred of mud by the operation of the sun, and the goddesses Isis and Venus,[18] her sexuality represents nature's divine fecundity. This image culminates in the image of motherhood: she is both the mother of her children, 'the memory of my womb' (3. 13. 193), and the mother of her country as monarch. The excess of her emotion, like the annual overflow of the Nile, which brings fertility, embodies the energy and vitality of nature. Like the ever-flowing Nile and its serpents, which take various forms, her 'infinite variety' becomes part of the constantly changing process of nature. Integrated with a vast, rich natural force, the characteristics Cleopatra shares with bad women not only evade Rome's moral judgement, but also reveal the limitations of such judgement.

Furthermore, the play is permeated with a Montaignesque sense of the fluidity of life, which transcends the control of human reason advocated by the Romans. Although evidence of the influence of Florio's translation of *Montaigne 'Essays'* on *Antony and Cleopatra* is inconclusive,[19] the play's vision of life as flux recalls Montaigne's concept of the universal stream of nature. It is first felt by Antony, when he is amazed at the changeability of both his own feelings for Fulvia once she is dead and the feelings of 'the slippery people' (1. 2. 171) who now support the once hated Sextus Pompeius. He later expresses this idea again, comparing his insubstantial grasp of his own identity to the changing shape of a cloud (4. 14. 3–25). Caesar describes the same feeling, referring to the instability of the service of the 'common body' (1. 4. 47); moreover, he embodies the fluidity itself when he confers magnanimous praise on Antony once he is gone (5. 1. 17–22). The Soothsayer in Act 1 Scene 2 epitomises the concept of the impotency of human reason before the proceeding of nature, in saying that 'nature's infinite book of secrecy' he can 'forsee', but can 'make not' (1. 2. 7: 13). The images of melting and water, which saturate the play (Knight, *The Imperial Theme*, 1965 231-8), and the incessant shifting of the short scenes also contribute to the evocation of an atmosphere of constant change (Emrys Jones, 1971 252). We are made to feel that, whatever men may contrive to shape the human situation, such attempts are eventually frustrated or absorbed by the larger reality of nature, with which Cleopatra is associated.

The limitations of Roman values are effectively shown in the contrast between Octavia and Cleopatra. Octavia is admired by the Romans as an epitome of female virtues; she possesses 'beauty, wisdom, modesty' (2. 2. 277), and, unlike Cleopatra's 'conversation' rife with sexuality and extravagant passion, hers is said to be 'holy, cold, and still' (2. 6. 140–1). Yet this 'gem of women' (3. 13. 131), a 'blessed lottery' (2. 2. 279) to the Romans, is made utterly helpless in the face of reality; she is neither able to keep Antony in Rome, nor achieve reconciliation between him and her brother, which the Octavia of Plutarch could manage.[20]

The disparaging report of Octavia given by Cleopatra's messenger in Act 3 Scene 3 points out her lack of liveliness; he describes her as 'a body rather than a life,/A statue than a breather' (3. 3. 28–9). One might smile at the Egyptian Queen's womanly rivalry towards Antony's new wife, when Cleopatra endorses the messenger's judgement in her favour by saying that he is able to say so because he has seen 'some majesty' (3. 3. 57). Yet it remains true that a sense of majesty is given to the human energy of spontaneous feelings. This energy is what the lovers admire each other for—an admiration testified to by the magnificence of their poetry—and it is just what Antony finds lacking in Octavia. In Rome, human energy is never fully liberated; just as men's impulses are subjected to political calculations, so women's impulses are fettered by the Roman ideal of good women, which, interestingly, corresponds to the

Jacobean ideal of womanhood. But the dictates of reason followed by the Romans are shown as incapable of comprehending the truth of life grasped by the lovers' impulses. Enobarbus follows reason in deserting Antony, yet dies of shame at the generosity of his master. Caesar's fulfilment of imperial ambition seems paltry in the face of the full realisation of the lovers' immense energy. Octavia's rational compliance with society's requirements of a good woman fails to match the highest sense of life emanating from Cleopatra; Octavia, 'the swan's down feather' (3. 2. 53), like the vagabond flag, can only swing on the tide of Roman society until it rots with motion.

But the impulses Cleopatra gives rein to are, in fact, controlled by her in order to retain her sense of self. As with Webster's Vittoria and the Duchess, it is the characteristic of Cleopatra's love that her selfhood is not totally subsumed in her passion. For these self-asserting Jacobean heroines, their love is of vital importance, not simply because of the truth of their feelings, but because they think that it embodies their selfhood, though maintaining their independence still; they do not see their relation to their lovers in terms of 'Fitnesse'. Such a kind of independent selfhood is to be found in some female characters created by Mary Wroth nearly twenty years afterwards in her pastoral comedy and prose romance. Cleopatra's sense of independence partly corresponds to her sense of royalty, but even this is unable to encompass her selfhood; as John F. Danby remarked, she 'always strives to make the political subservient to her' (Danby, 1952 142). She desires to fight at Actium, not because, as Robert Ornstein claimed, she wishes 'to be worthy of this Herculean Roman' (Ornstein, 1966 43), but because she wants to prove her independent self by appearing as a man, 'the president of my kingdom' (3. 7. 21).

Cleopatra's desire to maintain her independence prompts her to play-act so as to control her situation. She torments Antony because she knows that 'Fitnesse' is the 'way to lose him' (1. 3. 12). In order to ascertain her circumstances after the disaster at Actium, she pretends to welcome Caesar's messenger, which infuriates Antony. To beg a kingdom for her children, she acts the role of a submissive loser to Caesar, whom she calls the 'Sole sir' of the world (5. 2. 146). She also trifles with Seleucus in an attempt to 'outpolicy' Caesar. Her role-playing makes her true intentions elusive, keeping Antony wavering between trust and mistrust. Shakespeare maintains her detachment throughout the play, showing the paradoxical qualities of Cleopatra's self-assertion. It destroys Antony's Roman virtues, but just as Venus taught Mars the imperfection of military values (Waddington, 1966 210–27), her domination makes Antony a fuller man; his poetic sensibility grows, and he comes to see death in her way, that is, as a continuation of life after sleep and dreams. And as to where they will awake, moral orthodoxy seems irrelevant, for Antony will become her 'Husband' there (5. 2. 323).

The long-delayed suicide of Cleopatra, already planned at the end of Act 4, makes it clear that it should not be seen only in terms of her fidelity to Antony; her death must also be an act 'noble to myself' (5. 2. 226). Before she 'shackles up all accidents', she must express a sense of the integrity of her life completely opposed to moral orthodoxy. First, by refusing to be carted through the Roman streets and to be staged in the posture of a whore, she asserts her transcendence over the common image of bad women. Then, by turning her life into art, she makes her values immortal; she raises Antony into an image of a god in her poetic vision, and also fixes her own dignity by staging a tableau of herself in regal costume. Moreover, her sense of independent selfhood allows her to transcend the changing process of nature itself; her death is not a melting into the constantly changing Nile, but 'a change into changelessness' (Ornstein, 1966 44). Significantly, when she finally decides to do 'that thing' (5. 2. 5), she disclaims the fleeting moon of Isis, declaring herself to be 'marble-constant' (5. 2. 284). And after her death she is addressed as the fixed 'eastern star' (5. 2. 346). Caesar's final defeat by Cleopatra is thus two-fold. Not only does her suicide frustrate his ambition to make his triumph memorable by her presence in Rome; she also disproves his assumption that an aberrant woman like her can never attain integrity because 'Women are not/In their best fortunes strong' (3. 12. 34–5).

Some critics feel that Queen Elizabeth is reflected in various aspects of Shakespeare's portrayal of Cleopatra (Bullough ed., 1957–75, Vol. 5, 216–7; Kenneth Muir, 1967 197–206; Helen Morris, 1968–9 271–8). Elizabeth's violent temper was as legendary as her display of majesty, and Cleopatra's shrewish outbursts and physical violence towards her servant may have recalled the late Queen's fits of rage. Moreover, Cleopatra shows Queen Elizabeth's skills in play-acting. Elizabeth's duplicity kept ambassadors and her courtiers perplexed. Like Cleopatra, she was said to have assumed a masculine militancy with her troops at Tilbury in the Armada year.[21] Although one thus finds various possible analogies between the two magnificent queens, there is no conclusive evidence that Shakespeare's memories of his Queen affected his characterisation of his heroine. More significant is the fact that Queen Elizabeth embodied various female characteristics, some of which hardly accorded with the contemporary image of a good woman. The 'infinite variety' of the Queen's nature indicates that bad female characteristics, condemned by moralists and presented usually in bad characters in dramas at the time, could in reality coexist with human majesty and nobility. The real-life example of the late Queen, together with Montaigne's scepticism and the Cleopatra created by Shakespeare's art, is likely to have increased the Jacobeans' awareness of the complexity of womanhood, a complexity which their ideal, such as that described in Overbury's *A Wife*, failed to comprehend.

'Masculine Vertue' as a female virtue in Webster's *The White Devil*

> [Women] are vngratefull, periured, full of fraud, flouting and deceit, vnconstant, waspish, toyish, light, sullen, proud, discurteous and cruell, and yet they were by God created, and by nature formed, and therefore by policy and wisedome to bee auoyded. (Joseph Swetnam, *The Araignment Of Lewd, Idle, Froward, and vnconstant women* (1615), sig. C4v)[22]

Although even earlier dates have been suggested by various critics (E. K. Chambers, Vol. III., 509–10), John Russell Brown makes a convincing case for dating the first performance of *The White Devil* to early 1612.[23] Since Webster himself admitted in his address to the reader that he was a slow worker, taking 'a long time in finishing this Tragedy'[24] (Webster, 1995–2007 140), he must have been working on his first independent play from some time around the turn of the decade.[25] This period coincides with the time in which women's self-asserting acts began to draw attention as threatening forces in Jacobean society.

In Tudor times, under the influence of Renaissance emancipation and an enthusiasm for learning, the daughters of aristocrats were often given much the same education as the sons. Despite occasional protests against the cultivation of the female mind, most writers seemed to appreciate intelligent women and to accept learning for women as a good thing. Consequently, the Tudor age saw a number of learned and highly individualistic ladies come to prominence, such as Margaret Roper, Lady Jane Grey, Sir Anthony Cooke's five daughters, and, most important of all, Queen Elizabeth I.[26] But when the brilliant Queen was succeeded by King James I, who was wary around women, especially those with intelligence and independent minds, there was a reaction against the intellectual development of women and their sense of independence.[27] James's accession resulted in the reinforcing of the climate of anti-female self-assertion of the time (Rogers, 1966 131). Ironically, however, one of the characteristic aspects of King James' reign was the many Court scandals caused by aggressively self-assertive noble ladies.

(1) The Court Scandals in the Early Jacobean Period

One couple who created a grave scandal at the Court at the beginning of King James's reign were Lady Penelope Rich and Lord Mountjoy, Earl of Devonshire. When Lady Rich, Earl of Essex's sister and Sidney's Stella, was married against her will in 1581, she may already have pledged herself to Charles Blount (Falls, 1954 58). Her marriage was a typical Elizabethan arranged marriage, intended to recoup the fortune of the impoverished Essex family through ties with the richly endowed young lord. By 1590 her adultery with Charles Blount seems to have become public knowledge.[28] By 1597, though still going back to her husband occasionally, she had borne five illegitimate children to Charles. After Essex's death in 1601, Lady Rich virtually separated from her husband and lived openly with Charles Blount. The King and Queen connived in their illicit relation, receiving them at the Court with the highest honour. In 1605, Lord Rich, apparently tired of his position, obtained the dissolution of marriage and remarried. On 26 December 1605, William Laud, the Earl's chaplain, celebrated a private marriage between Lady Penelope and Blount at the Earl's country house in Wanstead. Since this marriage was against canon law, it offended both the King and Queen, and the Earl and Countess were forbidden to attend the Court.[29] The legality of Laud's act was questioned, and his preferment in the Church was much delayed as a result. It seems likely that none of them could have expected such a storm of indignation as a result of making such a long relationship legitimate. The Earl tried to justify his marriage to the King in a tract (Bradbrook, *John Webster*, 1980 65), but royal favour was never restored. In the event, the couple did not survive for long after this disgrace. On 3 April 1606, the Earl died at Savoy House in the Strand, and his Countess did not outlive him by many months.[30]

This remarkable couple lived in Webster's neighbourhood; while the Earl of Devonshire had at one time a house in Holborn, Lord Rich's London residence was within the priory of St Bartholomew. M. C. Bradbrook suggests that, for the characterisation of the Duchess of Malfi, Webster may have been inspired by the independent-minded Lady Rich (*John Webster*, 1980 68). However, her bold flouting of the institution of marriage also recalls that of Vittoria in *The White Devil*; the King told the Earl that he had married 'a fair woman with a black soul'.[31] Beauty and charm were constant attributes of Lady Rich, as written by Sidney in *Astophel and Stella*, and her love of literature was well known. John Florio dedicated Book II of his translation of Montaigne's *Essays* to her and the Countess of Rutland, Sir Philip Sidney's daughter. Both Lady Rich and the Earl of Devonshire were particularly fond of plays; at one party they stayed till the early hours of the morning watching two plays (Falls, 1954 64). According to Fynes Moryson, author of *Itinerary* and secretary to the Earl, the latter kept a Shakespearean wise fool on his estate (1967 xxxiv). At Wanstead he built a fine library containing playbooks for recreation. In the production of Ben Jonson's *The Masque of Blacknesse* at Whitehall on Twelfth Night 1605, Lady Rich was one of the twelve black nymphs, together with the Queen and other noble ladies including the Countesses of Suffolk, Derby and Bedford, and Lady Mary Wroth. Her strong personality was particularly evident in her great influence over her brother, the second Earl of Essex. The fact that this extraordinary pair, embodiments of Renaissance values in many respects, though living a life that violated the absolute moral standard of the time, had their breach long overlooked at the Court, must have suggested to a sensitive mind a different perspective on the illicit relationship than the homiletic condemnation of 'the outrageous sea of adultery'.

The public reaction to the couple's marriage, however, was unanimously condemnatory, reflecting the anger of the King and Queen. For instance, Chamberlain's letter, dated 5 April 1606, reports the Earl's death to Winwood thus:

> The earle of Devonshire left this life on Thursday night last, soone and early for his yeares but late enough for himself, and happy had ben yf he had gon two or three yeares since, before the world was wearie of him, or that he had left that scandall behinde him. (Vol. I. 226)

In contrast to this attitude, the young John Ford celebrated their romantic relationship in *Fames Memoriall, or the Earle of Deuonshire Deceased* (1606), an elegy published soon after the Earl's death. His dedication to Lady Penelope styled her as Countess of Devonshire, a title that was officially denied to her at the time.[32] Perhaps realising, though, that this might attract criticism, Ford defended his attitude by concluding his address to the readers with the words, 'I striue not to please many' (1606 sig. A3v).

Another great scandal that stirred Londoners at the time concerned the King's first cousin, Lady Arabella Stuart.[33] Her relationship with the King, as well as the late Queen, had always been precarious because she stood next in line to the English throne after the King and his children.[34] On 2 February 1610, Lady Arabella became engaged to William Seymour, whose descent from the Suffolk line made him especially disagreeable to the King as her consort.[35] When Lady Arabella and Lord Seymour were subsequently summoned before the Privy Council, they declared that they would never marry without the King's permission. On 22 June 1610, however, they were secretly wed, a fact that was soon discovered. On 9 July, Lady Arabella was committed to the custody of Sir Thomas Parry, while her husband was sent to the Tower. On 13 March 1611, she was placed under the charge of the Bishop of Durham, but through various excuses she just managed to avoid being taken away to Durham. On 4 June in the same year, she escaped, disguised as a page, boarded a French vessel in the Thames, and sailed for Calais. She was captured in the Straits of Dover, brought back, and imprisoned in the Tower. In the meantime, William Seymour succeeded in escaping from the Tower, landing at Ostend. In 1613, rumours spread that her husband was dead and that she was distracted.[36] On 25 September 1615, she died in the Tower, reportedly by starving herself to death.

While Webster was writing *The White Devil*, Lady Arabella's disastrous career seems likely to have stimulated much excitement amongst Londoners. The latter part of her tragedy—the false rumours of her husband's death, her distraction, and her death while imprisoned—remind us of the Duchess of Malfi's ordeals. Since Webster's tragedy was written earlier, the parallel offers a curious example of real life imitating art, but Lady Arabella's long-continued defiant attitude towards authority also resembles Vittoria's flaunting of authority, as is magnificently displayed in the trial scene. Flamineo's suggestion to Brachiano that they should escape to Padua by dressing Vittoria 'in a Pages suit' (IV. ii. 208), though such a disguise is a common device in contemporary drama as in the case of Innogen in *Cymbeline* (King's Men, 1609), may even have reminded the original audience of Lady Arabella's recent unfortunate attempt to escape.

Webster's original audience witnessed yet another embodiment of female defiance. This was Mary, Countess of Shrewsbury, who was Lady Arabella's aunt and a daughter of the celebrated Bess of Hardwick. She was committed to the Tower in 1610 on the charge of assisting in Lady Arabella's marriage. Her wilfulness and defiance of authority were commonly known at the time.[37]

Lady Anne Clifford was another prominent woman with much learning and independence of mind, whose self-asserting acts greatly annoyed King James during this period. Since the death of her father, the third Earl of Cumberland, in October of 1605, she had been constantly fighting her uncle, the fourth Earl of Cumberland, and his son, over the family estates in the north. She also fell out with her husband, Richard Sackville, Earl of Dorset, whom she married in 1609, since he urged her to forsake her claims to the estates in favour of a financial settlement in order to pay his debts. Although she was frequently at the Court and was a favourite with the Queen, many influential lords took the sides of her husband and repeatedly rebuked her for insubordination. Her feelings of frustration are betrayed in her diary, but she never gave way to the pressure exerted by these men of high position. After the death of Richard Sackville, she married Philip Herbert, the third Earl of Montgomery, thus becoming a relative of Mary Wroth and visiting Penshurst Place often. Finally, in 1643, after the death of her uncle and of his son, she inherited all the estates, where she lived for the rest of her days. Like the Countess of Shrewsbury, Lady Anne Clifford became to her contemporaries a by-word for female obstinacy.[38]

Jacobean moralists repeatedly preached against female wilfulness, but the determination demonstrated by these women points to a possible virtue in women's self-assertion. Their acts, though condemnable according to contemporary moral standards, are testament to human integrity in the courageous pursuit of truth to oneself, which is in Webster's terms, 'masculine vertue'. On the other hand, Jacobean people witnessed the purely dire consequences of female self-assertion, which the moralists had warned against, in the Countess of Essex's involvement in the murder of Sir Thomas Overbury, the most scandalous incident in the reign of King James.[39]

In December 1605, Frances Howard, daughter of Thomas Howard, the first Earl of Suffolk, was married to Robert Devereux, the third Earl of Essex. Soon after their marriage, the Earl was sent on a grand tour of the Continent, leaving his beautiful young wife with her parents at the Court. During his absence, she was attracted to Robert Carr, the King's favourite, and remained so after her husband's return in 1610. While Webster was working on *The White Devil*, the Countess had not yet publicly proceeded in her attempt to obtain annulment of her marriage with Robert Devereux, nor had the Howards started their plot to poison Sir Thomas Overbury, who bitterly opposed the marriage between his master, Robert Carr, and the Countess.[40] By 1612, however, rumours of the Countess's improprieties seem to have been widely circulated at the

Court.[41] Since Webster's family business was coachmaking,[42] he must have been familiar with gossip at the Court through his association with his gentlemen customers. Therefore, it is quite likely that, when writing *The White Devil*, Webster had knowledge of the Countess of Essex's adultery with the most powerful courtier of the time.[43]

(2) Vittoria as the popular image of a bad woman

Webster's motive for choosing recent Italian history as the subject of his first work of sole authority is not known, nor has any source been conclusively identified as that which he drew on in writing his play. Yet whatever version of the story of Vittoria Accoramboni he happened to know, it must have impressed the dramatist as material containing ample elements that would interest his audience. Even the barest outline of the affair offers the kinds of episodes that would suit the Jacobean image of Italy as being bloody and corrupt. Vittoria especially, one of the central figures of the affair, seems likely to have stirred Jacobean people's curiosity, since she, like Shakespeare's Cleopatra, afforded a perfect example of a bad woman as judged by contemporary standards. She was an adulteress whose husband, Francesco Peretti, was murdered on the orders of her lover, Paulo Giordano Orsino, Duke of Brachiano. She eventually managed to marry Brachiano, thus obtaining the title of Duchess. After Brachiano's death in 1585, however, she was pursued by the relatives of his first wife, Isabella Medici, and was murdered by Lodovico Orsini in Padua in December of that same year.

Various details in Webster's play diverge from both the historical facts and the contemporary accounts of Vittoria. Gunnar Boklund's researches have shown that Webster's main source may have been a lost Italian account on which an extant newsletter written for the Fugger banking-house was based, for this contains many details in common with the play (Boklund, 1957). A comparison of Webster's work with the Fugger document indicates Webster's conscious intent to underline Vittoria's evil; departing from the story as it is told in the newsletter, the dramatist suggests the possibility that Vittoria might have been responsible, though indirectly, for the murders of both her husband and Isabella.

Webster's intention to portray Vittoria as an obviously bad woman is made clear when some aspects of Vittoria's personality are compared with the qualities defined as typical female evils in contemporary writing such as Overbury's *A Wife*. Vittoria, for instance, fits perfectly well into the image of a bad woman presented by Joseph Swetnam in *The Araignment of Lewd, Idle, Froward, and vnconstant women*, published in

1615. Although this pamphlet was published later than Webster's play, it offers a commonplace image of a bad woman that had been prevalent in society for a long time before the play was written. Swetnam's pamphlet is an amalgam of the images of bad women commonly described in the preceding popular diatribes against women, such as *The Schole House of Women* (probably by Edward Gosynhyl),[44] published in 1541, and Dekker's *The Bachelor's Banquet*, published in 1603. The enormous popularity of Swetnam's pamphlet also suggests a general endorsement of the images of women depicted therein,[45] as well as popular amusement at these images.

Swetnam recurringly states that a beautiful wife is a cause of many disasters. Certainly, the 'fair wife', Vittoria, is depicted as the source of all the disasters in the play. Vittoria's beauty, provoking Brachiano's passion, leads to the murders of his wife and her husband, the fratricide of her brother, her mother's distraction, and finally to Brachiano's downfall and her own death.

Similarly, another of the targets of Swetnam's constant attack is female deceitfulness:

> A woman which is faire in shew, is foule in condition: shee is like vnto a glow-worme, which is bright in the hedge, and blacke in the hand [. . .] the fairest woman hath some filthiness in her. (Sig. C2v-3r)

The equation of a woman with the devil is frequent in Swetnam, and the gap between a woman's beautiful appearance and her ugly reality is frequently described through the contrasts between black and white, and between devil and angel (sig. E3v-4r).

In Webster's play, to show Vittoria's evil, the same contrasts are used not only by her foes, but also by Brachiano himself. Indeed, the oxymoron of the title of the play points to such a common image of female deceitfulness.[46]

Swetnam denounces any form of self-assertion by women, especially by wives. The ideal quality of a wife, Swetnam insists, as Overbury does in his writings, is docile submission to her husband's will. He advises young men, if they must marry, to take a wife of around seventeen years old, rather a maid than a widow, because

> a young woman of tender yeares is flexible and bending, obedient and subiect to doe any thing, according to the will and pleasure of her husband. (Sig. G3v)

Vittoria's drive for independence is at the core of her nature. Other people can never hold sway over her—neither her foolish husband, nor her brothers, either villainous or virtuous, nor her moralistic mother, nor even her glorious lover. Vittoria is exactly the type of self-assertive woman whom Swetnam strongly advises his young readers to avoid marrying.

While attacking women violently, Swetnam's pamphlet, like medieval satires, is rife with the male fear of women's power over men. Citing from history examples of great men destroyed by women, such as David, Solomon, Samson and Hercules, Swetnam warns against women who are conscious of their own power:

> thou shalt see the power of women, how it hath beene so great, and more preuailed in bewitching mens wits, and in ouercomming their sences, then all other things whatsoeuer. It hath not onely vanquished Kings and Keisars, but it hath also surprised castles & countries, nay what is it that a woman cannot do, which knows her power? (Sig. D3r-3v)

Vittoria, who is fully aware of the power of her charm over Brachiano, manipulates him, first to carry out their spouses' murders, and then to marry her, thus finally enabling her to attain the title of Duchess. Judged from the points of view given in Swetnam's pamphlet, Webster's Vittoria is indeed an epitome of 'Lewd, Idle, Froward, and vnconstant women'.

Despite this image of Vittoria's badness, and for all the unfavourable judgement passed upon her, not a few critics have found themselves attracted by her. They find her one of the most fascinating characters in Jacobean drama because of the integrity that, for all her evil acts, she maintains throughout the play (Bogard, 1955 57; Heinemann, 1980 174).

The most remarkable aspect of Vittoria's personality derives from Webster's method of showing her transcendence over the stereotype of a bad woman, despite the fact that she retains their attributes. As Shakespeare did with Cleopatra, by deliberately portraying Vittoria as a typical bad woman, Webster points out the complex reality of her womanhood, which eludes contemporary assumptions about women. This is particularly clear in four of the five scenes in which Vittoria appears: Act II Scene ii, Act III Scene ii, Act IV Scene ii and Act V Scene vi. Here, Webster employs the same technique of making other characters constantly apply to Vittoria common assumptions about a bad woman, but underlines the failure of these assumptions to define the complexity of her personality.

(3) The arraignment scene in Act III Scene ii

Webster's aforementioned technique is most effective in the arraignment scene (Act III Scene ii). The importance he attached to this scene is evident from the way it is arranged in the first Quarto of the play. Although this edition (1612) has no act and scene divisions, a special title, 'The Araignment of Vittoria' (sig. E2r), is prefixed to the scene.[47] The scene itself seems like a play within a play, with its audience not only that of the theatre, but also of 'lieger ambassadors' and other characters in the play. Thus, the whole dramatic energy is concentrated on the battle between Vittoria and authority, which, by applying to her common assumptions about a bad woman, tries to reduce her to a stock figure of a 'Whoore and Murdresse' (III. ii. 149).

From the start, authority is discredited by being represented by a foolish lawyer. Using Latin, the lawyer begins to accuse Vittoria of being corrupt, but she immediately undercuts him by demanding that he change the language to English, so that her charge can be clearly understood by the whole assembly. This obviously echoes the similar insistence by Katherine of Aragon in her trial.[48] Jacqueline Pearson (1980 73) has argued that Webster's device highlights Vittoria's fictional role by ironically contrasting her evil nature with the innocence of the real-life Queen, Katherine, who was prosecuted by the vicious Cardinal. Yet, in view of the satirical description of the lawyer in the scene, it seems more likely that Webster's intention was to draw a parallel between these two strong-willed women, both of whom refuse to be identified as bad women in an obscure language, as well as to point out the potential dangers of law hidden behind the façade of elaborate legal terms and procedures.[49] When Vittoria scoffs at the absurdity of the lawyer's pompous jargon, he counters her criticism by suggesting another common concept—that women are incapable of comprehending sophisticated arguments: 'the woman/Know's not her tropes not figures, nor is perfect/In the accademick derivation/Of Grammaticall elocution' (39–42). Vittoria's protest against being labelled as a bad woman by the lawyer in such a manner is justified, since even Francisco scorns his 'learn'd verbosity' (48), driving him out of the court. Webster stresses Francisco's scorn by his stage direction in the first quarto: *Francisco speakes this as in scorne* (45).[50]

Now Monticelso takes over the task of reducing Vittoria to a whore. Although she attempts to evade his accusation by casting doubt upon the Cardinal's authority 'To play the Lawier' (61), he links her spirited protest with an assumed characteristic of a whore, immodest language:[51] 'Oh your trade instructs your language!' (62). Monticelso's following tirades against Vittoria are wholly cliché-ridden. After pointing out her hypocrisy in much the same terms as Swetnam's,[52] Monticelso calls her a whore, on the evidence that she holds extravagant parties, which were commonly associated with 'whores' and courtesans.[53] When Vittoria asks him for the definition of a whore, Monticelso pronounces a long delineation in the form of the Character, like those Webster himself contributed to the 1615 edition of Thomas Overbury's *Characters*. Yet, the twelve figures Monticelso uses here are only vaguely related to whores, that is only in the general sense of deceitfulness and a threat to health and wealth. However, satisfactory his definition of whore may be by Jacobean standards, it certainly does not prove Vittoria to be one. Thus she can simply retort, 'This carracter scapes me' (102).

Monticelso proceeds with his accusation, now defining her as a murderess, drawing on the conventional concept that murder is the natural consequence of adultery.[54] Here, too, however, the only evidence that Monticelso can present is Vittoria's deviation from the conventional assumptions about a widow—her unwidowlike attire and scorne and 'impudence' in behaviour (127). When she denies any knowledge of the murder of her husband, he simply calls her 'conning' (124), which is another typical attribute of a bad woman.[55] Although Vittoria violently protests against the way in which her arraignment is conducted, Monticelso dismisses her objection, saying that 'Shee scandals our proceedings' (130).

So far, Vittoria has simply refused to allow for these assumptions to be applied to her, but now she starts to challenge the assumptions themselves. While reluctantly accepting society's expectation of traditional female virtues of 'modesty and womanhood', she must in the circumstances 'personate masculine vertue' (136) in order to defend herself. Masculinity in women, being a deviation from the traditional concept of womanhood, is almost always presented as a negative quality in Jacobean drama.[56] Here, though, she calls it a 'vertue' since it is her only means to save herself from 'a cursed accusation' (134).

Vittoria's following retort to Monticelso poses a challenge to common attitudes to women. When Monticelso shows Brachiano's letter as evidence of her adultery, she insists on her independence of others' conduct towards her:

> Grant I was tempted,
> Temptation to lust proves not the act,

> *Casta est quam nemo rogavit,*
> You reade his hot love to me, but you want
> My frosty answere. (198–202)

Then she points out the male selfishness of accusing women of men's love for them: 'Condemne you me for that the Duke did love mee?' (203). The denunciation that women allure men to love was common in contemporary tirades against women; in drama of the period, some male characters, including Brachiano and Antony of *Antony and Cleopatra*, also accuse women of their ruin, regardless of their own faults. Webster took this criticism of the male attitude from Tofte's *Honour's Academy*[57] and has Vittoria voice it. Vittoria's challenge reaches its climax when she denies the validity of the assumptions by which she is evaluated:

> Summe up my faults I pray, and you shall finde,
> That beauty and gay clothes, a merry heart,
> And a good stomacke to feast are all,
> All the poore crimes that you can charge me with: (207–10)

Even though the audience knows that Vittoria has sinned against orthodox morality and is telling lies here, her argument conducted so cleverly underscores the inappropriateness of the conventional criteria used to evaluate women. One cannot but agree with the English ambassador: 'Shee hath a brave spirit' (140).

Vittoria's cry of 'rape' (274), though ridiculous, seems justified, after we are made to observe the whole procedure of the distortion of justice in the hands of the Cardinal. She makes a final protest, if only to release her frustration: 'ô womans poore revenge/Which dwels but in the tongue' (283–4). Ever since medieval satires, a woman's tongue had been an object of attack, and it is also frequently satirised in Jacobean drama.[58] Vittoria challenges this attitude, saying that a woman's tongue is her only means of self-defence. Her oral revenge, however, is not successful since Monticelso immediately reduces her reaction to another stock female quality, 'fury' (278).[59]

Nevertheless, these common attitudes towards women are discredited in this scene, not only by Vittoria's brilliant challenge to them, but also by the corruption of the authority that advocates them. During the trial, Brachiano suggests the possibility that the Cardinal aimed to cheat Vittoria of her property, a possibility that the Cardinal does not deny. At the end of the trial Vittoria calls Monticelso 'devill' (280). This label at least turns out to be relevant, since he is later found to be both the holder of the black book that contains 'a general catalogue of knaves' (IV. 1. 60) and a man inciting Francisco to sinister revenge. Another representative of authority, Francisco, is a perfect Machiavellian prince. In inspiring Camillo's murder, Monticelso and Francisco are no less guilty than Vittoria, for they deliberately send him away to create an opportunity for Brachiano to pursue his desire for Vittoria and for her to rid herself of her husband.

The inhabitants of this world are inescapably infected by its evil and violence. Even Brachiano's virtuous wife, Isabella, as John Russell Brown has observed (*The White Devil* ed. liii–liv), not only reveals her hidden selfishness in her meek submission to her husband, but resorts to dissimulation in her attempt to mediate between him and her brother. And in feigning jealousy, she vents her true feeling of fierce hatred of Vittoria, while Vittoria's good brother, Marcello, leaves Francisco to follow his brother and thus to join Brachiano. Her puritanical mother tells a lie in trying to save Flamineo from his murder charge. Furthermore, the innocent Giovanni has already been said to bear Francesco's features. In the world where the distinction between good and evil is elusive, the conventional standards of female virtues are irrelevant. Yet the men in power employ society's assumptions, not as a means to consider the true nature of women, but as a means to pursue their own selfish desires. In such a situation, a woman can prove her integrity only through the assertion of her independence of these assumptions, as Vittoria magnificently does in this scene. Although she is defeated in the trial and dispatched to the house of convertites, her challenge is unabated; she refuses to surrender to weeping, which was considered a typical female reaction:[60] 'I will not weepe,/No I do scorne to call up one poore teare/To fawne on your injustice' (III. 2. 284–6).

(4) Vittoria's 'masculine vertue'

Although Vittoria has persistently refused to have herself judged by conventional standards in Jacobean England, the self-awareness she finally reaches at her death is not so unique, but her expression of it is characteristic of her complex personality: 'O my greatest sinne lay in my blood./Now my blood paies for 't' (V. vi. 235–6). In fact, Vittoria's uneasy awareness of her deviation from morality upsets her at times; for instance, she is greatly shocked by Cornelia's rebuke or curse on her, or when Brachiano denounces her as a 'whore' in the quarrel scene. And yet, this uneasiness does not lead to her acceptance of society's moral code. In the assessment of her own life, she simply acknowledges the consequence of having chosen to follow her own inner drive, 'blood'. Nor does her final utterance that she envies those who never saw the Court or knew great men (V. vi. 256–7) indicate her repentance; she simply expresses her recognition of the evils and dangers embedded in glorious Court life, though she herself would never have shunned it. Her final speech displays her courageous confrontation with the dislocation of her spirit, not any reconciliation with the conventional moralisation of death: 'My soule, like to a ship in a blacke storme,/Is driven I know not whither' (V. vi. 243–4).

Witnessing Vittoria's magnificent self-possession in the face of death, Flamineo finally realises that his sister has an individuality that transcends his cynical assumptions about women, which he had hitherto applied to her. For the first time, he recognises the integrity of her spirit, and calls it 'masculine virtue'. Although still cynically, he even tries to save her from being categorised as a bad woman due to her viciousness and guilt:

> Know many glorious woemen that are fam'd
> For masculine virtue, have bin vitious
> Onely a happier silence did betide them.
> Shee hath no faults, who hath the art to hide them. (V. vi. 239–42)

In a world, where law has degenerated to an absurd formality, and morality and religion to instruments of the Machiavellian prince and the venal prelate, women may be considered virtuous only when they are successful in hiding their faults. Isabella and Cornelia, embodiments of female virtues by conventional standards, are to be found, as has been mentioned before, hiding selfishness and viciousness under their virtuous appearances. If society's views of good women have no validity in the world of the play, the only way for a woman to prove her integrity here is through 'masculine virtue', an aggressive assertion of her selfhood, such as has hitherto been mainly a male preserve. Vittoria's challenge to common notions of women is thus recognised by her brother as a challenge to society's moral code, which sanctions these assumptions. It is significant that, after witnessing Vittoria's death, Flamineo's last words are his acknowledgement, though in his usual sardonic tone, of the inapplicability to his sister of the proverbial saying about women's invulnerability to death; 'Falce reporte/Which saies that woemen vie with the nine Muses/For nine tough durable lives' (V. vi. 249–51). This is the only speech in the play in which Flamineo admits, though jokingly, the irrelevance of common concepts of womanhood with regard to his sister.

(5) Vittoria's 'masculine vertue' and Jacobean England

The historical facts of some noble ladies' rebellion against authority, dealt with earlier in this chapter, indicate the growing sense of selfhood among some English women at the very time when Webster was working on his first independent play. These women began to conceive of themselves and of their role in society from an angle that differed from conventional views on women. Society's response to their actions was usually critical. However, Webster's dramatisation of Vittoria's drive for self-actualisation as 'masculine vertue' points to a positive aspect, as well as to the possible dangers and evils, of women's urge to satisfy their will.

The word 'masculine' was usually applied to women to criticise any form of their violation of social norms. In the early seventeenth century the issue of women's increasing masculinity had for some time been a matter of concern in society. Particularly, women's mannish aggressiveness was identified with their desire to copy men's dress. Towards the end of the sixteenth century, for instance, William Harrison wrote in his *Description of England*:

> I have met with some of these trulls in London so disguised that it hath passed my skill to discern whether they were men or women. (Qut. John Dover Wilson, 1949 165)

Women's fondness for dressing like men, which William Harrison observed among women of a special kind, 'trulls', as will be discussed in the final chapter of this book, had become a fashion prevalent in all social classes by the end of the second decade of the seventeenth century. This change in women's fashion of dress was a serious matter, for it reflected, or at least suggested, a change in the way women saw themselves in relation to men. Women's dressing like men was, therefore, interpreted as indicative of their refusal of the conventional gender role and was attacked severely as both a symptom and a cause of social disorder. Thomas Adams, for instance, in his sermon, 'Mystical Bedlam, or the World of Madmen' (1615), calls a masculine woman '*hic mulier*' and condemns this new fashion as evidence of feminine pride and a defacing of the image of God in which woman had been formed (Adams, 1861, Vol. 1 277–8). This anxiety over women's fashion and aggressiveness culminated in King James's proclamation of 1620, which will be examined in the final chapter of this book. In the same year, the pamphlet entitled *Hic Mulier: or, the Man-Woman* was published. The false Latin suggests that its title was most likely taken from Adam's sermon (Baines, 1978 ix). The pamphlet was accompanied by a fascinating companion-piece called *Haec-Vir: or The Womanish-Man*. *Hic Mulier* and *Haec-Vir* will also be discussed in the final chapter of this volume. Hic Mulier's assertion of her autonomous self echoes that of Vittoria. Yet it took nearly ten years after the production of *The White Devil* for such a bold declaration of women's independence to be printed.

It is noteworthy, however, that *The White Devil* is not the only play of the period that reflects changing attitudes towards women's desire for self-actualisation. Although the subject is never so profoundly explored as in Webster's tragedy, some other plays written around the beginning of the decade represent as somewhat justifiable women's defiance of common assumptions about womanhood. One interesting example of society's ambivalent feelings towards rebellious women is seen in the difference between Middleton's and Dekker's attitude in *The Roaring Girl* (Prince Henry's, 1608) and that of Nathan Field in *Amends for Ladies* (Queen's Revels (?), 1610–1611). Both plays centre on an actual contemporary Amazon in breeches, Mary Frith, commonly called Moll Cut-purseurse. Her eccentricity and criminal activities were well known at the time.[61] Chamberlain's letter of 12 February 1612 gives a critical description, though tinged with amusement, of her penance at Paul's Cross:

> this last Sonday Mall Cut-purse a notorious baggage (that used to go in mans apparel and challenged the field of divers gallants) was brought to the same place, where she wept bitterly and seemed very penitent, but yt is since douted she was maudelin druncke, being discovered to have tipled of three quarts of sacke before she came to her to penaunce. (Vol. I. 334)

Nathan Field denounces Moll as a bawd in his play, but Moll in *The Roaring Girl*, despite her refusal to play the normal roles of woman, is presented as essentially a virtuous woman, who helps the young lovers to marry. Moll insists that judging women by common opinion is wrong, and that eccentricity alone does not make a woman evil. She refuses marriage for herself:

> I have no humour to marry. I love
> to lie o' both sides o'th' bed myself; and again, o' th'other
> side, a wife, you know, ought to be obedient, but I fear me
> I am too headstrong to obey, therefore I'll ne'er go about
> it. [. . .]

I have the head now of myself,
and am man enough for a woman; marriage is but a chopping and changing, where a maiden loses one head, and has a worse i'th' place. (II. ii. 36–45)

The authors obviously intended to provide a different view of this 'notorious baggage', but *The Roaring Girl*'s sentimental characterisation of Moll prevents any deep probing into the significance of her self-assertion.

Evadne in *The Maid's Tragedy* (King's, 1610) is another outstanding female character. In the first part of the play she is charmingly independent in her callous exploitation of male sexuality, despising society's concept of a happy marriage. The evil in Evadne's self-assertion is also mitigated by the corruption and stupidity of the men surrounding her. Nonetheless, when Melantius, her brother, forces her into repentance, she loses both her independence and charm; she is subsequently transformed into another new female figure, a woman revenger, thus usurping the traditional male role of revenge plays. Yet her revenge is represented as a kind of female hysterical outburst, and her suicide, after Amintor, her husband, denies her his bed for ever, narrows the focus by underlining her sexual frustration, thus obscuring the issue of a woman's assertion of selfhood in a corrupt world.

Fletcher's *The Woman's Prize, or The Tamer Tam'd* (Unknown (King's in 1633), 1611) also suggests a new approach to women's assertion of selfhood. The play forms a parody on Shakespeare's *The Taming of the Shrew*. Petruchio's first wife, the tamed Kate, is now dead, and the wife he has just married, Maria, is determined not to subjugate herself to her husband's autocratic will, and so is refusing to consummate the marriage. Maria's fight to change the traditional concepts of marital role-playing receives powerful support from her cousin, Byancha, who sees it in a sociological and historical light:

All the several wrongs
Done by Imperious Husbands to their Wives
These thousand years and upwards, strengthen thee:
Thou hast a brave cause. (I. ii. 9)[62]

Maria presents Petruchio with her conditions for the consummation of their marriage, and all the women in the city stand up to support her and Byancha. In the end, Petruchio submits himself to Maria's demand of 'both sexes due equality'. This is probably the only play of the period that presents women acting for themselves to get freedom from their expected roles. And yet, Maria's conditions are conventional, and, without fully exploring the meaning of Maria's defiance of society's concept of women's roles, the play ends with the happy reconciliation of the couple.

The heroines of these plays all give precedence to their urge for their self-actualisation over their duty to observe the conventional codes in society. In presenting women's transgression in a sympathetic light, these authors before Webster seem to reveal their acknowledgement of the relevance of women's assertion of selfhood. Webster fully explored what they caught a glimpse of in *The White Devil*. Despite the obvious evil in Vittoria's ambition, Webster questions the validity of social assumptions about womanhood and presents the possibility of the integrity, as well as of the dangers, found in women's desire to insist on their will. Webster's understanding of the female mind may have been inspired by the actions taken by the contemporary aristocratic versions of Hic-Mulier. His play may signal the emergence of a new male attitude at around the turn of the decade, an attitude which, though well aware of its dangers, recognised that women's desire for self-fulfilment was an essential part of their humanity. At any event, in another decade, this attitude was to be developed, in *Haec-Vir*, into a forthright challenge to society's assumptions about womanhood. Furthermore, in 1621 Lady Mary Wroth published her original romance, *The Countess of Montgomery's Urania*, defying the ideal image of womanhood upheld in Jacobean society.

2
Female Selfhood and Ideologies of Marriage in Early Jacobean Drama: *The Duchess of Malfi* and *The Tragedy of Mariam*

The depressing norms for women within married life, as demonstrated in Thomas Overbury's *A Wife*, paradoxically seemed to offer women the opportunity to construct their sense of selfhood. Faced with the images of female roles in marriage as defined by orthodoxy, many women in early modern England became conscious of the gap between what they felt they were and what they were supposed to be, even though most of them did not dare to challenge their conventional roles, conforming instead to the passive roles assigned to them. Nevertheless, historical records do show some cases of women who, feeling their conflicts with the notions of femininity permeating their society, resorted to sexual transgression. These women, known from extant records, were mostly aristocrats, probably because personal histories of women of their standing had a better chance of being recorded than those of women lower down the social scale.[1] But, thanks to work on the records both of the ecclesiastical courts and of Bridewell Hospital in London, we now also know a great deal about the transgressions of less prominent women and men.[2] As has been explained in the previous chapter, Lady Penelope Rich, for instance, who was discontented with her arranged marriage with the wealthy Lord Rich, developed a long-standing adulterous relationship with Lord Mountjoy, later Earl of Devonshire, and, after bearing him five illegitimate children, finally married him, which caused a great scandal at the Court. Similarly, Frances Hatton was forced into an arranged marriage in 1617 with John Villiers, Buckingham's elder brother, by her father, Edward Coke, the Lord Justice of the King's Bench, despite the strong opposition of her mother, Lady Hatton. Eventually, Frances found a lover's solace in an extramarital relationship with Robert Howard and bore his child, whom she named Robert. She eventually deserted her husband.[3]

Among the women who defied the contemporary discourse on marriage, the most remarkable was Lady Mary Wroth (1587?–1651/1653), who had an adulterous relationship with her first cousin, William Herbert, the third Earl of Pembroke, and bore him two illegitimate children, Katherine and William, in around 1624.[4] Lady Mary Wroth was different from other adulterous women in the period in that she chose to become an author, exploring deeply in her works the significance of the gap created in female identity due to the social system of her time.[5] She was most probably the first Englishwoman to write a pastoral comedy, *Love's Victory* (c.1619), and to write a prose romance, *The Countess of Montgomerry's Urania* (1621), published with the appended sonnet sequence, *Pamphilia to Amphilanthus*. She also wrote the continued part of *Urania*, which was nearly two-thirds the length of the first part, but this was left unpublished until 1999. In all these works Wroth explores what a female self experienced as autonomous might signify in a society that denies women the availability of such experience. In particular, both parts of *Urania* abound with descriptions of women whose innermost thoughts contradict the contemporary discourses on marriage. (Chapter 3 will focus on the works of Lady Mary in view of Jacobean concepts of marriage.)

Another female writer in the period who pursued the issue of female selfhood in relation to the Jacobean ideologies of marriage was Elizabeth Cary (1586–1639), Viscountess of Falkland. Although, unlike Wroth, Cary did not engage in sexual transgression, in *The Tragedy of Mariam* (c.1603, published in 1613), the first-known tragedy written by an Englishwoman, she dramatises the heroine's way of constructing her selfhood by examining Cary's own feeling of incompatibility with the conventional notion of wifehood.[6] Cary also describes the problem of female sexual transgression in her portrayal of Queen Isabel in *The History of the Life, Reign, and Death of Edward II* (c.1626), which, if the attribution of this work to her is correct (as seems likely to be the case), is the earliest historical writing by an Englishwoman.[7]

Many male playwrights in the English Renaissance also dealt with wives' marital unhappiness and sexual transgression. Their approaches to the issue on the whole are quite different from those of the female writers. Rather than exploring the significance of a woman's sense of contradiction with the orthodox concepts of marriage, most male writers present the wife's adultery as stemming from what they regard as innate female weakness or monstrous sexual assertiveness, qualities that had been attributed to womanhood in misogynistic writings since medieval times.

Male characters created by male playwrights in Jacobean drama are often portrayed as considering female identity in terms of consistency and wholeness, as something that can be wholly displayed on the surface and that conceals no innermost self. On the other hand, a discrepancy between appearance and selfhood demonstrated by the female characters is usually depicted as female duplicity, which harms the men around them. Wroth and Cary, in contrast, both represent female identity as constituted of plural aspects. In their works the gap between female feelings and outward appearance is presented as something that women of integrity cannot help but experience within themselves, and yet they are forced to hide it underneath the mask of conventional female behaviour in order to avoid their ruin in society.

Some female characters in the works of Wroth and Cary try to keep these views private and prevent men from knowing them—especially if the male attempt to gain access to these thoughts is associated with violence. What the female characters consider to be their autonomous selfhood may actually be, as Catherine Belsey argued in *The Subject of Tragedy*, the product of the cultures they live in, even though they are not conscious of this fact; the construction of what they regard as their selfhood may be deeply affected by the very social assumptions about womanhood from which, ironically, they are trying to free themselves. And yet, their sense of the discrepancy between what society expects women to be and what they consider themselves to be is still highly significant in the light of the long-term history of changes in women's self-consciousness. Women's sense that they possess an autonomous selfhood interacts with various elements in culture, creating a new concept of womanhood in society.

In English Renaissance drama, when male characters realise that underneath a woman's appearance there exists an area that they cannot dominate, they exhibit jealousy, often inflicting physical violence by torturing her body, or psychological violence by treating her as mad. What distinguishes male writers' treatments of this problem from those of Wroth and Cary is their tendency to incorporate grotesque elements in their representations of violence inflicted by male characters.[8] In contrast, Wroth and Cary both present the gap within female identity not through images of grotesqueness, but in terms of theatricality: they demonstrate female identity as constituted of both a woman's performance of her assigned role and of what she regards as her autonomous self.[9] Women in their works are either good or bad at performing their conventional roles, while concealing their inward feelings.

The first part of this chapter examines John Webster's *The Duchess of Malfi*, focusing on the theme of a female assertion of selfhood in the context of marriage and male violence. Then the female viewpoints on marriage are addressed as expressed in Elizabeth Cary's *The Tragedy of Mariam*. This chapter also looks briefly at the representation of Mariam's sense of self by Thomas Lodge, a translator of *Famous and Memorable Works of Josephus* (1602), on which Cary drew heavily for her play.

In order to highlight the characteristic features in English Renaissance drama with regards to female desire and marriage, this chapter also examines a well-known Kabuki play, *Musume Dojoji (A Maiden at Dojoji [Temple])*. The female roles in Kabuki have been traditionally played by men, as in the plays in the English Renaissance,[10] but the representations of female assertive power function in different ways.

Representations of female selfhood and male violence: *The Duchess of Malfi*

In *The White Devil* Webster dramatised the possible virtue of masculinity in women in a degenerated world, but left unexplored the significance of the agency of women when they were placed in such a world. In *The Duchess of Malfi*, written about a year later, Webster's emphasis shifted from masculinity in a woman to a woman's insistence on her agency in the context of marriage.

Having witnessed the Duchess's secret marriage, Cariola, her chambermaid, is at a loss as to how to understand her mistress's audacious act:

> Whether the spirit of greatnes, or of woman
> Raigne most in her, I know not, but it shewes
> A fearfull madnes; I owe her much of pitty. (I. 1. 487–9)

Cariola's words effectively summarise the central issue of the play. She does not know whether the Duchess is under the control of an heroic spirit of defiance or of blind female passion, which was inveighed against so often by contemporary moralists. Whichever it may be, to Cariola the Duchess's flouting of social decorum seems to be 'A fearfull madnes'. Webster's original audience must have shared Cariola's ambivalence, for, seen in the social context of 1613–4, when the play was most probably first performed, the Duchess's remarriage with a social inferior raises complicated moral problems.

Elizabethan and Jacobean moralists often voiced objections to a widow's remarriage, objections inherited from Humanists like Vives.[11] The thirty-two characters added in the 1615 edition of Overbury's *A Wife*, which are generally attributed to Webster, include passages entitled '*A vertuous Widdow*' and '*An ordinarie Widdow*'. 'A vertuous Widdow' gives a clear image of how Webster's contemporaries generally thought of an ideal widow. She is compared to:

> the Palme-tree, that thrives not after the supplanting of her husband. For her Childrens sake she first marries, for she married that she might have children, and for their sakes she marries no more. [. . .] To change her name were, shee thinkes, to commit a sin should make her asham'd of her husbands Calling: shee thinkes shee hath traveld all the world in one man; the rest of her time therefore shee directs to heaven. (Overbury's *New Characters*, 1615 sig. L8R)

In a similarly conventional manner, 'An ordinarie Widdow' is likened to:

> the Heralds Hearse-cloath; shee serves to many funerals, with a very little altering the colour. The end of her husband beginnes in teares; and the end of her teares beginnes in a husband. (Sig. M1R)

The revival of Chapman's *The Widow's Tears* in 1613 also indicates the predominant contemporary sentiments against widows' remarriage.[12] While her husband was 'alive', Cynthia is said to have denounced a widow's remarriage thus:

> as being but a kind of lawful adultery, like usury permitted by the law, not approved; that to wed a second was no better than to cuckold the first; that women should entertain wedlock as one body, as one life, beyond which there were no desire, no thought, no repentance from it, no restitution to it. (Yamada ed., 1975 II. iv. 27–32)

The complexity arises when these sentiments are considered in relation to the social realities in England in the sixteenth and seventeenth centuries. In the case of widows of high social status, the realities surrounding them—their relatives' political calculations and property interests—made it almost impossible for them to remain unmarried for long.[13] Innumerable contemporary instances of prominent widows' remarriages—sometimes they had a succession of husbands—demonstrate that these sentiments went almost unheeded among the upper class. The Duchess's remarriage itself, therefore, though Webster's original audience must have felt a certain sympathy with her brothers' fierce objections, might have been accepted simply as the way of the world.

However, the Duchess's choice of husband in her second marriage suggested to the Jacobean audience a serious defiance of their shared values.[14] In most cases, members of the Elizabethan and Jacobean nobility and gentry, whether in a first or subsequent marriage, chose their partners from their own rank of society. The reason for this choice was not simply their respect for pedigree; political and material concerns were equally involved (Stone, 1977 627–32). At the time when a prominent real-life widow's marriage with a man beneath her station, such as Lady Hatton's marriage to Edward Coke, caused a scandalous stir,[15] a duchess's marriage with a commoner, let alone with her servant, must have seemed an outrageous act. Webster's original audience still by and large held the view, established in the Middle Ages and stoutly maintained since, that a 'noble lady marries a commoner against the will of her relatives and great calamities ensue' (Boklund, 1962 67). Actual cases in recent history of ill-matched marriages must also have reinforced the objection. Some of Webster's audience, for instance, must still have remembered the tragic outcome of Lady Mary Grey's marriage; like the Duchess, defying her royal blood, she secretly married Queen Elizabeth's sergeant porter in 1565 and was severed by the Queen from her husband for the rest of her life (Rickman, 2008 17).

The Duchess's marriage involved yet another serious offence by being conducted in secrecy. Since she and Antonio exchanged their marriage vows with Cariola standing behind the arras as a witness, her marriage was legal, being a marriage *'per verba de praesenti'*. Yet it was a marriage conducted in defiance of the Church, which, though it would recognise such an exchange of vows as legal, forbade consummation until the Church's blessing had been bestowed. Morally, a secret marriage was considered evil largely on three grounds: First, it commonly flouted parental authority, or other authority equivalent to it. Second, it was keeping from the state a fact that the state considered itself entitled to know. The third reason was the possibility that a secret marriage might not receive religious sanction.[16] From any of these orthodox points of view, the Duchess's secret marriage could be seen as evil.

What is amazing, however, is that here again there existed a great gap between social norms and social realities. Despite the condemnation by ecclesiastical and moral authorities, a considerable number of secret marriages did indeed take place among aristocrats in the Elizabethan and Jacobean periods. Some of Queen Elizabeth's maids of honour managed to marry secretly even with men who were the Queen's favourites.[17] Yet, at the same time, Webster's audience must have been well aware of the great risks involved in the offence. Queen Elizabeth, in most cases, severely punished the rebellious couples, often by imprisoning the bridegrooms, as in the cases of the Earl of Southampton and Sir Walter Raleigh. In December, 1601, John Donne, while secretary to the Lord Keeper, secretly married his master's niece, Anne More. As punishment he was put in the Fleet Prison on charges of conspiracy to violate the civil and common law (Bradbrook, 1980 150). Later, as has been argued, the secret marriage of the Earl of Devonshire and Lady Rich in December 1606 provoked King James's rage, resulting in their fatal disgrace. In particular, when one of royal blood married without the sovereign's consent, the results were extremely serious.[18] Queen Elizabeth's severe punishment of Lady Catherine Grey, who secretly married Lord Edward Seymour in 1560, is paralleled by King James's punishment of his first cousin, Lady Arabella Stuart, for her secret union with Lady Grey's grandson, William Seymour.[19] Vicious and corrupt as the Aragonese brothers are in the play, the Duchess, by secretly marrying Antonio, flagrantly defies the conventions that the Elizabethan and Jacobean authorities forcefully sustained.

Contemporary attitudes towards the story of the Duchess of Amalfi

When Webster wrote his play, the story of the unfortunate Duchess of Amalfi was already known in England. The accounts of her tragedy are included in the two most popular story collections of the time: William Painter's *The Palace of Pleasure* (1566–7), translated from Belleforest's versions of Bandello's novella, and Simon Goulart's *Admirable and Memorable Histories* (1607), translated by Edward Grimeston. Even though briefly, the story of the Duchess of Amalfi is also mentioned in Thomas Beard's *The Theatre of Gods Iudgements* (1597), George Whetstone's *An Heptameron of Ciuill Discourses* (1582), Robert Greene's *The Carde of Fancie* (1587), and *The Forest of Fancy* (1579). For people with a knowledge of French and Italian, the original versions of Bandello and Belleforest were also available; some people, like Webster himself, may even have known Cinthio's account of the incident (Boklund, 1962 1–55). Naturally, some spectators would have recognised Webster's deliberately different approach to the story. In *The White Devil*, by making use of his audience's common assumptions about bad women, Webster explores the significance of Vittoria's assertion of selfhood. Likewise, in his later tragedy, by depending on his audience's awareness of their predecessors' attitudes towards the Duchess's marriage, Webster highlights his own vision of its meaning.

It is generally agreed that, for the plot and details of his play, Webster mainly drew on the Painter–Belleforest account. In *The Palace of Pleasure* the author's attitude towards the lovers is somewhat ambiguous; his severe moralising is interspersed with admiration for Antonio's heroic virtues, sympathy for the lovers' plight, and condemnation of the brothers' cruelty. However, Painter's purpose in telling the story is obviously to set forth a moral lesson on the lovers' breach of propriety: 'pollicie requireth order in all and eche wight ought to be matched according to their qualitie'. The motivations for their marriage are unequivocally described as lust in the Duchess and ambition in Antonio; their secret marriage is criticised as 'a Maske and couerture to hide her follies and shamelesse lusts' (Painter, 1566–67).[20]

Webster's use of other episodes in Goulart's *Histories*[21] indicates his knowledge of Goulart's account of the Duchess's marriage, itself based on Belleforest's version. Goulart presents a rigorously moralistic interpretation of the lovers' behaviour:

> this widowe being young and fayre, hauing regarded him with a lasciuious eye, she desired him: but to couer her fault, shee sought the colour of marriage: and after many vaine discourses in her thoughts, insteed of flying to the councell and good aduise of her Bretheren, and honorable Kinsfolkes, (whereof she had many) and to accept a partie fitte for her qualitie [. . .] transported with her desire, she discouers her thoughts vnto this Gentleman, who drunke with his owne conceite, and forgetting the respect which hee ought vnto his Ladye and to her house, neither yet remebring his owne meane estate [. . .] being presumptuous and lust-full, he yeelded to ioyne (vnder the vaile of a secret marriage) with her who had long before cast vnchast lookes at him and with whome he had rashly and against all dutie fallen in loue. (1607 364–5)

In his extremely popular book, *The Theatre of God's Iudgement*, Thomas Beard refers to the story in a chapter against secret marriage, entitled *'of whoredomes committed under colour of Marriage'*. The reference itself seems too brief to have exerted any substantial influence on Webster. Nonetheless, this chapter is useful here, since it starts with the author's condemnation of secret marriage in general:

> Seeing that oftentimes it falleth out that those which in shew seeme most honest, thinke it a thing lawfull to conuerse together as man

and wife by some secret and priuat contract, without making account of the publicke celebration of marriage as necessarie, but for some worldly respects according as their foolish and disordinate affections mispersuadeth them, to dispence therewith: It shall not bee impertinent as wee goe, to giue warning how vnlawfull all such conuersation is, and how contrarie to good manners, and to the laudable customes of all ciuill and well gouerned people. For it is so farre from desweruing the name of marriage, that on the other side it can bee nothing but plaine whoredome and fornification. (1597 sig. X4r)

As an example of God's punishment for a secret marriage, Beard invokes the story of the Duchess of Amalfi. In his account, even while denouncing the Cardinal's cruelty, Beard regards him as a scourge of God (sig. X4v-5r) in punishing the guilty couple.

Whetstone's reference to the story in *An Heptameron of Ciuill Discourses* is also so short that it is unlikely that it affected Webster's treatment of the subject in any important way. Yet Whetstone's 'The fift Daies Exercise', in which the tragedy of the Duchess of Amalfi is mentioned, contains an interesting discussion among Queen Aurelia's courtiers about unequal marriages, especially a servant's marriage with his great lady. Soranso starts his defence of such a match on two grounds. First, the levelling power of love is upheld with romantic ardour: 'loue spareth no degree, transgresseth euery law & bringeth the mightiest in bondage to the meanest' (1582 sig. Q2r). Soranso's democratic views on degree are opposed by Dondolo, who recalls the possibilities of fearful revenge sought by the wife's family for their stained family honour. Citing the Cardinal's revenge upon the Duchess of Malfi and her husband, Dondolo even gives voice to the Cardinal's justification for his own ruthless act:

> he had done no iniurie to Nature, but purged his House of dishonour: for Nature (quoth he) is perfect, and who blemisheth her is a monster in Nature, whose head, without wrong to Nature may be cut off. (1582 sig. Q2v)

Soranso argues against Dondolo by reminding him of the world's condemnation of the Cardinal's cruelty and the rarity of actual cases of such revenge. Dondolo still disagrees with Soranso, saying that a servant's marriage with a great lady would result in the wife's dominance, which would entail various kinds of domestic troubles. Dondolo's view receives firm support from others. As in *An Heptameron*, sympathetic views of the Duchess are carefully qualified in *The Forest of Fancy* and *The Carde of Fancie*. These contemporary accounts indicate the pervasive critical view of the Duchess's marriage, though different ways of looking at it are sometimes glimpsed.

The crucial point here again is that, despite the conventional attitudes upheld in these accounts, marriages that were highly offensive to society's norms actually took place in Elizabethan and Jacobean England. Lady Arabella Stuart, for instance, was still imprisoned in the Tower of London for the offence of her secret marriage and rumours of her madness and her husband's death had started spreading[22] when Webster's tragedy was first performed at the Blackfriars. Lawrence Stone argues that, in the early seventeenth century, widows were eager to marry again, not only because of their severe disadvantage in coping with the problems of daily life, but because of their anxious hope to secure the domestic felicity that had hitherto been denied them: 'they openly voiced the opinion that "all the riches in the world without content is nothing—for this liberty I will take to myself, that is, to make choice of one as I afecte"'. Stone cites the actual cases of some unfortunate widows who married in hope of love, only to find themselves shamelessly exploited; the chief reason for their unhappy remarriage lay in common law, which left the financial condition of women almost entirely in the power of their husbands (1977 622–3). All this is not to suggest that Webster intentionally alluded to any particular historical examples of unhappy remarriages. It is, however, an important factor that the story Webster chose to dramatise was located in an area of ideological ambivalence for a contemporary audience. In this respect, as Gunner Boklund said, the story itself 'possessed great vitality' (1962 69).

Popular images of widows and Webster's portrayal of the Duchess

In presenting the Duchess's individuality, Webster employs the same method as he used to characterise Vittoria. The people surrounding the Duchess—mostly male—try to impose on her common assumptions about womanhood, while her responses indicate the limits of these reductive views. Soon after the opening of the play, for instance, conflict emerges when the departing Aragonese brothers warn their sister against remarriage. Their exhortations, however repulsive the expressions they use, reflect to a great extent contemporary attitudes towards widows. Their concepts of a 'lusty Widowe' (I. 1. 326) indulging in 'chargeable Revels' (I. 1. 319), of women who 'are most luxurious' to 'wed twice' (I. 1. 284–5) and whose 'livers are more spotted/ Then *Labans* sheepe' (I. 1. 285–6), echo the suspicions about widows' virtue commonly expressed in contemporary writings.[23] Ferdinand's command to the Duchess to forbear 'chargeable Revels' also recalls the moralists' usual advice to widows that they should conduct themselves with extreme modesty so as to guard themselves from the charge of being 'lusty'.[24]

The brothers' objections to the Duchess's possible remarriage, though couched in strong language, thus reflect current sentiments against the remarriage of widows. The Cardinal's cynical response to the Duchess's vow never to marry—'So most Widowes say:/But commonly that motion lasts no longer/Then the turning of an houreglasse' (I. 1. 289–91)—represents the very theme of Chapman's *The Widow's Tears*. Similarly, the brothers' damning comment on secret marriage, 'Such weddings, may more properly be said/To be executed, then celebrated' (I. 1. 309–10) recalls Thomas Beard's condemnation of such unions quoted above.

However, Webster gravely undermines these common attitudes by having them advocated by the corrupt Aragonese brothers. Right at the beginning of the play, Webster establishes the princes as unambiguously evil, though neither Painter nor Belleforest does so until the brothers resort to their cruel revenge. For example, as soon as Antonio finishes his opening speech on 'a fix'd Order' (I. 1. 6) reinstated in the French Court, Bosola, the 'onely Court-Gall' (I. 1. 23), enters. Demanding that the Cardinal reward him for the murder that he committed by the Cardinal's commission, Bosola likens the brothers to 'Plum-trees' that 'grow crooked over standing-pooles' (I. 1. 48–9). Furthermore, in sharp contrast to the integrity of the French King, as described by Antonio, the brothers' evil comes to take on threatening implications: obviously the world of this play is poisoned 'neere the head' (I. 1. 14). On the other hand, the common assumptions about widows, as insisted upon by these powerful princes, become indicative of the tremendous pressure society imposed on widows.

The Duchess's ability to resist this pressure is, though, implied from the beginning. She displays great vitality not only in maintaining her self-composure during her brothers' terrifying threats, but also in transforming them into jests: to her brother's condemnation of her remarriage, she responds, 'Diamonds are of most value/They say, that have past through most Jewellers hands' (I. 1. 286–7). Moreover, no sooner have her brothers gone than she asserts her autonomy openly, by declaring her defiance of their threats:

> Shall this move me? If all my royall kindred
> Lay in my way unto this marriage:
> I'll'd make them my low foote-steps: (I. 1. 327–9)

Although later, in wooing Antonio, the Duchess may become carelessly optimistic in thinking that 'time will easily/ Scatter the tempest' (I. 1. 456–7), at this moment Webster does not present her, as Clifford Leech thought, as showing 'a rash defiance of the accepted code' (1951 69). On the contrary, she is well aware of the risk of the 'dangerous venture' (I. 1. 334) she is entering upon. She is fully conscious that her rebellion against her brothers' authority equals a fight against the whole world surrounding her, and that she is, therefore, venturing upon 'Almost impossible actions', such as only 'men in some great battailes/By apprehending danger, have atchiev'd' (I. 1. 330–4). The Duchess also hints at her awareness of the general public's likely objection to her breach of propriety, though she chooses to ignore these objections: 'Let old wives report/I wincked, and chose a husband' (I. 1. 334–5). She sees her insistence on autonomy of her self as an attempt to enter upon a new world in which she can depend upon no existing norms:

> I am going into a wildernesse,
> Where I shall find nor path, nor friendly clewe
> To be my guide— (I. 1. 344–6)

The rest of the play explores the consequences and significance of her attempt.

The Duchess and the men surrounding her

The audience's response to the Duchess's audacious act depends on their assessment of Antonio, whom the Duchess deeply loves. The widely divided opinions of critics about him[25] partly stem from the inconsistency of Webster's characterisation of this man. In the beginning of the play Antonio is presented as a man who deserves the Duchess's admiration of him as 'a compleat man' (I. 1. 421). His praise of the reformed Court of the French King shows him to be a man of Renaissance idealism, with a firm belief in the 'fix'd Order' in the Court. His intelligent evaluation of the reality around him appears clearly in his portrayals of the Arragonese princes and of Bosola. Moreover, the wordplay on the ring in Ferdinand's first speech draws attention to Antonio's ability as a man of action as well as to his virility. Embodying the Renaissance ideal of horsemanship, Antonio tells Ferdinand that this skill is the origin of 'the first Sparkes of growing resolution, that raise the minde to noble action' (I. 1. 135–6).[26] Ironically, though, it is these 'first Sparkes of growing resolution' that Webster denies him in the rest of the play. It is always the Duchess who initiates actions, while Antonio meekly follows her decisions. Although her dominance over her husband is by no means an unpleasant one, Dondolo's warning against marriage with a great lady in the *Heptameron* seems to have some relevance.

In wooing Antonio, the Duchess ardently claims her humanity, urging him also to show a human reaction:

> Sir, be confident,
> What is't distracts you? This is flesh, and blood, (Sir,)
> 'Tis not the figure cut in Allablaster
> Kneeles at my husbands tombe: Awake, awake (man) (I. 1. 438–41)

As F. L. Lucas remarked, the Duchess's allusion to her alabaster figure at her husband's tomb ominously foreshadows the end of her present happiness (1966 Vol. II. 140). More importantly, however, she is protesting here against her identity being reduced to an alabaster monument, a dehumanised image of a virtuous woman that society forces upon widows, such images of saintly women as are projected by Antonio and upheld in a 'vertuous Widdow' in Overbury's *Characters*. The Duchess's insistence on her humanity—on being 'flesh and blood'—is repeated later in the bedchamber scene, when she attempts to justify her remarriage by telling Ferdinand that she refuses to be treated 'like a holy Relique'. In contrast, the Duchess's proposal of marriage makes Antonio kneel trembling, and she has to awake the man in him. Even while they are in each other's arms, his fear recurs: 'But for your Brothers?' (I. 1. 453). In contrast to his wife's defiant resolution, Antonio is constantly fearful of the consequences of their marriage. Although this has the effect of increasing the oppressive atmosphere of the play, it is also presented as being responsible for his inefficiency and his failure to cope with his situation.

The problem of Antonio is that, though possessing gentility and humility, virtues advocated by contemporary moralists, he has neither a clear sense of his own selfhood nor the strength to establish it. Without fully understanding the meaning of his own actions, he fearfully follows the Duchess's ardent pursuit of self-fulfilment. While the earlier part of the play depicts Antonio's fear, the latter part shows the outcome of his uncertain self-identity; separated from the Duchess, his personality falls apart (Pearson, 1980 90).

When we see Antonio again in Act V, he has lost any positive attitude towards life. Despite the fact that he is still unaware of the death of his wife and children, he already regards life as 'a poore lingring life', thinking that it is 'better fall once, than be ever falling' (V. 1. 62: 73), perceiving that he has lived 'a mockery, and abuse of life' (V. III. 48). Antonio's expression of his sense of the futility of the life he has lived is sharply contrasted with the Duchess's magnificent affirmation of her selfhood in the face of death. Moreover, his dying wish, 'let my Sonne, flie the Courts of Princes' (V. IV. 71), indicates that he has also abandoned his belief in the 'fix'd Order' of the Court, a belief that he had so ardently advanced at the beginning of the play. Through the dissolution of Antonio's personality, Webster seems to suggest that the virtues praised by contemporary moralists and embodied in Antonio are insufficient to enable a man to attain nobility in a corrupt world. Unlike the Duchess, the virtuous but 'womanish, and fearefull' Antonio cannot dare to do 'what is just'; he thus fails to transcend the 'deepe pit of darknesse' (V. V. 100–3) of the gloomy world in the play.

As in the case of Vittoria and Flamineo, despite the great difference in their personalities, the Duchess and her brothers take the same general attitude towards themselves. They insist on an unconstrained assertion of their will, whereas Bosola, Antonio and the other characters in the play are essentially submissive, simply reacting to the situations created by these great people of will. As M. C. Bradbrook said, 'Ferdinand, the Cardinal and the Duchess are born to rule; their imperious tempers are innate' (1980 38). The Duchess's self-assertion differs from her brothers' only in that what she gives full rein to is the feminine urge in her, while they assert an absolute egoism.

The Duchess's marriage to Antonio, both in her flouting her brothers' opposition to her marriage and in her choosing an unsuitable partner, challenges the brothers' self-created image of being absolute, thus threatening even their sense of self. The sense of their absoluteness being challenged develops, though, in different directions in the two brothers; Ferdinand's intemperate rage shifts to a ferocious sadistic urge, whereas the Cardinal, who can be angry without such open frenzy, hides his vindictiveness, though ultimately this is just as cruel as Ferdinand's.

The driving force in the Duchess, which spurs her on in the pursuit of her will, is at first associated with the creative forces of nature. By contrast, the evils of the brothers and the pressure they exert on the Duchess are linked with the destructive elements of nature through images of disease, brutal animals, noxious worms and poisonous plants in which the play abounds. Webster eliminated Painter's reference to the Duchess's 'libidinous appetite', but a healthy female sexuality is one of the defining qualities of his Duchess. As Shakespeare does with

Cleopatra, Webster associates her sexuality with nature's generative energy.

Act III, for example, opens with Antonio's description to Delio of the Duchess's vitality as an excellent 'Feeder of pedigrees' (III. i. 6). The first half of the following bedchamber scene gives a glimpse of the happiness that results from the fulfilment of the Duchess's feminine urge. Although Antonio declared his preference for the single life in Act 1, he has now completely reversed his view, trying to dissuade Cariola from living single. The happiness of his married life is couched in terms that symbolise the richness of nature, such as 'Oliffe, Pomgranet, Mulberry', 'Flowres, precious Stones, or eminent Starres' (III. ii. 31–2).

The Duchess, though only half-consciously, wishes to create an alternative order to the orthodoxies embodied by her brothers. During her private marriage ceremony, she twice makes defiant references to the established Church represented by the Cardinal: 'What can the Church force more?' (I. i. 471) and 'How can the Church build faster?' (I. i. 474). Refusing 'all vain ceremony', she insists on a new order that will allow her to pursue 'simple vertue, which was never made/To seeme the thing it is not' (I. i. 433–4). For example, when she jokingly suggests that Antonio should adopt the new fashion of the French Court and wear his hat before his prince, she really is challenging authority, thus obliquely justifying her marriage to a commoner. She also hopes that the mode of her marriage will become a custom; she wishes that like Antonio, 'Noble men shall come with cap, and knee,/To purchase a nights lodging, of their wives' (III. ii. 4–6).

When Ferdinand secretly intrudes into the Duchess's bedchamber in Act III Scene ii, these two sets of values directly collide. The Duchess's immediate protest—

> Why might not I marry?
> I have not gone about, in this, to create
> Any new world or, custome. (III. ii. 110–12)

—shows her failure to realise that what she has actually embarked on through her marriage is indeed an attempt to create a 'new world', one that is ruled by an entirely different system of human values from that upheld in her brothers' world. The cause she puts forward to justify her marriage is her right to be human:

> Why should onely I,
> Of all the other Princes of the World

Be cas'de-up, like a holy Relique? I have youth,
And a litle beautie. (III. ii. 137–40)

The Duchess's use of the simile of 'a holy Relique' is probably an echo of the 'Relique' in 'a vertuous Widdow' in Overbury's *Characters*, where the image of a selfless, saintly woman devoting herself to the memory of her deceased husband is presented as the ideal image of a widow:

> No calamity can now come neere her, for in suffering the losse of her husband, shee accounts all the rest trifles: she hath laid his dead body in the worthyest monument that can be: Shee hath buried it in her owne heart. To conclude, shee is a Relique, that without any supers[ti]tion in the world, though she will not be kist, yet may be reuerenc't. (Sig. L8v)

While the image of 'a Relique' in Overbury's *Characters* is used to represent the steadfast, unworldly figure of 'a vertuous Widdow', the Duchess employs the same image to point out the unnaturalness and inhumanness of forcing such a concept on her. Ferdinand, however, has no understanding of her viewpoint, condemning her remarriage because of her failure to live up to this ideal, calling her 'a bare name' (III. ii. 74) and 'no essentiall thing' (III. ii. 75).

The defeat of the Duchess's insistence is inevitable because of the great power her brothers hold in their world. When the Cardinal takes away her wedding ring at the Shrine of Our Lady of Loretto, virtually nullifying her union with Antonio, her defeat is visually completed. Even the Duchess herself comes to accept the impossibility of pursuing her belief in the world she inhabits; that is, she recognises the difference between herself and the birds in the field, which can choose their own mates (III. v. 17–20). After she is banished from Ancona, whenever she is associated with nature, it is no longer through her generative energy, but only through her vulnerability and helplessness. For example, when Bosola captures her, he compares her to a silly bird allured to the nets (III. v. 98–100). Predicting her imminent death, the Duchess equates herself with the caged robin and nightingale (IV. ii. 13–14).

Nevertheless, the fact that the Duchess's spirit remains unbreakable, despite Ferdinand's persistent persecution, confirms the unquenchable power of nature within her. Even Ferdinand acknowledges the occasional subordination of a man-made law to the law of nature, when he admits parents' affection for their bastards (IV. i. 34–7). The Duchess's display of her maternal instincts in the face of her death once again emphasises her close relation to nature. Whereas, in Painter's account, it is the Duchess's son by her first husband who inherits the duchy, Webster makes Delio bring on Antonio's son at the end to be instated as the Duke 'In's mothers right' (V. v. 112). Although Antonio at his death wishes differently, it is his son, the product of the Duchess's assertion of her female desire, who ultimately is to nourish new life.[27]

Ferdinand's desire to reduce his sister to despair and madness may be interpreted from the Anglican point of view as a devilish urge to drive a person to damnation.[28] At the same time, his desire may also be seen as his unconscious attempt to restore the lost sense of his identity as absolute self. If the Duchess were to fall into despair and madness, and thus lose her sense of selfhood, her self-assertion would prove after all to be only a momentary outburst of 'the spirit [. . .] of woman', not a serious challenge to his absolutism. Such a development would restore his confidence in his absolute power. Ironically, however, as Ferdinand continues his persecution, the Duchess's spirit rises. She manages to confront the consequences of her self-asserting act with open eyes:

> I am not mad yet, to my cause of sorrow.
> Th'heaven ore my head, seemes made of molt[o]n brasse,
> The earth of flaming sulphure, yet I am not mad: (IV. ii. 24-6)

It is her brothers who cannot endure to face the consequence of their own acts. At the sight of his dead sister, Ferdinand's eyes dazzle and he goes mad. Similarly, after the death of the Duchess, the Cardinal suffers from a persistent guilty conscience, getting 'puzzell'd in a question about hell' (V. v. 1). And at his death he hopes that he may 'Be layd by, and never thought of' (V. v. 89). These great men not only fail to perceive the illusion of their absolutism, but also come to lose their very sense of selfhood, ending as 'a kind of nothing' (V. v. 78).

Bosola, employed by the brothers, is Webster's great invention, created out of Painter's brief reference to 'Thys newe Iudas and pestilent manqueller', a 'bloudy beast' named Danile de Bozola. As the play progresses, Bosola becomes, with the Duchess, the central interest of the play, not only because he is a product of profound psychological study, but also because his relationship with the Duchess throws into relief various aspects of her selfhood. As is the case with Flamineo in *The White Devil*, role-play constitutes the essence of Bosola's being. Throughout the play, he acts various roles—a melancholic court railer, an intelligencer, a persecutor, a bellman, a tombmaker, an assassin and, finally, a revenger. We also hear that he has played yet other roles before, such as a 'fantasicall scholler', a 'speculative man' (III. 3. 50: 57), a soldier, a murderer and a slave who served in the galleys. To put one's talents into full practice was a Renaissance form of self-realisation, but the problem for men of intellect and will, but of humble birth, was that they had no way to exercise their ability except through their connections with men of power.[29] Like Flamineo, Bosola had accomplished qualities suitable for advancement at the Court; he studied at the University of Padua, was a valiant soldier, and even had experience of 'travel'. Like Flamineo and Vittoria, though, he is fully aware that his humble position in the social order allows him no chance to realise himself on his own, and so he has entered the service of the Cardinal, one of the most influential men in their world.

What distinguishes Bosola from Flamineo is that, for all his cynicism, he still clings to the ethics of feudal loyalty. For example, when he criticises the Duchess's feigned act of expelling Antonio from her household, he asserts this principle; even though he evidently intends to search out the Duchess's true motive, his assertion sounds serious:

> You shall want him,
> For know an honest states-man to a Prince,
> Is like a Cedar, planted by a Spring,
> The Spring bathes the trees roote, the gratefull tree
> Rewards it with his shadow: (III. ii. 261–5)

As Robert Ornstein rightly noted, Bosola is a 'feudal liege man brought up to Jacobean date' (1960 144). Service to the Cardinal has committed him even to playing the roles of murderer and slave in the galleys. Although he has loyally discharged these duties, the Cardinal attaches no significance to his service. While attempting to obtain freedom to be himself by acting roles for great men, Bosola, like Flamineo, has lost all sense of self-identity except in his relationships with men of power. Since he cannot find the meaning of his own life, he must find it in others' recognition of his service. It is this urge, as well as his need for money, that compels him to pursue 'rewards' and to accept Ferdinand's employment as his intelligencer, even though he knows that it will lead him to hell.[30] Webster makes this point explicit by having Bosola reverse the meaning of Montaigne's passage: 'The reward of wel doing is the doing, & the fruit of our duty is our dutie' (II. xvi.), devaluing the proverbial view that virtue is its own reward: 'Miserable age, where onely the reward/Of doing well, is the doing of it' (I. i. 31–2).[31]

Although his essential personality remains unchanged until the end, all his characteristics of negative thinking undergo a considerable change in the course of his contact with the Duchess. Bosola's disillusionment with the world is shaken first upon hearing the Duchess's confession of her secret marriage with Antonio, which he takes as an example of a prince advancing an obscure man solely for his worth. While elated to have obtained the vital information that he knows will please Ferdinand, he seems serious in admiring her act:

> Do I not dreame? can this ambitious age
> Have so much goodnes in't, as to prefer
> A man, meerely for worth: without these shadowes
> Of wealth and painted honors? (III. ii. 276-9)

Bosola sees the Duchess's choice of her partner as symbolising the revival of the old ethics: 'some preferment in the world can yet/Arise from merit' (III. ii. 285-6). Although his tone is his usual sardonic one, he explicates at length the social significance of the Duchess's marriage—its significance to neglected people in society, such as the 'unbenific'd Scholler', dowerless maids, soldiers or 'neglected Poets' (III. ii. 283-91). For the first time, Bosola experiences a moral conflict between his loyalty to his master and his admiration for the Duchess. Nevertheless, the experience does not affect his professionalism and, to ensure her capture, he even suggests that she might feign a pilgrimage to Loretto. And yet, he begins to recognise in the Duchess's self-asserting act of marrying Antonio a possibility of human integrity that he had thought had ceased to exist. From then on, while playing his various roles as Ferdinand's creature, he constantly tests this possibility in the Duchess, by trying to deprive her of meaning to her life and by confronting her with reductive views of human existence. By dramatising the Duchess's responses to Bosola's futile trials, Webster throws light on the significance of her assertive power from various angles. Webster's method is rightly admired by Gunnar Boklund as 'one of the greatest achievements of Elizabethan kaleidoscopic characterization' (1962 143).

Bosola's testing of the Duchess's mental strength, which produces grotesque effects, is highlighted in Act IV4. The entire act presents the process in which, by faithfully executing Ferdinand's order to bring her to despair, Bosola gradually takes away from the Duchess everything that makes life meaningful to her, until she is left with nothing but her sense of selfhood. Her suffering in her imprisonment is so nobly borne that Bosola admires it at the beginning of the scene. But when the wax figures of her supposedly dead husband and children are shown, her grief drives her to the verge of despair. Thinking that her existence has now become utterly meaningless, she wishes for a quick death, even cursing the stars. This scene brings about uniquely grotesque effects; though the Duchess's sorrow is genuine and tragic, these figures are fake wax objects.[32] For example, when Bosola speaks his famous line, 'Looke you, the Starres shine still' (IV. i. 98), he asserts the absolute indifference of the supernatural to human affairs, thus attempting to deprive her of any ideological justification for her suffering. Now that she thinks that all the meaning of life has been lost to her—husband, children, her own freedom, even ideological support—she appears to Cariola only like her 'picture in the gallery,/A deale of life in shew, but none in practise', or like 'some reverend monument/Whose ruines are even pittied' (IV. ii. 31-4). And yet, despite her agonies, she still preserves her spiritual strength, and though her speeches in this scene betray some mental imbalance, she can still proclaim that she is not mad.

Bosola employs another grotesque means to destroy the Duchess's spirit.[33] He lets madmen enter the room exhibiting antimasque-like capering, but his attempt fails to destroy the Duchess's mind. After the madmen's antimasque fails, Bosola reappears disguised as an old man, informing the Duchess of her approaching death. In *The White Devil*, in the face of her death Vittoria undertakes one final battle against society's conventional assumptions about womanhood. The Duchess's last fight is on a still larger scale: it is not merely against society's reductive views of womanhood, but also against conventional concepts of the futility of human existence, concepts that Bosola has constantly asserted. When the Duchess asks the disguised Bosola a very existential question, 'Who am I?' (IV. ii. 114), he defines her identity in conventional terms of *de contemptu mundi*: 'Thou art a box of worme-seede, at best, a salvatory of greene mummey' (IV. ii. 115-16). Then, by drawing on the proverbial idea that the soul is imprisoned in the body, he attempts to show the meaninglessness of the human soul because of the limits of its knowledge, employing the familiar metaphor of a lark in a cage (IV. ii. 120-3). Yet, the Duchess still insists on her transcendence over Bosola's definitions of human existence: 'I am Duchess of *Malfy* still' (IV. ii. 131). Bosola then attempts another assault upon her sense of integrity by indicating the futility of the glory of her status. Nevertheless, Bosola's attempts to destroy her spirit all fail. Challenged by the full range of these reductive views of humanity, and confronted by the realities of death—executioners, coffin, rope and bell—the Duchess still declares that 'it affrights not me' (IV. ii.159).

For all the suffering she has gone through, she herself does not think that her life has been 'a *generall mist of error*' (IV. ii. 174), as described in the dirge sung by Bosola disguised as a bellman. At her last moment, in contrast to the men who surround her, she reveals neither regret nor cynicism over the life she has chosen to live. Showing consideration for others—her children, Cariola, even the executioners—she kneels in the face of death, adopting a Christian gesture of humility.

When Bosola is denied any reward by Ferdinand after the Duchess's death, he tearfully repents. But his repentance, as has been said, is motivated not by his sense of justice, but by his anger at being again neglected. It is this anger that makes him decide to go to Milan, where he 'will enact' something 'Worth my dejection' (IV. ii. 361–2). He now begins to think that he can prove his true selfhood by playing yet another role, this time for Antonio, as revenger upon the two brothers. Bosola thinks that he can be absolved from all responsibility for his previous acts and can prove his goodness simply by changing sides from the persecutors to the victims. Only after his accidental murder of Antonio does he realise for the first time the absurdity of playing roles for others and decide to be 'mine owne example' (V. iv. 82). Now, though, he has nothing with which to prove his selfhood except his old trade of murder. After killing the Aragonese brothers, he faces his own death with the same self-satisfaction as Flamineo shows at his death; to the amazed onlookers, he explains the murders as 'Revenge, for the Duchesse of *Malfy*', 'for *Antonio*', 'for lustfull *Julia*', and only finally for himself (V. v. 80–4). His explanation indicates that he still sees even his final action mainly in terms of a role played for others. Bosola, thus, having lost his selfhood in the various roles he has played for others, fails to become 'my own example'. At death, Bosola's view of the world still remains deeply pessimistic and sceptical. Yet his last words indicate that through his contact with the Duchess his cynical views of humanity have been somewhat modified. Bosola now seems aware that, after all, there exist some 'worthy mindes' who can rise above 'this gloomy world', though the great majority of its inhabitants including himself, are mere examples of 'womanish, and fearefull' mankind (V. v. 101).

Social significance of the Duchess's assertion of self-actualisation

The Duchess of Malfi holds a unique position in Jacobean drama in that it explores a tragic vision through a woman's insistence on her selfhood, a selfhood that is not entirely absorbed in her passion for those she loves. It is true that the Duchess's femaleness is most clearly embodied in her love for her husband and children. In this sense Catherine Belsey is right in seeing the Duchess's motherhood and family-oriented attitudes as representing the emergence of the new seventeenth-century ideal of the affectionate nuclear family (1985 199–200). However, the Duchess's assertion differs in one vital point from the mere female desire for domestic happiness, which was advanced by liberal humanism. Her self-assertion is constantly depicted as representing a woman's claim to her humanity freed from the fictional images of womanhood created and imposed by society. Such recognition of the possibility of human integrity in a woman's self-assertion was a strikingly new attitude in the drama written by male playwrights at the time.

The vital issue is how Webster dramatises the transformation of his heroine from a transgressor of Jacobean social and moral norms at the beginning of the play into the 'sacred Innocence' (IV. ii. 342) as described by Bosola after her death. The brothers' diabolical revenge focuses the audience's attention on their evils, making her offence seem less serious. It is the Duchess's profound sense of the importance of her selfhood, in spite of her recognition of its tragic outcome, that enables her to transcend not merely the Jacobean concept of female self-assertion, 'the spirit [. . .] of woman', but also the reductive views of human existence she is constantly presented with by Bosola. The Duchess's famous assertion that she is 'Duchess of *Malfi* still' indicates her pride, not in her political position, as interpreted by Bosola, but in her having remained faithful to the imperatives of her inner thoughts despite the tragic consequences. It is also important to note that the Duchess's submission to Divine will at her death does not necessarily show the final dissolution of her self. Although she accepts her helplessness in front of the supernatural and thus shows humility, she still maintains her belief in the rightness of her action. For her, 'th'other world' is where she will 'meete such excellent company' (IV. ii. 199), the 'eternal Church' where she will never be parted from her family; it is a place where the dictates of her self will finally be fulfilled.

In the meantime, as Jacqueline Pearson demonstrated, the play's world cannot maintain this high tragic level achieved by the Duchess (1980 90–5). Act 5 shows the dissolution of this tragic vision of human existence into a satirical vision of a 'gloomy world' inhabited by 'womanish, and fearefull' mankind. Yet the play offers the audience the opportunity to reflect upon the significance of one woman's insistence on human integrity. It is indeed Webster's great irony that the only character in the play that proves not to be 'womanish' is a woman.

The Duchess's rejection of the Jacobean ideal of the widow and her insistence on her individuality foreshadows the claims later articulated by Hic-Mulier in *Haec Vir: Or The Womanish-Man* (1620), a pamphlet published several years after the first performance of Webster's play. Although Hic-Mulier's assertion of her humanity centres on a specific issue, that is, women's right to dress themselves in unconventional mannish fashions, the basic principles advanced in her argument recall those voiced by the Duchess in defending her remarriage and her unconventional choice of partner. Both women long for the realisation of a new order, one in which, freed from established laws and social customs, they can pursue 'simple vertue, which was never made/To seeme the thing it is not'. (A detailed examination of the significance of Hic-Mulier's assertion can be found in Chapter 5 of this book.)

In the actual cases of contemporary women flouting marriage conventions, Webster may well have seen the possibilities of female claims to autonomous selfhood as are to be proclaimed by Hic-Mulier. Instead of condemning women's self-assertive drive simply as 'the spirit [. . .] of woman', as was commonly done both in contemporary drama and society, Webster explored in *The Duchess of Malfi* its positive aspects. The vision is presented as tragic, for, though such a drive might lead to the affirmation of human integrity, it would also cause the destruction of the person because of the ferocious reactions it would raise in men of power and the disruption it would cause to society. That such a tragic vision was not merely fictional is shown by the actual ordeals suffered by contemporary self-assertive women, such as Lady Arabella Stuart and Lady Penelope Rich. The Duchess's tragedy lies in that, in the world she inhabits, her assertion of her selfhood can never be realised due to the many restrictions upon her. As Ferdinand says in the bedchamber scene, only a woman of lower status, such as a shepherdess, is allowed to pursue her will in her choice of a marriage partner. Yet, several years after the play, even a middle-class woman, like Hic-Mulier would claim her dignity in following the dictates of her self.

Representations of female desire in Kabuki: *Musume Dojoji*

The characteristic features of the representations of a female assertion of self in *The Duchess of Malfi* become even clearer when they are compared to one of the well-known Kabuki pieces called *Musume Dojoji (A Maiden at Dojoji [Temple])*. The story of a maiden at Dojoji is dramatised in both Kabuki and Noh plays.[34] These two versions of the story are basically the same, though in the Kabuki performance more emphasis is placed on actions in the dancing. The story itself derives from various sources, mostly texts whose purpose was to disseminate the teachings of Buddhism, dating from the eleventh century onwards. The Kabuki version of the story narrates that a young priest, Anchin, encounters the heroine, Kiyohime, during his pilgrimage to the sacred shrine of Kumano, in a southern part of the mainland of Japan. They are attracted to each other, but since Anchin is on his pilgrimage, he leaves her, pledging that he will come to visit her on his way home. However, realising that his further commitment to Kiyohime will prevent his pursuit of the truth of Buddhism, upon his return he breaks his promise, passing the area where she lives without making contact with her. When she learns that Anchin has failed to fulfil his promise, she runs after him, turning herself into a serpent in order to cross the Arita River, and catches up with him when he has reached a temple called Dojoji. To escape from her, he hides himself inside the great bell of the temple. Suspecting this, Kiyohime, who still has the appearance of a serpent, destroys the bell with flames that issue from her mouth, in the process burning Anchin to death.

Actually, the Kabuki play starts at the point when, hundreds of years afterwards, a ceremony to inaugurate a new holy bell is about to take place in Dojoji. While the priests are praying for the successful installation of the new bell, a female professional dancer enters the site of the ceremony. Since women are prohibited from taking part in such a holy event, particularly since the former bell was destroyed in a tragedy caused by a woman, at first she is dismissed by the priests. Nonetheless, impressed by her ardour, the priests finally admit her to the site on the condition that she will dedicate her sacred dance to the inauguration of the bell. While dancing, she is transformed into a serpent, and thus it is revealed that the dancer is in fact the spirit of Kiyohime. The aesthetic highlights both in the Kabuki play and in the Noh version of the same story occur at the moments when the heroine expresses her hidden vindictiveness and sexual frustration. In the Kabuki version, Kiyohime, transformed into a serpent (this is shown by her silver-coloured kimono with a pattern of scales), looks from the top of the bell over the frightened priests, and the transformation from her innocent-looking beauty as a young dancer to the beauty of a frustrated mature woman is considered to be the most enjoyable moment for the audience. Thus, while the sources of the story emphasise the dangers of a female desiring a man who is dedicating himself to the teachings of Buddhism, the characterisation of Kiyohime places in the foreground the aesthetic aspects of female desire as well.

At the same time, the monstrosity of female desire is also made explicit through the representations of a snake crawling around the bell in the final scene. But the significance of this is complicated, partly because this scene constitutes the climax of the play, presenting ultimate beauty as combined with monstrosity, and partly because the role of the heroine is actually played by a man and, thus, the whole narrative of female desire is rendered as a fiction. And yet the uncontrollable quality of female desire hidden in a woman is stressed when the beautiful dancer turns into a fire-breathing serpent, an embodiment of desire and revenge.

Both English Renaissance plays and Kabuki plays represent theatrical traditions in which female roles are enacted by men and in which, therefore, the female desire represented on the stage is a fiction created with full consciousness of the male gaze; and in both of them female desire is presented as a potential threat to the social order or to a male sense of identity. When *Musume Dojoji* was written and first performed in the Edo period of the early nineteenth century, patriarchal power as a social system was too strong and stable for any female power to overturn. Nevertheless, privately, female power was still a threat for men who wanted to dedicate themselves to the pursuit of religious truth. The attraction men continued to feel for female eroticism despite its disruptive power seems to be embodied in the combined form of beauty and grotesque monstrosity in the climactic scene of *Dojoji*. English Renaissance plays, on the other hand, were performed at a time when women began to feel that their selfhood was no longer entirely constrained in the notion of womanhood as defined in their society, and when some women, like the Duchess of Malfi or others such as those dealt with earlier in this chapter, dared to take socially disruptive actions to assert their desire for self-actualisation. Female self-assertiveness, in particular their sexual drive, could thus be an actual threat to male authority in seventeenth-century England in a way that was not possible in early nineteenth-century Japan. It is interesting to note, however, that, due to an awareness of the male gaze in the audience, as well as of the audience's sense of distance from the authenticity of a female character's feelings created through the body of a male actor, both English Renaissance plays and some Kabuki plays tend to use grotesque elements to present a female self-assertiveness uncontrollable by men, a tactic that has the effect of belittling female power.

Elizabeth Cary's *The Tragedy of Mariam*

Elizabeth Cary's *The Tragedie of Mariam, the Faire Queene of Iewry* was published in 1613, but had been written much earlier in around 1603.

In 1602, at the age of seventeen, Elizabeth married Sir Henry Cary, later Viscount Falkland. After their wedding, Sir Henry went to fight in the Netherlands in 1603. While her husband was away, Elizabeth lived first at home with her authoritarian parents, and then with her mother-in-law, Lady Katherine Cary, with whom she soon found she was incompatible.[35] She probably started writing *Mariam* either while she was still living with her parents or when she was already with her exceedingly domineering mother-in-law. The play consists of a clash between Mariam's strong, though often contradictory, sense of self and the dominant ideologies of marriage, which correspond to those in early seventeenth-century England. Lewalski and many other commentators have pointed out the parallels with Cary's personal life (Beilin, 1987 158; Lewalski, 1993 190–1; Wray, 2012 3–11). As shown in the biography probably written by her surviving son,[36] Cary's whole life was marked by a constant struggle against domestic and social pressures that acted to keep her within the confines of the contemporary female ideals of wife and mother. Her struggle eventually led to her conversion to Catholicism in 1626, which resulted in domestic, social and even political turmoil.

Elizabeth Cary's father, Sir Lawrence Tanfield, was a successful lawyer who, after 1607, became Chief Baron of the Exchequer. Her mother was Elizabeth Symondes, descended from country gentry. Elizabeth was their only child and grew up in Burford, Oxfordshire. She was a precocious child who loved learning and voraciously read books, probably including Florio's translation of Montaigne's *Essays*, from her father's library; she mastered five foreign languages on her own when very young. Her fondness for learning was not necessarily approved of by her parents, especially by her mother, so she had to bribe her servants to bring her candles so that she could read at night. When she was twelve, her father gave her Calvin's *Institutes* to read, to which she made many objections, pointing out various contradictions in Calvin's argument. Sir Lawrence is said to have been bemused by his daughter's aversion to Calvinism (R. S., 1861 7). During the time that Sir Henry was away in the Netherlands, Elizabeth's mother, apparently considering her daughter incapable of composing a properly wifely letter to her husband, hired someone to ghost-write letters on her behalf to Sir Henry. We do not know how Elizabeth reacted to this humiliating arrangement by her own mother, which denied her authorship of her personal letters to her husband, but Sir Henry seems to have been quite impressed by the letters she herself wrote to him later on (R. S., 1861 8–9).

As she had been a person of such intellectual independence since childhood, her new status as wife, and the new circumstances of her life with Sir Henry, who is said to have been 'absolute' (R. S., 1861 14), and with her autocratic mother-in-law, must have caused her to question contemporary ideas of wifely submission. Yet, ironically, even such repressive patriarchal situations sometimes lead to an unexpected result. We are told that because her mother-in-law opposed Elizabeth's fondness for learning and took all her books away from her chamber, she started writing verses (R. S., 1861 8). As its author was 'governed' by the values of her society in many ways, *The Tragedy of Mariam* is replete with gender anxieties and statements of stereotypical ideas of womanhood. Furthermore, Mariam's emerging sense of self is presented as contradictory in various respects. These aspects of the play have led some critics to see it as chiefly endorsing the dominant ideological system of marriage.[37] Catherine Belsey interprets Mariam's vacillating attitudes as evidence that she has not yet quite established her selfhood (1985 171-5). On the other hand, critics such as Lewalski and Beilin stress the significance of the subversive elements in Mariam's rebellion against her husband's authority. And yet these critics see Mariam's resistance mainly in relation to the intellectual or religious milieu of the time. Lewalski notes its parallel with contemporary French Senecan dramas and with histories in the Tacitean mode, which allow for the conflict of ideological positions and for sympathetic attitudes towards resistance (1990 190-201).[38] Beilin sees Mariam's resistance and her execution by Herod as a Christian allegory, the martyrdom of Christ (1987 159-60).[39] Yet, more attention should be paid to the significance of the play's structure, which points to the emergence of a new discourse on womanhood.

The play is structured in such a way that each scene presents itself as a site of the clash between a woman's selfhood and various conventional ideologies concerning womanhood. When the play opens, the Jewish people are faced with the possibility of a great change in their society due to the news of the death of their tyrannical King, Herod. People react differently to this new situation, but the most complicated reaction comes from Mariam, Herod's beloved and beautiful wife. The play begins with Mariam's soliloquy, in which she eloquently articulates her own baffling psychological state. The play shows her constantly trying to analyse her inner state by means of the dominant ideologies of marriage in society. First of all, she has come to consider it wrong to condemn the changeability of the human mind, for her feeling for Herod has suddenly altered at the news of his death. She hated Herod, who, despite his infatuation with her, had murdered her brother, Aristobolus, and plotted against her grandfather, Hircanus, in order to ensure his own political power. Furthermore, when, on a previous occasion, he was called to Rome by Antony, he left secret orders with Josephus, the former husband of his sister, Salome, to kill Mariam if he failed to return, so that no one else could marry her. Josephus, however, revealed this secret to her. On Herod's return, Mariam protested against his command, but, at the suggestion of Salome, Herod executed Josephus immediately on the false charge of his having had a liaison with Mariam. When Herod was again called to Rome, this time by Octavius Caesar, who had recently triumphed over Antony, he not only left the same command with his servant Sohemus, but also imprisoned Mariam in a room with Sohemus as her guardian. Out of pity for the great Queen, Sohemus revealed Herod's secret order about her. Indeed Mariam had good reasons to hate her husband:

> When *Herod* liu'd, that now is done to death,
> Oft haue I wisht that I from him were free:
> Oft haue I wisht that he might lose his breath,
> Oft haue I wisht his Carkas dead to see. (1. 1. 17–20)[40]

However, for all her hatred of Herod, to her embarrassment she suddenly feels love for him, remembering the ardent passion he bestowed upon her while he was alive. Now she cannot stop her tears, and realises that, contrary to the general assumption about human nature, the mind can feel 'both griefe and ioy' (1. 1. 12) for the same person. Cary's representation of Mariam's unstable emotions may have come from the concept of changing human emotions argued in Florio's Montaigne.

Seen from the perspective of the post-modern theories of Jacques Lacan and Michel Foucault,[41] the complex feelings Mariam suddenly finds in herself for the supposedly dead Herod are obviously the unstable drive of desire, which springs from her lack of fulfilment at his death. Yet, having no access to such theories, Mariam, or rather the author, has no discourse to elucidate this complicated feelings in herself. Instead, Mariam tries to explain her contradictory state of mind by drawing on the dominant ideologies of womanhood in the society in which she lives. First, she tries to rely on the stereotypical idea of irrational female passion, blaming herself for having neglected Herod's love because of her rage against him. Then she brings in the ideology of wifely submission, which leads her to consider her hatred for him as a failing in her wifely duty: 'Hate [. . .] kept my heart from paying him his debt' (1. 1. 23–4). She also tries to excuse herself for this failure through another stereotypical idea, that of women's intellectual weakness:

> My Sexe pleads pardon, pardon then afford,
> Mistaking is with vs, but too too common. (1. 1. 9–10)

Nevertheless, Mariam is not entirely convinced by her own explanations. She still feels love for Herod and, at the same time, extreme anger against his possessiveness, which she thinks denies her personal independence:

> And blame me not, for *Herods* Iealousie
> Had power euen constancie it selfe to change:
> For hee by barring me from libertie,
> To shunne my ranging, taught me first to range. (1. 1. 25–8)

Mariam considers Herod's command to kill her in the event of his own death so exorbitant that not only her hatred for him but even her adultery with another man could be justified, though, bound up by the contemporary dictate of wife's fidelity, she does not dare to resort to such a deviant retaliation:

> But yet too chast a Scholler was my hart,
> To learne to loue another then my Lord: (1. 1. 29–30)

Thus Cary talks about conventional ideologies of womanhood not to endorse them, but to examine whether or not they can explain Mariam's confused state of mind. As a result, it can explicate neither her love for Herod nor her strong hatred of him. Cary can provide no discourse to systematise Mariam's complicated feelings. And yet, this absence itself denotes a failure in the power of the contemporary ideologies of the marriage system, and thus points to the emergence of subversive forces in Mariam's self-consciousness, which could have led to an alternative view of womanhood in society.

Like Elizabeth Cary herself, Mariam is 'governed' by ideologies in society. This is most clearly shown in the scenes that focus on her, her mother and Salome, Herod's sister. At the close of her soliloquy in the first scene, Mariam temporarily comes to terms with her divided self, deciding to dismiss her hatred for Herod on the grounds of the norm of wifely submission:

> And more I owe him for his loue to me,
> The deepest loue that euer yet was seene: (1. 1. 57–8)

However, right after this, her mother, Alexandra, enters and starts to impose other ideologies upon Mariam, trying to make her look at her problems from these perspectives. She insists on the inappropriateness of Mariam's lament for Herod's death for three reasons: first, their familial obligations to Aristobolus and Hircanus, whom he murdered, and the consequent necessity of revenge against him; second, Herod's racial inferiority to them; third, the unreliability of men's affection, which might cause Herod to go back to his former wife, Doris, whom he divorced in order to marry Mariam. Moreover, resorting to the common idea that women can obtain power only through their relationships with powerful men, Alexandra regrets that she did not send Mariam's portrait to Antony when he was in power. If she had done so, Alexandra thinks, Antony would have forsaken Cleopatra, thus avoiding his tragic defeat by Caesar, and in the celebration of Antony's triumph over Caesar, Mariam might have been set in the place of honour instead of Cleopatra.

Mariam can respond to most of these conventional arguments only in conservative ways. She does not have an available language that would allow her to deliver a more radical retort to her mother. Yet her flat denial of the possibility of her becoming Antony's mistress indicates her strong sense of self in terms of chastity:

> Not to be Emprise of aspiring *Rome*,
> Would *Mariam* like to *Cleopatra* liue:
> With purest body will I presse my Toome,
> And wish no fauours *Anthony* could giue. (1. 2. 204–7)

Here again, Mariam's sense of personal integrity is based on the stereotypical virtue of female chastity, but unlike the chaste wives depicted by male Renaissance playwrights, she insists on maintaining the purity of her body not for the sake of her husband's honour, but for her own integrity. Here we can observe a woman's emerging sense of self, independent of her husband, which underlines a potential to challenge the husband's authority.

At the same time, it is not only Alexandra but also Mariam who is represented as preoccupied with notions of race and class. Like Alexandra, Mariam articulates her strong sense of superiority over Herod and his ancestors. In Act 1 Scene 3, Mariam and Alexandra on one side, and Salome on the other, start bickering. Mariam's response to Salome, who falsely slanders her as unfaithful, is charged with the prejudice against race and class found in Elizabethan and Jacobean England, though here they are transported to the Palestinian context of the play:

> Though I thy brothers face had neuer seene,
> My birth, thy baser birth so farre exceld,
> I had to both of you the Princesse bene.
> Thou party Iew, and party Edomite,
> Thou Mongrell: issu'd from reiected race,
> Thy Ancestors against the Heauens did fight,
> And thou like them wilt heauenly birth disgrace. (1. 3. 240–6)

Salome refutes Mariam's insult from an egalitarian point of view:

> Still twit you me with nothing but my birth,
> What ods betwixt your ancestors and mine?
> Both borne of *Adam*, both were made of Earth,
> And both did come from holy *Abrahams* line. (1. 3. 247–50)

Again, faced with a new concept of race, Mariam has no language to argue back. She therefore shifts the point, blaming Salome for having in the past made false allegations of a love affair between her and Josephus, Salome's former husband. Alexandra is worse. She even refuses to continue her conversation with Salome on the grounds of her inferiority in race and class: 'let vs goe: it is no boote/To let the head contend against the foote' (1. 3. 267–8).

Despite the difference in race and class, Salome makes an interesting parallel with Mariam. Drawing on the Biblical description of Salome (Fischer, 1985 235) rather than on Josephus's account, Elizabeth Cary makes her a foil to Mariam, portraying her as an utterly wicked woman whose sexual indulgence destroys not only her husbands, but many others around her. Through the conventional use of the difference in their complexions, Cary makes the contrast between them. As Dympna Callaghan has pointed out, whether the real colour of the historical Mariam, who was a Jew, was white is uncertain, but Cary portrays her throughout the play as a traditional female beauty, symbolised by her white complexion with 'rosy' cheeks (1994 163–77). The blackness of Salome's complexion, on the other hand, is stressed throughout the play. Salome is described as a woman who is constantly driven by desire. Once her sexual urge, whether for Josephus or Constabarus, was fulfilled through marriage, she was driven by desire for another man; she is now plotting to get rid of Constabarus in order to marry Silleus. However, Salome's constant sexual drive is basically the same as the love that Mariam suddenly feels for her supposedly dead husband, as stressed in Florio's Montaigne, both arising from the unpredictability of desire. Moreover, the way in which Salome defies the social code recalls Mariam's refusal to submit herself to wifely obedience. Furthermore, both women are blamed by others for being too outspoken. Salome's outspokenness is harshly criticised by her present husband, Constabarus (1. 6.), whereas Sohemus is afraid that 'Vnbridled speech is *Mariams* worst disgrace' (3. 3. 1186). Thus, the contemporary notion of race and class presented by Cary is, in fact, deconstructed in the text through the similarities between Mariam and Salome.[42]

What makes a great difference between Mariam and Salome is that since the latter is characterised as a wicked woman, the author gives her a language in which to expound her desire and justify her breach of the moral code. Having killed her first husband by manipulating Herod, Salome finds no meaning whatsoever in the value system of society; she no longer feels that a sense of shame or honour is important to her. She even challenges the unfairness of society in which women cannot initiate divorce:

> Why should such priuiledge to man be giuen?
> Or giuen to them, why bard from women then?
> Are men then we in greater grace with Heauen?
> Or cannot women hate as well as men? (1. 4. 315–18)

Under Jewish law at the time, women were strictly forbidden to initiate a divorce (Lewalski, 1990 195). Yet Salome's challenge has a wider implication here, since it has relevance to marital conditions in early seventeenth-century England. Although divorce in the modern sense was unknown at that time, it was possible, albeit difficult, to secure an annulment on the grounds that a supposed marriage had actually been void. A judicial separation was possible on the grounds of adultery or the cruelty of either party. In practice, men tended to sue on the grounds of adultery, and women on the grounds of cruelty (Ingram, 1987 171–88; Stone, 1990). That not all English women in this period were satisfied with this legal system can be illustrated by a few actual cases in which women obtained annulment or judicial separation on the evidence, though dubious, of their husbands' physical impotence; the most notorious case was Lady Frances Howard's annulment suit against the third Earl of Essex in 1613.[43]

It is also interesting to note that Salome's challenge to the authority of the husband invites an accusation of her masculinity, which recalls typical Jacobean reactions against female self-assertion, such as those observed in King James's order against women wearing mannish clothes in 1620, or in contemporary pamphlets against female masculinity such as *Hic Mulier*. Constabarus, Salome's second husband, criticises Salome's assertion of autonomy in such terms:

> Are Hebrew women now trāsform'd to men?
> Why do you not as well our battels fight,
> And weare our armour? Suffer this, and then
> Let all the world be topsie turued quite. (1. 6. 435–8)

Thus, while Salome, since she is a wicked character, is given a language that can accommodate a woman's sense of an independent self, Mariam's self-awareness is presented only through the incompatibility between what ideologies in society define as femininity and what Mariam actually feels as a woman.

This is also the case in Act 3 Scene 3, in which the Chorus delivers its criticism of Mariam's decision not to submit to Herod upon hearing the news of his safe return. The unsteady drive of desire Mariam felt for Herod immediately disappears at this unexpected news. She decides never to subject herself to his authority, even forswearing his bed. She knows that she can captivate Herod with her charming smiles and gentle words; she also knows that if she does not accept the role of wifely submission, Salome and her mother, taking advantage of the discord between Mariam and Herod, will plot against her. Neither of these thoughts convinces Mariam to conform to the conventional concept of wifehood. Placed in parallel with Salome's similar decision, Mariam's bold decision makes clear her emerging sense of selfhood, which, like Salome's actions, challenges the contemporary ideologies of womanhood and of a husband's authority. But here again, unlike her portrayal of Salome, Elizabeth Cary does not furnish Mariam with any alternative discourse to articulate her state of mind. Instead, she makes Mariam prove her personal integrity by asserting confidentially her 'innocence', a vital element in the contemporary notion of goodness in women:

> Oh what a shelter is mine innocence,
> To shield me from the pangs of inward griefe:
> Gainst all mishaps it is my faire defence,
> And to my sorrowes yeelds a large reliefe.
> [. . .]
> Let my distressed state vnpittied bee,
> Mine innocence is hope enough for mee. (3. 3. 1174–83)

'Innocence' is, however, not an appropriate term for describing Mariam's feelings here. It can be interpreted as her innocence of the false charge of her liaison with Sohemus. It can also be seen, as argued by Belsey and Fischer (Belsey, 1985 172–3; Fischer, 1985 234), to imply her innocence of hypocrisy, a hypocrisy in hiding the discrepancy between her true feelings and her acceptance of wifely submission. Yet, in either interpretation, the term 'innocence' is not quite adequate to explain the situation she is in. What makes Mariam decide to defy Herod's authority is her belief that she is doing nothing wrong in the situation she is in; she is 'innocent', she insists, in challenging the traditional concept of wifehood. This must have been the most subversive attitude possible for a woman in sixteenth- and early-seventeenth century England; wifely obedience constituted the cornerstone of the whole patriarchal system at the time, by virtue of the analogy between kingly and divine authority and that of the husband.[44] Elizabeth Cary had no language—except for the conventional word 'innocence'—to explain the exceedingly subversive attitude Mariam is taking towards her husband. In the meantime, the author imposes the conservative concepts of wifehood on Mariam through the Chorus, thereby showing that Mariam's selfhood cannot be contained by these views.

The Chorus at the end of Act 3 Scene 3 first advocates an Elizabethan and Jacobean commonplace that a woman must keep herself spotless, and that it is equally important for her to keep herself free from suspicion. Therefore, she should not disclose her private feelings to a man other than to her husband, as Mariam did to her custodian, Sohemus. Then the Chorus asserts one of the most important dictates for a woman at the time: that, once married, a woman should entirely submit herself to her husband's authority and that, to possess her own sense of self constitutes a usurpation of his right—

> When to their Husbands they themselues doe bind,
> Doe they not wholy giue themselues away?
> Or giue they but their body not their mind,
> Reseruing that though best, for others' prey?
> No sure, their thoughts no more can be their owne,
> And therefore should to none but one be knowne. (3. 3. 1237–42)

Some critics take these views expressed by the Chorus as the author's endorsement of contemporary ideologies. Considered in the whole dramatic context, however, the Chorus's speeches function to highlight

Mariam's subversive attitude: she acts against their ideas of wifehood, such as 'Fitnesse' according to Overbury's term.

In the next scene, when Herod comes back, ardently wishing to see his beautiful Mariam, she appears in a sombre dress and demonstrates her resistance to his authority. He gets extremely upset, but tries to appease her in various, though silly, ways; he promises her titles, land or wealth, without even trying to understand her feelings. Cary presents this point clearly by making Mariam blame him for not caring for her as a person, but simply treating her as a beautiful object:

> No, had you wisht the wretched *Mariam* glad,
> Or had your loue to her bene truly tide:
> Nay, had you not desir'd to make her sad,
> My brother nor my Grandsyre had not dide. (4. 3. 1376-9)

In plays written by male playwrights during the English Renaissance, we often hear men claiming their wives as 'my goods, my chattels',[45] but rarely have a chance to know women's reactions to this treatment. By juxtaposing the ideologies of wifehood articulated by the Chorus and embodied in Herod's attitudes towards Mariam on the one hand, and Mariam's reaction towards them on the other, the author shows that these contemporary concepts are not relevant to a woman's sense of personal integrity. This dramatic dynamism, produced by the complicated interactions between characters, is one of the qualities that make English Renaissance drama particularly energetic and stimulating. According to her relatives, Elizabeth Cary liked theatre-going in the earlier years of her marriage. In the dramatic structures of these scenes Cary might have been influenced by the plays she saw in the theatres in early Jacobean England. It has been generally said that she wrote her play without any intention of actual performance, but in view of her construction of dramatic structures, she might have intended her play to be performed in some way.

At this point it is useful to compare Cary's representation of Mariam's selfhood with portrayals by male contemporary writers. Thomas Lodge, in his translation of Flavius Josephus, *The Famovs and Memorable Works of Josephus* (1602), on which Cary drew heavily for her play, depicts Mariam's assertion of self simply as a fault:

> she was both chast and faithfull vnto him; yet had she a certaine womanly imperfection and naturall frowardnesse, which was the cause that shee presumed too much vpon the intire affection

wherewith her husband was intangled; so that without regard to his person, who had power and authoritie ouer others, she entertained him oftentimes very outragiously: All which he endured patiently, without any shew of discontent. But *Mariamne* vpbraided and publikely reproched both the kings mother and sister, telling them that they were but abiectly and basely borne. (quot. Extract From Flavius Josephus, *The Famous and Memorable Works* (1602) in *The Tragedy of Mariam*, ed. Ramona Wray, Arden Early Drama, 2012, 210)

Philip Massinger also used Thomas Lodge's translation of *Famovs and Memorable Works of Josephus* as one of the sources for *The Duke of Milan* (1621), though he transported the whole scene into Renaissance Italy. Centring his play on the infatuation of Lodovico Sforza, the Duke of Milan, for his beautiful wife, Marcelia, Massinger presents the tragic turning point in the play as the moment when Marcelia hears from Sforza's right-hand man, Francisco, that her husband commanded him to kill her at the news of his own death, so that no one else could possess her affection. As Philip Edwards pointed out, Sforza seems to believe that even in heaven he can enjoy his wife sexually (2008 40–1). Marcelia is shocked to discover the possessive nature of her husband's passion, which does not acknowledge her as a person, but only as a beautiful sexual object:

> that my Lord, my *Sforza* should esteeme
> My life fit only as a page, to waite on
> The various course of his vncertaine fortunes,
> Or cherish in himselfe that sensuall hope
> In death to know me as a wife, afflicts me [. . .] (3. 3. 58–62)[46]

Like Mariam, Marcelia protests against her husband's demand for her self-effacement through both her words and actions, which results in her death. However, unlike Elizabeth Cary, Massinger does not specifically present the cause as a clash of the heroine's sense of self with the contemporary ideologies of wifehood, simply treating the issue as a problem of possessive male love.

Elizabeth Cary did not have a language in which to put forward a new concept of womanhood. Probably only someone like her, who had constantly struggled against domestic and social pressures, could present a woman's sense of self in such a unique way, a way in which the heroine tests her feelings and thoughts against the orthodox ideologies of marriage and then perceives that they do not accommodate her sense of self.[47]

In the face of her execution, Mariam realises that her sense of integrity, derived from her confidence in her chastity and in Herod's love for her, has taken no account of the importance of the humility society requires of women: it has not been able to make her live 'wisely':

> Had I but with humilitie bene grac'te,
> As well as faire I might haue prou'd me wise:
> But I did thinke because I knew me chaste,
> One vertue for a woman, might suffice
> That mind for glory for our sexe might stand,
> Wherein humilitie and chastitie
> Doth march with equall paces hand in hand,
> But one if single seene, who setteth by? (4. 8. 1833–40)

These lines illustrate another example of the contradiction in Mariam's sense of self. Although the speech expresses regret, and appears to endorse the importance of the humility required of women, these are not Mariam's final words: she immediately makes clear her sense of integrity independent of the concepts of womanhood in society:

> tis my ioy,
> That I was euer innocent, though sower:
> And therefore can they but my life destroy,
> My Soule is free from aduersaries power. (4. 8. 1841–4)

Then, according to the messenger, she died nobly. Herod regrets that he has executed Mariam and laments her death in almost the entire final scene of the play. Cary presents female integrity through Mariam's constancy to what she has perceived as right even in the face of her death, and despite her acknowledgement of the importance of the ideological requirement for humility in women. Even though, as shown in the previous section, Webster in *The Duchess of Malfi* portrays the Duchess's sense of integrity in a similar way, his play was written a decade later than Cary's play. Since Cary's play was published in 1613, slightly earlier than the production of Webster's play, we cannot deny a possibility that Webster was influenced by Cary's play in some aspects of his characterisation of the Duchess.

Male writers both of English Renaissance drama and of Kabuki plays had a tendency to use unnatural combinations of ludicrous, bizarre elements in representing the limitations of male violence as a means of attempting to subjugate female assertive power. In *Musume Dojoji*, female assertiveness is presented in terms of desire, and male violence is inflicted upon the mental state of the heroine, as is also the case in *The Duchess of Malfi*. These male-authored plays vary in their descriptions of the nature of female assertiveness and of the ways in which men exercise violence directed towards women. However, a special theatrical condition both of English Renaissance drama and of Kabuki, a condition in which female characters were enacted by male actors, seems to have created a special mode of representation of the relation of female selfhood to male violence, a mode of employing grotesque elements.

3
Lady Mary Wroth and Ideologies of Marriage in Late Jacobean England

Mary Wroth is quite different from Elizabeth Cary in her way of representing a woman's sense of self. In all her works—the pastoral comedy *Love's Victory*, her published prose romance, *The Countess of Montgomery's Urania* and its continuation, and her sonnet sequence—Wroth persistently explores the issue of female selfhood by making use of the genre of pastoral. To borrow Gary Waller's phrase about Petrarchan love poetry in general, Wroth's pastoral works embody 'the major dynamics' of desire (1993 146). And yet, when she presents a discourse on desire it departs from the pastoral conventions established by male writers, particularly by her uncle Sir Philip Sidney.

Love's Victory (c.1619): representations of female agency

Love's Victory frequently recalls plays written by Wroth's male contemporaries, especially Shakespeare, in its theme and settings (see Figure 3.1). As in *A Midsummer Night's Dream*, the characters are completely under the control of superhuman figures of desire, in this case Venus and Cupid, who, like Oberon and Puck, provide the framework for the actions by entering at the beginning and the end of each act.[1] All the characters, except for the aged mother of Musella, are driven by sexual passion, which, again as in *A Midsummer Night's Dream*, is presented as a constant state of unfulfilled inadequacy.

Philisses and Musella are in love with each other, but Philisses is in deep despair, thinking that she loves his best friend, Lissius, while Philisses himself is loved and pursued by several other women. Musella is also desired by many other men. Towards the end of the play she is almost married off to a silly but rich shepherd, Rustick. Silvesta, who used to pursue Philisses, finding it impossible for her desire ever to be

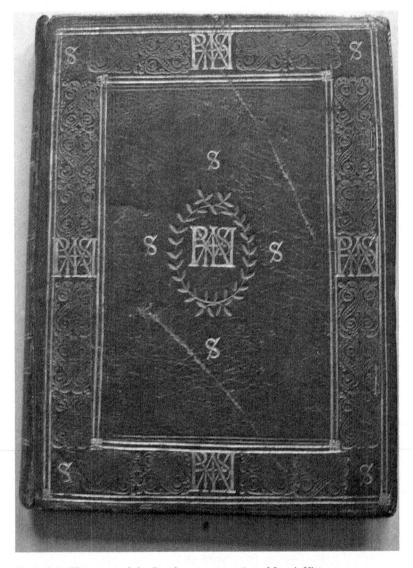

Figure 3.1 The cover of the Penshurst manuscript of *Love's Victory*
Source: By kind permission of Viscount De L'Isle from his private collection at Penshurst Place, Kent, England.

fulfilled, has sworn eternal chastity, and yet she is passionately desired by Forester. Lissius, who has disdained such irrational erotic desire in human beings, is punished by Venus for his defiance of her authority, and is suddenly awakened to passion for Simeana, Philisses' sister. She, on the other hand, at first accepts Lissius's love, but soon comes to be possessed by strong jealousy as a result of the intrigue of a villain, Arcas, who feels threatened by assertive women and also hates to see other people's happiness. These aspects of Arcas remind us of some characteristics of Iago, though the motivation for the latter's viciousness is much more complicated and obscure. Thus, the pastoral world in the play, which is called 'Arcadia',[2] is in a state of confusion caused by the unstable and destabilising drive of desire that emanates from Venus and her son, Cupid. Like the lovers in *A Midsummer Night's Dream*, the lovers in *Love's Victory* have to undergo trials and difficulties before their libidinous energy finally finds its right object.

A major difference between Wroth's play and the pastoral plays written by her male contemporaries is, as Ann Rosalind Jones argued with respect to *Urania*, the absence of Court life or even courtiers (*The Currency of Eros*, 1990 119-22). Drawing on Louis Adrian Montrose's view of the pastoral in the English Renaissance, Jones thinks that in England the pastoral was seen 'as a potentially critical and satirical genre' (*The Currency of Eros*, 1990 123, 141-2),[3] which offered discontented courtiers a chance to express their criticism of the current state of the Court. This certainly was the case with many writers of pastoral romance and poetry in Elizabethan England, such as Philip Sidney and Edmund Spenser. In these writings women are usually represented in Petrarchan terms, either as a symbol of perfect beauty which enhances male virtues or as a cruel mistress who denies the fulfilment of male desire, and love often functions as a means by which men articulate their unfulfilled ambition for political power. Similarly, in the case of Sidney's sonnet sequence *Astrophel and Stella*, as has been pointed out, we hear a great deal about Astrophel's frustrations with political affairs at the Court through his portrayals of Stella, whereas we hardly ever know what she really feels or thinks (Jones and Stallybrass, 53-68).

By contrast, in *Love's Victory*, Wroth eliminates all elements of Court life, presenting a pastoral world that centres on desire.[4] The framework of the play created by the goddess of desire and her son makes this point clear. The characters cannot escape into a life where love is only a peripheral concern, as is the case in pastoral writings by men. Some male characters, such as Philisses and Lissius, still retain Petrarchan concepts of love. The female characters, on the other hand, are free from these courtly values and candid in admitting their own desire. They are also more seriously committed to their passion than the male characters, although they are not always accepted by the men they love; and their situation is made more difficult by the conventional concepts of womanhood in early seventeenth-century England, which defined as deviant women's sexual approaches to men.

Many female characters created by male playwrights, such as Shakespeare's Cressida in *Troilus and Cressida* (Chamberlain's, 1602) or Helena in *All's Well That Ends Well* (King's, 1604), find their situations extremely frustrating due to the requirement that women should not take the initiative in their relationships with the men they love. Although Wroth's female characters live in a pastoral world, they are also quite conscious of this code of female propriety. For instance, Musella feels sorry for Philisses, who is suffering from the delusion that she loves Lissius, and wants to confess her love to him, but thinks it improper for a woman to do so:

> Somtimes I faine would speak, then strait forbear
> Knowing itt most unfitt; thus woe I beare. (Act 3, 77–8)

Silvesta agrees with Musella: 'Indeed a woman to make love is ill' (Act 3, 79). Yet, they are resourceful enough to devise a situation in which Musella can reveal her love to Philisses without breaching this code. Although outspoken in admitting their love, the female characters in the play continue to share friendship and mutually support each other despite their rivalry in love; Silvesta is still the best friend of Musella in spite of her unrequited love for Philisses, and guides them to marriage by helping them to resolve their problems. Furthermore, the female characters in *Love's Victory* do not play tricks upon men to titillate their desire by frustrating their passion, something that female characters often do in plays or love lyrics written by male writers. Dalina, who is called '*a fickle lady*' in the cast list of the play, mentions this strategy to keep men's love (Act 3, 268–70), but even she is portrayed as simply being frank in admitting the imperative of her desire (Act 3, 134–49: 153–61), not as a destructively promiscuous woman, such as the Countess in Marston's *The Insatiate Countess* or Middleton's Beatrice-Joanna.

It is also important to note that in *Love's Victory*, as in *Urania* I and II and the sonnet sequence, Wroth presents women as sexually autonomous. In *Urania*, some women, like Limena, are driven into forced marriages that cause them great misery, but at the same time they are always capable of loving someone they themselves have chosen. Moreover, they often articulate their sexual attraction to male beauty, and thus men are sometimes made objects of their gaze. For instance, the opening scene of *Urania* presents an interesting contrast to Philip Sidney's *Arcadia*. In the latter the shepherds, Strephon and Claius, lament the disappearance of a beautiful shepherdess, Urania, uttering their admiration for her in Petrarchan terms. In contrast, Urania at the beginning of Wroth's pastoral is presented as a woman searching for her self-identity; she has been deeply depressed as she was told by the couple whom she had thought her parents that actually they were not. And yet, a little later, she is described as expressing in elegantly simple language her admiration for the male beauty and sexual attractiveness of the young Prince, Perissus, whom she has just found in a cave (1997 15). Another example is found in the passage in which Urania turns her gaze on the two youths who have rescued her from a wolf:

> faces of that sweetnesse, as *Venus* loue could but compare with them, their haire which neuer had been cut, hung long, yet longer much it must haue been, had not the daintie naturall curling somewhat shortned it, which as the wind mou'd, the curles so pretily plaid, as the Sunne-beames in the water. (*Urania* I 19)

These are by no means the only examples of male beauty being subjected to the female gaze in *Urania*.

Women's sexual autonomy also characterises *Love's Victory*. Here men like Philisses and Lissius still talk of their love in the Petrarchan terms established by male tradition, but the author underlines the irrelevant aspects of these male attitudes towards love. For instance, Philisses's love for Musella is like Orsino's passion for Olivia in *Twelfth Night*; he is in love with the concept of being in love. Right after his first entrance on the stage, Philisses laments his unrequited love for Musella. Yet, soon afterwards Philisses learns from Lissius, whom he has regarded as his rival in love for Musella, that Lissius does not love her, but does love his sister, Simeana. And yet Philisses continues to lament his unrequited love. Even after having confirmed with Musella herself that she loves him, he is still drowning in melancholy. Moreover, in his song in the Act 2, he divides love from reason in Petrarchan terms, insisting that reason should control human passion (Act 2, 213–24). Nevertheless, it is Philisses himself whose passion overrules his reason, being at the mercy of the illusion that Musella and Lissius are in love with each other.

The women in the play, by contrast, do not create a dichotomy between love and reason. They accept desire as integral to the human constitution. Thus Wroth, influenced probably by Montaigne's views on sexuality, launches an alternative discourse to the traditional description of humanity that divides the human constitution into body and soul.[5] She makes it clear in her play that women are subjects of desire, not objects, and thus tries to present the possibility of female integrity through honesty to their own desire. This concept of desire is explored in more depth and greater detail in the two parts of *Urania*.

These presentations of women's sexual autonomy in Wroth's works can be seen as the author's intentional defiance of the conventional notions of womanhood, which defined obedience, chastity and silence as the prime female virtues. Mary Wroth's own life story embodies her defiance of these norms. Not only did she breach the code of women's silence by publishing in 1621 *The Countess of Montgomery's Urania*, which caused a great scandal at the Court, but she also bore two illegitimate children to her first cousin, William Herbert, the third Earl of Pembroke, in around 1624.[6]

What differentiates Lady Wroth's play from Shakespeare's pastoral comedies is the fact that she assigns to female characters roles as agents and initiators of action. As is also the case in both parts of *Urania* and the sonnet sequence (Ann Jones, *The Currency of Eros*, 1990 141), the male characters in *Love's Victory* who function as agents of change are notable by their absence. It is the goddess, Venus, rather than the King of the Fairies, Oberon, who manipulates the characters' amorous situations. It is Musella, Silvesta and Simeana, not the central male characters Philisses or Lissius, who are resourceful and resolve their amatory entanglements. It is especially interesting to see how Wroth often reverses Shakespeare's allocation of male and female roles by assigning to the women in her play the roles usually given to men in the works of her male predecessor. In Act 4, for instance, thanks to Silvesta's stratagem, Musella, like Romeo in the balcony scene, has a chance to overhear Philisses confessing his love for her. In the forest scene, Silvesta ponders the nature of love, as Orlando does in *As You Like It*. The final scene presents the faked death of Philisses and Musella, which is designed to avoid the latter's forced marriage to Rustick. This situation obviously recalls a similar scene in *Romeo and Juliet*, but it is Silvesta, not the Priest of the Temple, who reminds us of Friar Laurence by furnishing the lovers with the potion that causes their pretend death. In fact, Silvesta is portrayed as carrying out her work with much more efficiency than Laurence.[7]

Moreover, although patriarchal power is still accepted as absolute even in this pastoral world, it is Musella's mother, not her father (who, being dead, is absent throughout the play), who directly represents that power by trying to force Musella into a mercenary marriage with Rustick. However, Wroth displaces the responsibility for the actions of Musella's mother onto her absent husband. Musella tells Silvesta that her mother is forcing her into marriage because of her father's will (Act 5, 11–14), whereas in the final resolution scene her mother apologises to her by saying: 'Pardon my fault, injoye, and blessed bee,/And children, and theyr children's children see' (Act 5, 501–2). The blame is also located onto the male villain, Arcas, who has told Musella's mother that, 'Musella wantonly/Did seeke Philisses' love' (Act 5, 391–2).

Thus, in *Love's Victory*, the women are always practical and initiate actions, while the men are incapable of resolving problems or of bringing about happiness; Philisses and Lissius limit themselves to deploring their predicaments through the medium of Petrarchan poetry, and Arcas plots to destroy others' happiness, while the insensitive Rustick shows no interest in anything other than country affairs.[8]

Unlike Elizabeth Cary, who could not provide a language to articulate female sexuality in *The Tragedy of Mariam*, Mary Wroth, who wrote her play nearly twenty years later, succeeded in presenting a discourse on female desire in *Love's Victory* by making use of the popular literary genre of pastoral.

Urania Part I and Part II: female divided selfhood in marriage and male violence

Wroth's *Urania* is different from other romances written in the period in that, as has been mentioned above, it employs the technique of dramatic communication between the characters. And yet, since it was not originally designed for the public stage, Wroth did not have to depend on the male body to represent female selfhood. Likewise, since Elizabeth Cary did not write *The Tragedy of Mariam* for actual performance in a public theatre, she probably did not consider the possibility of her heroine being embodied by men. The fact that these women writers did not have to fictionalise the issue of female self through the male body seemed to enable them to pursue the issue of gender in more realistic ways without using the appalling, bizarre images frequently found in contemporary male playwrights' representations of female self-assertiveness.

As in Florio's Montaigne, Wroth portrays female desire as a necessary component of female identity in *Love's Victory* as well as in both parts of *Urania*. She explores the ways in which a woman can construct authenticity in her sexual assertiveness without losing her integrity in a male-dominated society that denies female desire. Unlike male authors of the English Renaissance, Wroth does not present the threat of female desire to men through bizarre images, though she subverts conventional notions of gender-specific behaviour themselves. For instance, in *Urania* in contrast to social assumptions about women's vulnerability to weeping, it is Amphilanthus who often displays his emotional weakness, weeping in departing from Pamphilia, whereas she manages to control her emotions.

Mary Wroth also differs greatly from her contemporary writers both in the depth of her exploration of a female sense of identity and in representing female desire as having the potential to be a positive human value. In this respect, her authorial position recalls that of John Webster. And yet she carries out this investigation in her characteristic way by considering female identity in terms of theatricality. This technique probably derived from Wroth's own awareness of the strategies necessary for a woman to survive in society without losing her sense of self.[9] At the same time, her work reveals an author well acquainted with the drama of the period, from the Court performances to performances at public theatres, which she may have learned about through published texts and word of mouth, especially because she took part in Queen Anne's Court masque, *The Mask of Blackness*, in 1605.

Women in both parts of *Urania* can be divided largely into two groups, depending on how successful they are in the performance of their theatrical selves.[10] The tale of Limena is one of the episodes in which Mary Wroth presents clearly her notion of the split within female identity, a split between female selfhood and female outward appearance. Limena's husband, Philargus, suspects that his wife still loves Perissus, with whom she had pledged love before her marriage. He repeatedly tortures her to make her confess her true feelings for her former lover. As Elizabeth Hanson has argued, a torturer assumes the existence of a truth hidden within the body of the tortured, and the torture is an attempt to draw this truth out from the body of the tortured by inflicting violence (2000 24–54). In the case of Philargus, two conflicting issues complicate his situation: since in the contemporary discourse of marriage his sense of identity as a man and husband depends on his wife's fidelity in both a mental and a physical sense, the success of his torture will lead to the loss of his own sense of identity. What is more, to his embarrassment and fury, despite his repeated and increasingly cruel violence on her body, Limena not only rejects Philargus's definition of her as a faithless wife, asserting that she has not betrayed him sexually, but also declares the impossibility of his gaining possession of her inmost self. In her concept of her identity, she distinguishes her selfhood from her tortured body. In a letter she narrates to Perissus what she said to her husband:

> This wretched, and unfortunate body, is I confesse in your hands, to dispose of to death if you will; but yet it is not unblest with such a mind as will suffer it to end with any such staine, as so wicked a plott, and miserable consent might purchase [. . .] I will with more willingnesse die, then execute your minde; and more happily shall I end, saving him innocent from ill, delivering my soule pure, and I unspotted of the crime you tax me of, or a thought of such dishonour to my selfe. (*Urania* I, 13)

When she and Perissus meet later and she tells him about the torture, her narrative points to her agency in two respects. First, in disclosing the violence that her husband has inflicted upon her body and her defiance of it, she tries to demonstrate an autonomous self that eludes Philargus's authority as a husband. Furthermore, even in talking to Perissus, she does it in such a way as to evoke his admiration for her as well as his erotic attraction to her:

> he [Philargus] opened my breast, and gave me many wounds, the markes you may here yet discerne (letting the Mantle fall againe a little lower, to shew the cruell remembrance of his crueltie) which although they were whole, yet made they newe hurts in the loving heart of Perissus, suffering more paine for them, then he had done for all those himselfe had received in his former adventures [. . .] (*Urania* I, 87)

In the episode of Limena, Wroth not only enables Limena to maintain her autonomous self in the face of the physical pain inflicted by her husband, but also allows her to dominate Perissus by narrating the torture in such a way as to awake his desire. In her married life, Limena succeeds to a certain extent in her performance of her theatrical self by concealing her passion for Perissus underneath the appearance of being an obedient, chaste wife. Yet her performance is not entirely successful, since her husband suspects that her appearance may not reveal her whole selfhood. When Philargus starts to torture her, trying to force her to confess her true feelings, she stops performing her theatrical self by confessing her love for Perissus and her hatred for her husband, thus exposing to him the split that has existed within her.[11] Moreover, she openly rejects Philargus's claim as husband to be entitled to access her inmost thoughts. In this sense Limena is not an entirely successful performer, but the author enables her to obtain happiness in the end; after having tortured his wife, Philargus dies of remorse, allowing Limena and Perissus to be united after all.

Few women who have a divided self in *Urania*, however, can obtain such happiness. Bellamira, who is generally regarded as a partially autobiographical portrait of Wroth herself, also experiences a divided self,[12] when, despite having a lover, she is forced to marry Treborius:

> the marriage followed: what torture was it to mee, standing betweene my love, and Treborius, when I was to give my selfe from my love to him? How willingly would I have turned to the other hand: but contrary to my soule I gave my selfe to him, my heart to my first love. Thus more then equally did I devide my selfe. (*Urania* I, 388)

Unlike Limena, Bellamira cannot be united with her lover. Moreover, even while her husband Treborius is alive, she is pursued by the King of Dalmatia, and after Treborius's death, she is forced to renew her affair with the King. Thus she is portrayed as a woman who endlessly suffers a split within herself.

Among these heroines, Pamphilia experiences the most complicated inner split throughout the work; before her marriage to Rodomandro, King of Tartar, she goes through a split between her desire for Amphilanthus and her frustration for this ever-changing man. After marriage she experiences one between her love for Amphilanthus and her wifely duties for Rodomandro. Her case is presented as much more complicated than the cases of other women in *Urania* because other issues, such as gender, race and politics, interact with the issue of marriage. Before and after marriage she maintains the inward split between being a woman in love and the Queen ruling the Kingdom of Pamphilia.

The notion of a husband's right to possess his wife's selfhood, a notion deeply rooted in the ideology of marriage in Renaissance England, is one of the main assumptions that women writers in the period, especially Mary Wroth and Elizabeth Cary, question in their works. In *The Tragedy of Mariam*, as discussed in Chapter 2, Elizabeth Cary makes the Chorus insist on this conventional claim and blame Mariam for her refusal to reveal her inner thoughts to her husband,

Herod. Cary makes it clear that this articulation by the Chorus contrasts sharply with Mariam's own sense of self. Herod assumes that his wife's body hides the 'truth', that is, her desire for Sohemus, and, being unable to draw out of her a confession, he executes her. Nevertheless, like Webster's Duchess, Cary's heroine ends up victorious despite her death. Furthermore, like Philargus in *Urania*, Herod deeply repents what he has done to his wife, and though, unlike Philargus, he does not die at the end, he becomes half mad, wishing for Mariam's restoration to life. Thus, both Wroth and Cary locate the basis of a female construction of selfhood in a woman's acknowledgement of a split within herself, a split between her inmost thought and her external duty to others.

Male authors in the period also deal with the gap between female appearance and female feelings, but in most cases quite differently. They usually represent it as a sign of female duplicity, which was conventionally regarded as a characteristic feature of femininity. This female duplicity is usually linked with a wife's sexual transgression, and even with the murder of a husband. For instance, Alice in *Arden of Faversham* (Unknown, 1591) is portrayed as being discontented in her married life with Arden, who is an ambitious, wealthy landowner, but she successfully disguises both her discontent and her desire for her lover, Mosby. Arden does not notice the gap that exists within his wife between her appearance and her desire, entertaining no suspicion of her betrayal, let alone her intention of murdering him. Thomas Middleton also takes a similar approach to women in most of his plays. In *Women Beware Women* (King's (?), 1621), Livia is described as an epitome of female duplicity, whereas Isabella is a young woman who comes to adopt duplicity as a strategy in order to continue her affair with her uncle, Hippolito. Bianca, on the other hand, is presented as duplicitous from the very beginning. Although she looks like an innocent, obedient, well-bred daughter of the Venetian aristocracy, she agrees to elope to Florence with Leantio, a man of much lower social status. Her duplicity is fully displayed in her attitude towards Leantio as she attempts to hide her desire for the Duke, who raped her. Female duplicity of this kind is usually dramatised as leading to a bizarre, chaotic ending of the play. Thus, English Renaissance drama frequently centres on female desire, especially as enacted in a wife's adultery, but most male playwrights present the problem as being caused by a duplicity arising from supposedly innate female weakness or the fierce power of female desire, both of which were assumed to be common attributes of femininity. As has been discussed in Chapters 1 and 2, the few exceptions to this stereotypical representation of female desire include Shakespeare's *Antony and Cleopatra* and Webster's *The Duchess of Malfi*.

In plays written by men, when male characters notice a gap within a woman's identity, they often inflict physical or psychological violence on her in order to eliminate this gap, thereby attempting to deprive the woman of her autonomous self by means of torture.[13] In particular, in scenes where male characters find it difficult to subjugate the power of the self-assertiveness of female characters, as has already been argued in Chapter 2, male playwrights in the English Renaissance, tend to use grotesque elements in their representations of torture. The monstrously hybrid nature of the cruelties enacted on the stage—at once ferocious, bizarre, and absurd—has the effect of revealing the male characters' desire to belittle the significance of women's resistance to the demands of male authority, as in the case of the tortures inflicted on the Duchess of Malfi by Ferdinand or by Bosola.

Another example of grotesque elements in the representation of male violence inflicted upon self-assertive women may be observed in Shakespeare's *Titus Andronicus* (Pembroke's, Sussex's, 1594). In his revenge upon Tamora, who incited her two sons to rape and mutilate his daughter Lavinia, Titus serves Tamora and her husband, the Roman Emperor Saturninus, a meat pie made of her sons' flesh. Although Shakespeare draws this episode from his source, the effect of the stage representation of this scene is certainly ridiculous and bizarre—or in other words, grotesque.[14] This incident, while truly appalling for Tamora herself, usually invites laughter from the audience. In punishing the uncontrollably assertive Tamora, whose affair with Aaron shows that she refuses to contain her desire to stay within the domain of her husband, Saturninus, Titus cannot rely on a more ordinary manner of revenge. Thus, as in the case of Webster's *The Duchess of Malfi*, the grotesque elements in Titus's revenge function to underscore Tamora's assertive power as well as his efforts to belittle it. Titus, like Ferdinand, realises that in dealing with a woman who took her self-assertion to an evil extreme, only grotesque actions can be effective to break her sense of self. These men know that in the case of women like the Duchess or Tamora the force and resilience of their personalities are so powerful that it is impossible to subjugate them to male authority through ordinary means of torment.

The introduction of grotesqueness in the representation of female assertive power is not limited to plays written by male writers of the West. A similar method is used to the utmost degree in a well-known ghost play in Kabuki, *Tokaido Yotsuya Kaidan* (*The Ghost Story of Yotsuya*), written by Tsuruya Nanboku (1755–1829). The play was based on a real-life murder case, which took place in Edo (now Tokyo), and was first performed in 1825. The heroine, Oiwa, was once a beautiful woman in love with Tamiya Iemon, a man of the warrior class. She married Iemon because he promised to take revenge for her sake on the murderer of her father, but unbeknown to Oiwa, the murderer was actually Iemon himself. Iemon is also adored by the grand-daughter of a man of high social rank, and, in order to climb up the social hierarchy through marriage with this woman, he has Oiwa murdered in the cruellest way. While Oiwa was alive, she was a docile, submissive wife, despite Iemon's most selfish and unreasonable actions; but once she is dead and has become a ghost, she becomes an extremely aggressive and defiant figure. Totally ignoring gender ideology in society, she constantly haunts Iemon and his accomplices, displaying her body grossly deformed by the effects of the poison administered by them, and expressing the resentment and grief she feels on account of their cruel betrayal and murder of her. In *Yotsuya Kaidan*, both morals in patriarchal society and men in authority are portrayed as totally corrupt. By showing the grotesquely deformed body of Oiwa onstage, the author asserts the absurdity of the social situation that allows such violence to be perpetrated on the female body.

The evils in society embodied by Iemon and his accomplices are described as so horrifying that anyone who wants to challenge such malicious energy needs even more tremendous power. For this purpose, the author used an extremely bizarre image for the damage done to the female body in the appearance of Oiwa's ghost. In Kabuki plays, although a male actor's body usually represents female beauty, in this play it presents the grotesque deformity of a woman's mutilated body. The grotesqueness in this play, however, unlike the meat pie in *Titus Andronicus* or the wax corpses in *The Duchess of Malfi*, does not simply signify a male inability to subjugate female challenges to male authority. It is also a sign of the unusually powerful energy required to challenge the absurdity and corruption in society. At the same time, the author also indicates in this way the interior energy concealed in the body of the docile Oiwa, an energy that cannot be contained by the gender ideology of the time. Being liberated from the conservative gender concepts in society after her death, she takes revenge upon her torturers in the most aggressive manner.

In recent years many important issues relating to the significance of boys playing female roles in English Renaissance drama have been discussed in both social and sexual terms. Little attention, however, has been paid to the problem of male writers' incorporation of grotesque elements in describing female assertive power through the body of a male actor. In plays both in the English Renaissance and in Kabuki, the audiences' awareness of the fictionalisation of actions on the stage, that is, their awareness that they were watching a fiction of the female produced through the bodies of men, seemed to create a distance in the audience's sense of reality that allows outrageously grotesque representations of female power onstage. Although the social implications of plays in the English Renaissance are different from those of the Kabuki play, it must be noted that male writers in both theatres deploy qualities of grotesqueness in expressing the power of female selfhood that a man cannot control in married life.

By contrast, neither Mary Wroth nor Elizabeth Cary depends on grotesque images in describing the strength of female self-assertiveness, which cannot be subsumed in the gender ideologies of society. Instead, they deeply explore the significance of the split that women feel between their selfhood and the outward appearance they try to adopt. As has been argued, among those women Wroth presents in both parts of *Urania*, the best performer of her theatrical self is Pamphilia. Her identity has many facets: she is the Queen of Pamphilia; an obedient daughter of the King of Morea; a woman passionately in love with Amphilanthus, the King of Naples; and later, wife of Rodomandro, King of Tartar. Because of Amphilanthus's faithlessness, she constantly suffers inner pain, but claims a constant self by maintaining her faithful love for him. She grieves over his repeated betrayals, but in the presence of other people, she feigns happiness by effectively masking her true feelings with behaviour in line with her assigned roles. The success of her theatricality allows Pamphilia to preserve her authority, but at the same time, as Heather Weidemann pointed out, it places her in a situation in which she constantly suffers from the gap within herself (1991 particularly 199–207). Urania at one point tells Pamphilia to disavow her constancy to Amphilanthus, whose name signifies 'the louer of two' (*Urania* I 250), since there is no use in her victimising herself for a faithless lover. Pamphilia, however, insists on the construction of her own selfhood through her insistence on the authenticity of her constancy, regardless of Amphilanthus's inconstancy:

> To leave him for being false, would shew my love was not for his sake, but mine owne, that because he loved me, I therefore loved him, but when hee leaves I can doe so to. O no deere Cousen I loved him for himselfe, and would have loved him had hee nor loved mee, and will love though hee dispise me; this is true love [. . .] Pamphilia

must be of a new composition before she can let such thoughts fall into her constant breast, which is a Sanctuary of zealous affection, and so well hath love instructed me, as I can never leave my master nor his precepts, but still maintaine a vertuous constancy. (*Urania* I, 470)

Wroth thus located Pamphilia's selfhood in her maintenance of constancy to her beloved, not to her husband as in the usual patriarchal discourse, underlining her independence both from Amphilanthus's changeability and from a world concerned only with conventional female outward appearance. Therefore, although, as Weidemann argued, Pamphilia's selfhood is delimited by her theatricality, she still demonstrates her agency in constructing her sense of self.[15]

Wroth inscribes her feelings within herself in her poems, in particular, the sonnet sequence,[16] or in her narratives of other women's painful stories that parallel her own experience in *Urania*. Since she inherited both her chosen literary forms—sonnet sequence and romance—from her male predecessors, above all from her male family members, such as her uncle Sir Philip Sidney or her father Robert Sidney, some critics think that Wroth was unable to establish female identity in any unconventional manner.[17] However, throughout both parts of *Urania* she subverts conventional notions of womanhood, especially the norms specified in the contemporary ideologies of marriage, presenting Pamphilia as capable of successfully performing her theatrical self while maintaining the integrity of her selfhood underneath her appearance. In view of the historical context of women in early seventeenth-century England, the most important point is that Wroth portrayed her female characters as capable of choosing men to love, not as simply succumbing to men who approached them, and presented this capacity in women as constitutive of their selfhood.

Gender and representations of mixed-race relationships in *Urania* Part II

Among the various causes of unhappy marriages represented in English Renaissance drama, one of the most striking is the set of problems that can arise when the husband and wife are of different races. A typical example is depicted in *Othello* (King's, 1604). In this play, whatever excellent quantities 'the noble Moor' is said to have embodied in the battles in which he fought before his clandestine marriage to Desdemona, Shakespeare dramatises the main causes of the tragedy as being derived from people's consciousness of Othello's race, including both Desdemona's and Othello's own consciousness of this matter. In this respect, in the second part of *Urania* Mary Wroth deals with the mixed-race marriage between Rodomandro, King of Tartar, and Pamphilia, the main heroine of the romance, from an entirely different point of view. It is noteworthy that none of the people at the Court of Pamphilia's father at Morea raises the issue of racial difference or comments on the difference of skin colour between the two when Pamphilia's engagement to marry Rodomandro is proclaimed. The only person who mentions his blackness as a mark of inferiority is Rodomandro himself. In his marriage proposal to Pamphilia he repeatedly refers to the blackness of his skin:

> 'Devine Lady', sayd hee, 'the Tartarians are noe Orators, butt plaine blunt men. Our harts are rich in truthe and loyalltie. Prowde indeed wee ar, butt onely of Ladys favours, knowing our sunn-burnt faces can butt rarely attaine to faire ladys likings. And therin is our ambition (especially I must confess mine) in presuming, nott onely to the fairest and lovliest, butt to the most machles and incomparable of any. Nor seeke I soverainitie over love, as that way to master, butt to bee a meanes for mee, poore mee, to bee accepted and receaved by you.' (*Urania* II, 271)

In fact, in this episode, Wroth clearly draws attention to Rodomandro's blackness. Although it was commonly supposed in Renaissance England that Tartary was the name of a large area covering the whole of Central Asia and extending as far as India (Roberts, *Urania* II, 484: note 42. 23), Wroth describes Tartar as being located somewhere around the Black Sea—the area that Henry Blount called 'petit Tartar' in his travel narrative (Blount, 1638 484). In reality, the inhabitants of this area were not black, but Wroth describes Rodomandro as black, as a way of stressing his cultural otherness. It is worth noting that Zoylo, a prince of Tartar, in Margaret Tyler's translation of *The Mirrour of Princely Deeds and Knighthood* (1575) also has a complexion that is described as being the 'colour of tawnie' (153). In *A Midsummer Night's Dream*, in her quarrel with Helena, Hermia tries to disdain her, calling her 'Tawny Tartar' (3. 2. 268). Wroth, in contrast, does not present the blackness of Rodomandro as a quality that stains his beauty. Rather, at the Court of Morea, people are struck by the handsome appearance and civilised manners of this black Tartarian:

> A brave and Comly Gentleman, shaped of body soe curiously as noe art cowld counterfett soe rare a proportion, of an excellent

stature neither to high nor of the meanest stature, his hands soe white as wowld have beecome a great Lady, his face of curious and exact features, butt for the couler of itt, itt plainely shewed the sunn had either liked itt to much, and soe had too hard kissed itt, ore in fury of his delicacy, had made his beames to strongly to burne him, yett cowld nott take away the perfect sweetnes of his lovelines. His diamound eyes (though attired in black) did soe sparcle gainst his rays as made them in ther owne hardnes knowe strength against his beames, and power to resist his strongest burning heat; and soe certainly had the conquest, for though black, yett hee had the true parfection of lovlines, and in lovelines the purest beauty. (*Urania* II, 42)

After having been shipwrecked in the course of his travels, Rodomandro visited the Court of Morea, but there, according to the narrator, he came to experience 'a worse-shipwreck' (*Urania* II, 42), a shipwreck of the mind, for he fell desperately in love with Pamphilia. Thus, he became Amphilanthus's great rival. Even though he was fully conscious of the fact that his blackness put him at a disadvantage in his attempt to win Pamphilia, he never expressed any sense of inferiority to Amphilanthus or any of the other knights with white complexions. In this triangular relationship, it was Amphilanthus, not Rodomandro, whom Wroth portrayed as suffering from jealousy; as soon as Amphilanthus met Rodomandro at the Court, he became intensely jealous of the brave and good-looking King of Tartar. In the case of the triangular relationship of Tamora, Saturninus and Aaron in *Titus Andronicus*, Saturnius, the Emperor of Rome and Tamora's husband, never becomes aware of Tamora's love affair with Aaron, her black servant. Shakespeare ingeniously avoids highlighting the problem of the jealousy the white male feels for the black male.

Later, Rodomandro, deciding to propose this mixed marriage to Pamphilia, first ask the consent of her father, King of Morea. The narrator reported that, having observed Rodomandro's excellent qualities, the King found 'noe obstacle' (*Urania* II, 270) and gave his permission, while making only one condition: that the marriage should be to Pamphilia's liking. The King showed no concern about his daughter's marriage to a man of a different race, but instead strongly advocated the concept of companionship marriage, which was emerging at that time in Renaissance England,[18] telling Rodomandro that 'force can never bee companionated with love' (*Urania* II, 270). Moreover, the King of Morea tried to persuade his daughter to accept Rodomandro's proposal.

Although Pamphilia's subsequent polite refusal of his marriage proposal might merely be a display of her courtly manners and diplomatic tact, it is nevertheless interesting to note that she started her speech by referring to his superiority to her, to his 'worthe farr beeyound my merritt' (*Urania* II, 271). Then, not even hinting that she might be hesitant due to Rodomandro's 'otherness', she expressed her preference for her life of solitude in which she could devote herself to reading: 'a booke and solitarines beeing the only companions I desire in this my unfortunate days' (*Urania* II, 271).

Together with Amphilanthus, Rodomandro had rescued her country from a Persian invasion. Of course, the reader knows that Pamphilia's depression was caused by her grief over the death of her brother, Philarchos, who had died in the battle against the Sophy of Persia. The reader is also well aware that the reason for Pamphilia's refusal is deeply related to her desire for Amphilanthus, whom she had secretly married in a ceremony witnessed only by some of their close friends (*Urania* II, 45–6).

Yet it is quite unusual in English Renaissance literature for a woman to be described as announcing that her preference for solitude and reading is her reason for declining a marriage proposal, especially since Pamphilia's intention was not to withdraw into religious life. Wroth represents Pamphilia's pursuit of solitude and reading as an alternative to the married life that women at the time were supposed to be destined to; as has been discussed, the contemporary discourse of marriage did not allow women to possess a sense of self independent of their husband. To Pamphilia's surprise, Rodomandro said that he was not only willing to accept her continued independence, but that he would protect her so that she could fully engage in her intellectual pursuits:

> Love your booke, butt love mee soe farr as that I may hold itt to you that, while you peruse that, I may Joye in beeholding you; and som times gaine a looke from you, if butt to chide mee for soe carelessly parforming my office, when love will by chance make my hand shake, purposely to obtaine a sweet looke. For surely you can nott bee soe cruell as that love will nott with all sweetnes shine in thos cleerest lights. Bee solitarie, yett favour mee soe much as that I may butt attend you. When you waulke in deserts and woods, I will serve you as a guard to keepe you from all harmes may proceed from serpents and venimous beasts. I will keepe att what distance you please, butt still in your sight, els how shall I serve you? (*Urania* II, 272)

When Pamphilia, keeping her *de praesenti* marriage with Amphilanthus secret, finally accepted Rodomandro's marriage proposal because of his ardour and her father's persuasion, Wroth stresses Pamphilia's grief at being united, not to Amphilanthus, but to a man not of her own choice: 'Pamphilia against her owne minde (yett nott constrain'd, for non durst attempt that) had sayd "[aye]"' (*Urania* II, 274). Her wedding, the narrator claims, is for her 'the most undesired wedding when her hart was longe before married to a more beeloved creature' (*Urania* II, 276).

Although Wroth repeatedly describes Pamphilia's deep sorrow after her marriage, she represents Pamphilia's sadness as being caused neither by Rodomandro's 'otherness', nor by his inferiority to Amphilanthus in any sense. In various episodes presented throughout the two parts of *Urania*, the cause of an unhappy marriage is often ascribed to a husband's inferiority. For instance, Lisia, who was forced by her father to marry the rich Duke, found her husband 'no more esteeming her, nor indeede understanding her worth then a Beast, or one of his Goats [. . .] and is, as dull a piece of flesh, as this, or any Country neede know' (*Urania* I, 556–9). In contrast to the distress created by such a marriage, Pamphilia's grief is described as not caused by her husband's inferiority or incompatibility, but simply by her desire for Amphilanthus.[19]

In fact, when the two men are compared, it is Amphilanthus, not Rodomandro, who is described as inferior, despite the abundant admiring words conferred upon him throughout *Urania*. Even before Pamphilia gave her formal agreement to her marriage with Rodomandro, Amphilanthus had married the Princess of Slavonia; he was tricked by his former tutor, Forsandurus, and the Queen of Candida into believing that Pamphilia had already been betrothed to the King of Tartar. Moreover, his marriage was largely motivated by the fact that the Queen of Candida, who had dallied with him during his visit made after his *de praesenti* marriage with Pamphilia, had grown tired of him. Despite such subsequent developments of the story, Wroth makes it clear that it is Amphilanthus who ardently desired the secret marriage with Pamphilia because of his jealousy of Rodomandro.

In depicting the episode of Amphilanthus's jealousy, Wroth seems to be quite conscious of the portrayal of mixed-race marriage in *Othello*, and deliberately departs from Shakespeare's approach to the issues of both race and gender. Most strikingly, it is the white Amphilanthus, the greatly admired King of Naples, who was tormented by his jealousy of the black Tartarian. At the banquet given by Pamphilia's father, the King of Morea, in honour of his guest Rodomandro, soon after he noticed Rodomandro paying intense attention to Pamphilia, he found himself incapable of staying in this visitor's company, and, making some excuse, retired from the banquet. In the meantime, Pamphilia was aware of the whole situation, but to avoid suspicion from other guests she stayed there for a while. Then she excused herself and went back to her chamber.

On her way there, she kept thinking about how to calm Amphilanthus's jealousy. In her chamber, she found Amphilanthus lying on her bed, sighing deeply. Pamphilia asked him about the reason for his desperation:

> what is the cause that you thus sigh? Alas, what can procure sadnes in you when all harts, especially mine, are and is soe truly yours? (*Urania* II, 45)

As Naomi J. Miller has remarked, this scene strongly reminds us of the beginning of Act 5 Scene 2 of *Othello*, except that the gender roles are reversed. While in *Othello* it is Othello who is preoccupied with 'the cause', and looks down at Desdemona in bed, in *Urania* it is Pamphilia who was much concerned about the cause of Amphilanthus's jealousy, and she looked down at him on the bed (Miller, 1991 162–3).

His answer to her enquiry was that 'though hee was assured of her love, yett his [love] was soe infinite to her as hee grudged any eyes showld feed on that rich fruit of her beauty butt his owne, and onely his' (*Urania* II, 45). Here Wroth foregrounds the egoistic male desire for possession that constitutes the core of Amphilanthus's love for Pamphilia. In response to Amphilanthus's possessive desire, Pamphilia asserted her selfhood independent of the male gaze, and, furthermore, pointed out the possibility that there was a double standard underlying Amphilanthus's attitude:

> [E]yes are wanderers, and fasting will seeke to feed on any food, especially if neere in ther way, and soe itt may bee some may endlesly enough looke on mee. Harts are alsoe travelours and seeke for harbour, yett as oft refused entertainment as taken in; and all this while noe hurt dunn, for if a lady looke on you ore sue to you for pitty, you can looke of[f] and refusingly frowne. May nott a lady doe the like, especially my self, your faithfull friend? (*Urania* II, 45)

Amphilanthus, however, still did not understand Pamphilia's insistence on her independent self, and asserted that the bond of marriage was the only way to prevent his jealousy:

[W]hile wee are butt lovers I ame suspitious, love never having the true heigth of Zeale in love till the knott never to bee untide bee tied; therfor knitt that, and noe more shall you see mee suspect, nor indeed is ther perfect love with out a pretty little Jealousie. (*Urania* II, 45)

As if often the case with male characters in English Renaissance drama, Amphilanthus thought that marriage would ensure his sole ownership of the one he loves and will, therefore, remove his jealousy: '"That will take away all cause of suspect or Jelousy," sayd hee, "when I am sure possessor of what I most desire"' (*Urania* II, 45).

Throughout *Urania*, Pamphilia is often described as retreating to a private space in order to engage in reading or writing poetry. Thus, it is made evident that Pamphilia is an individual of great creativity, one whose sense of self cannot be possessed by any man even by means of marriage. In his attitude towards her wish to keep her independent selfhood, Rodomandro made a great contrast to Amphilanthus. As has already been mentioned, in his marriage proposal, Rodomandro said that he would allow her to have her own independent space in which she could devote herself to her intellectual pursuits, and which he promised never to interfere with, except for looking at her from a distance. Amphilanthus, by contrast, was so far from being able either to acknowledge Pamphilia's selfhood or to allow her to maintain her independence, that he fell prey to jealousy if any man other than himself paid special attention to her. In order to remove Amphilanthus's jealousy, however, Pamphilia agreed to a secret marriage with him, and the ceremony was conducted in front of their friends the next morning.

It is interesting to note that in previous episodes Wroth has introduced the idea that jealousy derives from an individual sense of unworthiness. Dacia, a place where men maintain absolute dominance over women, for instance, is described as 'a strict place', where 'a hard hand is held over the woemen, the men having are an naturall knowing unworthnes about them, which procures too much hatefull Jealousy' (*Urania* II, 14). This concept of male jealousy is also forcefully expressed in Part I of *Urania*, where the jealousy of Lisia's husband, who is totally incapable of esteeming her worth, is explained in terms of its 'roote being selfe knowledge of unworthynes' (*Urania* I, 556).

While Othello's jealousy can be attributed to his unconscious sense of his being 'unworthy' of the beautiful white Desdemona, especially in comparison with Cassio, a fair Florentine, Amphilanthus's jealousy of Rodomandro can be said to be motivated by his own sense of 'unworthiness' when faced with the beautiful, courageous black Tartarian. Furthermore, as mentioned before, in view of his acceptance of a female asserting selfhood, Rodomandro is described as much more understanding than Amphilanthus, whom, rather ironically, people constantly admire throughout *Urania*.

There is a puzzling aspect to these portrayals of the two kings, however, since in other descriptions of blackness in *Urania*, as has been pointed out by Kim Hall and other critics, rather negative feelings are articulated. To express her constant love for Amphilanthus despite his repeated betrayals, Pamphilia said to herself: 'I rather would wish to be a Black-more, or any thing, more dreadfull, then allure affection to me, if not from you' (*Urania* I, 465). Also, in the Throne of Love, where, drinking from the magic stream, the travellers including Pamphilia, Urania and Parselius, all became confused, Urania's servant had a hallucination in which she saw her beloved, Allimarlus, embracing a black woman: 'Allimarlus in the second Towre, kissing and embracing a Black-more: which so farre inraged her, being passionately in love with him, as she must goe to revenge her selfe of that injurie' (*Urania* I, 49).

Critics are divided in their explanations of the significance of this sudden and brief appearance of a 'Black-more'. Josephine A. Roberts regards the figure as a dream symbol that 'serve[s] physically as a double for the maid, allowing her to view her subservience from the outside and eventually to become conscious of her own self-abnegation' (1991 188). On the other hand, Kim Hall thinks that the blackness of the woman whom the maid saw in Allimarlus's arms symbolises women's fear of the foreign women their beloved men would encounter in their adventures (1995 188–9). These interpretations, though different in specific aspects, share the notion that blackness is seen as something undesirable. Also, in Part II of *Urania*, a black knight called Follietto appears. He complains of 'what feminine fairnes doth among ladys. My tanned, scorchd face cowld gain noe thing.' (*Urania* II, 60).

What differentiates these people with black complexions from Rodomandro, apart from his social status as King, is that he is never called a Moor, but rather is called 'the great Cham'. As has been said, Wroth situates Tartar somewhere in the region of the Black Sea, and seems to regard Rodomandro's race as Asian, not as African. Benedick, complaining to Don Pedro about Beatrice in *Much Ado About Nothing*, refers to the great Cham when he hyperbolically expresses his wish to be sent away so as to escape from her sharp tongue: 'Will your Grace command me any service to the world's end? I will go on the slightest errand now to the Antipodes that you can devise to send me on; I will fetch you a toothpicker now from the furthest inch of Asia, bring you a length of Prester John's foot, fetch you a hair off the great Cham's beard, do you any embassage to the Pigmies, rather than hold three words' conference with this harpy' (2. 1. 183–8). While Shakespeare uses the term 'the great Cham' in a comical representation of the total 'otherness' of remote areas, Wroth does not introduce any pejorative implication in describing the 'otherness' of Rodomandro. The Tartarian masque Rodomandro presented on his first visit to the Morean Court is described as being performed in an entirely dignified manner, the only differences from other masques being the costumes and styles, which were totally Tartarian.

In her description of Rodomandro, Wroth never uses the term 'Moor', though forcefully foregrounding his blackness. Here it seems that Wroth intentionally avoids using the word, preferring to use the expression 'the Cham' in order not to invoke the negative image of blackness attached to the term 'Moor' at that time. The 'great Cham', the fierce Mongolian leader, had threatened both Christian and Islamic regions with invasion in the thirteenth century. Although Christopher Marlowe may have this Mongolian warrior in mind in dramatising Tamburlaine the Great, Mongolian military power no longer posed a serious threat to Christian territories in the Renaissance period, and had simply come to embody cultural otherness. Thus, by portraying Rodomandro as black, though not as a Moor but rather as the 'Cham', Wroth tries to present the possibility of there being beauty and attractiveness in cultural otherness, though she invokes negative images of the blackness of Moors in other parts of *Urania*.

However, even in the case of Rodomandro, it is true, as Kim Hall mentioned, that he is always put in a secondary position to Amphilanthus. Admiration for his beautiful looks is often modified by expressions such as 'though black'. Also, the whiteness of Rodomandro's hand is emphasised in order to make up for the blackness of his face (Hall, 1995 189). This is also the case with another good-looking black man in *Urania*, Follietto:

> Wee must goe with Follietto in such rage and distraction for having his handsomnes disgraced (which hee held most deere) and more than in truth deserved. Yett he was, to speake truthe, tollerable and soe enough to bee commended for a Very handsom black man, well-shaped for strength, wel-featured of face, butt ill-complexiones; yett had hee exceeding white hands, and they showed a hope his skinn was answerable. For the rest, his minde was only to haughty; els indeed, hee was a gallant man. (*Urania* II, 61)

Follietto, being 'Cholorick', can be said to be an immature version of Rodomandro. Although he was 'to haughty' and had no patience, he is described as having some good qualities, the only problem being that he had not yet learnt how to use them (*Urania* II, 61). Though rejected by Denia, with whom he was in love, he was proud of his complexion: '"Farewell, sweet Lady," sayd hee, "and the next scurched face you meet with, remember mee. I am sunn burnt; itt came from heaven, and therfor I ame contented"' (*Urania* II, 60). As Josephine Roberts notes (*Urania* II, 489, note 60. 24), because of his immaturity, Wroth puns on folly and his name, but as in the case of Rodomandro, never calls him a 'Moor'. Generally speaking, it seems that the race/gender system in Renaissance England never allowed the cultural otherness of a Moor to be associated with attractiveness, though a very few travellers to Islamic countries seem to have recognised the cultural otherness they found there not as inferior but simply as different, as a culture of 'another kind of civility, different from ours' (Blount, 1638 484).

If Rodomandro is placed in a secondary position to Amphilanthus, this is not due to his blackness. Not only Rodomandro, but any man who falls in love with Pamphilia, is placed in a secondary position and rejected by Pamphilia. Even Steriamus, the beauty of whose white skin was so admired in *Urania* (*Urania* I, 19–20), was flatly refused by Pamphilia, once he began to confess his love for her:

> 'If you have', said she, 'any busines, I shalbe ready to do you any service in it: but if it be concerning your glasse discovery, know this, you shall doe best to bee silent; for a greater offence you cannot doe mee.' (*Urania* I 70)

Likewise, Leandrus's suit to Pamphilia was rejected. Although she accepted her father's recommendation of the young King on the grounds of 'his worth, and the fitnese of his estate' (*Urania* I, 262), she put him in a secondary position in relation to her country. In a further argument against her father's recommendation of Leandrus as a potential husband, she expressed her lack of love for and suspicion of the young King, who, she insisted, desired her only for the purpose of expanding his territory (*Urania* I, 262). Amphilanthus told him that he had heard her saying that 'she was already bestowed upon her people, and had married her selfe to them' (*Urania* I, 264).

The greatest puzzle is over understanding why Pamphilia continued to be obsessed by her desire for Amphilanthus, in spite of his repeated betrayals and of her acknowledgement of the black Tartarian King's personal integrity as well as his military prowess. It seems that here again Wroth was faced with the constraints of the race/gender discourse in English Renaissance society; she lacked any language to assert her heroine's integrity other than the one provided by the contemporary discourse that identified female constancy to a white male as female integrity.

It is true that Pamphilia and Amphilanthus shared their pleasure in writing and reading poetry and admired each other's works. And yet, due to the constant change in Amphilanthus's love, Pamphilia's desire for his constant love for her was never fulfilled. This is particularly the case after her marriage with Rodomandro and Amphilanthus's marriage with the princess of Slovania. However, whenever she felt deep frustration and sorrow over her desire, her creativity was awakened and she resorted to reading and writing poetry. Thus, Wroth presents Amphilanthus's inconstancy and Pamphilia's constancy to him as leading to the latter's construction of a sense of self through writing. Furthermore, Pamphilia's constancy is by no means defined as the usual patriarchal one, for she is described as constant to her beloved, not to her husband.

In conclusion, the representation of the mixed-race marriage between Pamphilia and the attractively black Rodomandro is groundbreaking in that it upsets the conventional discourse of marriage in Elizabethan England in terms of both gender and race. First of all, in contrast to the orthodox view of marriage, it is made evident that Pamphilia's selfhood could not be subsumed by her husband or by her much admired lover, who was white; yet her sense of unfulfilled desire led to the construction of her sense of self through writing. At the same time, though in other parts of *Urania* Wroth describes negative aspects of blackness, to most of which she applies the term 'Moor', her portrayal of Rodomandro, who is called 'the Cham' rather than being characterised as a Moor, presents the possibility of blackness being attractive and of even having superior qualities to those of white males.[20] Because of the lack in Renaissance England both of a discourse that associates blackness with attractiveness and integrity, and of a discourse that defines female integrity in terms other than female constancy, Wroth's portrayal of Pamphilia may at first glance look rather conventional in terms of her constancy to her first beloved, who is a white, good-looking, and brave King. In fact, Wroth's portrayal of a mixed-race marriage poses a question about the prevalent discourse on the superiority of white males both to females and black males. Thus, both in terms of gender and race, the representation of mixed-race relationships provided in *Urania* is a strikingly unusual one in English Renaissance literature, and suggests a new way of looking at mixed-race marriage in the society of early modern England.

The representations of illegitimate children in *Urania* Part II

In *Urania* II there appear some illegitimate children who bear important roles in terms of the development of the story and the political context. It is helpful to examine the significance of Wroth's representations of illegitimate children in comparison with Shakespeare's portrayal of the Bastard in *King John* (Chamberlain's, 1590–91).

Among Shakespeare's history plays, *King John* occupies a unusual position. The character to whom the author assigns the largest role is not a real monarch in history but a dramatic invention, the Bastard. Though fictional, the Bastard is made a much more compelling character than the King who gives the play its title.

The Bastard is a natural son of Lady Falconbridge, another fictional character, by King Richard Coeur-de-lion. The Bastard has much in common with self-serving illegitimate characters in Shakespeare's later plays, such as Don John in *Much Ado About Nothing* and Edmund in *King Lear*, but he is portrayed as sympathetic, intelligent, courageous and witty, as well as ambitious for advancement. Furthermore, the Bastard is not merely a commentator, a role that is often given to an outsider of the realpolitik in Shakespeare's history plays. He fights fiercely for the English cause, greatly contributing to sustain the English force against the French amidst the ever-shifting situation of the war. The warrior that King John trusts most is apparently the Bastard, to whom he assigns 'the ordering of this present time' (5. 1. 79) and asks to support his son Henry after his death. It is also the Bastard who, swearing his 'faithful services/And true subjection' (5. 7. 108–9) to the new King, delivers the final speech of the play.

Another unique quality of the play is the strong presence of women; they aggressively interfere with politics both on the English and French sides. In Shakespeare's English history plays, there appear some powerful women who assume the traditionally male roles of leading politics and wars, such as Queen Margaret and Joan la Pucelle in *Henry VI, Part I* (1590, Strange's). Women in *King John* do not take such radical actions, but unlike most of the female characters in Shakespeare's other history plays, they are not simply the victims of the ruthless and absurd human situations created by the male politicians and warriors. In particular, Queen Elinor and Lady Constance heavily involve themselves in politics, each forcefully insisting on the legitimacy of her son's claim to the

English crown. They slander each other fiercely onstage, calling their opponent's son 'bastard' (2. 1. 129).

Lady Falconbridge is a woman with the least power who has the briefest appearance on the stage. The only scene in which she appears is Act 1 Scene 1, in which she verifies to the Bastard that he is the product of her adultery with King Richard Coeur-de-lion, not the elder son of Sir Robert Falconbridge. Although at first she is reluctant to admit her marital infidelity, once the Bastard tells her that he has given up his legal legitimacy as a Falconbridge, yielding to his younger brother Robert the title and the lands of Sir Robert, she proudly admits the truth (1. 1. 255–60).

It is Queen Elinor, not King John, who first recognises the Bastard's resemblance to King Richard Coeur-de-lion, and offers him the position of 'the reputed son of Coeur-de-lion,/Lord of thy presence and no land beside' (1. 1. 137–8), which the Bastard accepts with great joy and gratitude. Rendering legitimacy of every kind utterly meaningless, Queen Elinor tells the Bastard: 'I am thy grandam, Richard; call me so' (1. 1. 169). The Bastard endorses her defiance of legitimacy, saying 'I am, howe'uer I was begot' (1. 1. 176). Once official legitimacy is sidestepped, Lady Falconbridge is proud of having given her son the father who epitomises ideal manliness. Trying to remove his mother's sense of shame with tenderness, the Bastard thanks her for creating him: 'Madam, I would not wish a better father' (1. 1. 262). After this scene, Lady Falconbridge appears no more on the stage.

Thus, by inventing forceful dramatic figures, the Bastard and his mother, Shakespeare presents as meaningless and powerless every kind of orthodoxy, such as legitimacy, inheritance and female fidelity to the marriage bond, which had great significance in the actual history of early modern England. On the other hand, male potency inherited from a biological father is treated as of utmost importance in the play. The Bastard, though illegitimate, not only bears the physical resemblance to, but also embodies all the fine male qualities of, King Richard Coeur-de-lion.

Queen Elinor overrules King John, even interrupting his official talk with the French ambassador Chantillon (1. 1. 5). To legitimise her son's rule, she invents a new ideology of legitimacy based on his 'strong possession' rather than 'right' (1. 1. 40). However, after her ranting against Constance over the legitimacy of the kingship of their sons in Act 2, Scene 1, and as King John's lack of political capability is being exposed, the Queen's presence is gradually diminished. Her death is simply announced by the messenger (4. 2. 121–3), though King John is emotionally shaken by the news.

In the play, where every source of authority, including ethics and royal genealogy, is made ambiguous, and therefore official legitimacy is reduced to a fiction created by each side—English and French—what is meaningful is only the male power represented by the body of the Bastard. Even Lady Falconbridge's illicit sexuality is connived thanks to the playwright's creation of the Bastard, though, as Howard and Rackin argue, it indicates the potentiality of women's power to subvert the patriarchal social order, which is based on 'men's genealogical continuity and their genealogical claims' (Howard and Rackin, 1997 131). Lady Falconbridge, who is powerless by herself, becomes a woman who has a possibility of getting involved in politics through the power of her natural son.

Alison Findlay thinks that the death of Arthur signifies the turning point for the meaning of bastardy in the play (1994 204–8). With Arthur's death, the order of legitimacy in the play is completely broken down. Philip, now Sir Richard, recognises such a desolate situation:

> How easy dost thou take all England up!
> From forth this morsel of dead royalty.
> The life, the right and truth of all this realm
> Is fled to heaven; and England now is left
> To tug and scamble, and to part by th' teeth
> The unow'd interest of proud-swelling state. (4. 3. 148–153)

The irony is that in the play world of this English history, all kinds of patriarchal authority are disrupted, not only by powerful female historical figures who openly challenge them, but also by a fictional woman of lesser power, Lady Falconbridge. She embodies the contradiction of patriarchal succession, as well as a woman's possibility to get involved in politics by giving birth to an illegitimate son by a great man.

On the other hand, the Bastard in *King John* is an exceptional case. In Shakespeare's other plays, the typical attributes of bastardy are associated with wickedness and subversion (Neill, 2000 127–48). The foremost example is Edmund in *King Lear*. As B. J. and Mary Sokol argue, the public attitude towards bastard-bearing became increasingly intolerant at around the time when *King Lear* was written. The Sokols think that the more austere attitudes, and with these a rapid fall in the rate of illegitimacy can be attributed to the combined effects of advancing Puritanism and the Elizabethan Poor Laws of 1576 (2003 161–2). This historical fact may have been reflected in the unfavourable depictions of bastards not only in Shakespeare's later plays but in the plays in the seventeenth century in general.[21]

The date of the composition of *King John* is still open to question, but can be considered to be between 1590 and 1591. England in this period was ruled by Queen Elizabeth, who had been declared a bastard when Henry VIII's marriage to Anne Boleyn was annulled; some people still considered her to be illegitimate. Elizabeth's possible bastardy and femininity both ran counter to the orthodox patriarchal concepts of national history. Moreover, the country was worried about who would succeed to the throne when the ageing Queen died, whose legitimacy was after all not unequivocally accepted. The Earl of Essex, of course, was not the legitimate heir, but was ascending greatly in power both at the Court and among the public especially after his successful attempt to sack Cadiz in 1596.

Alison Findlay thinks that the Bastard's final words, 'Nought shall make us rue,/If England to itself do rest but true' (5. 7. 121–2), would have encouraged Shakespeare's original audience to acknowledge the reality that 'a woman and a bastard was ruling the country' (1994 208). If so, the Bastard's speech could have worked both to undermine and uphold Elizabeth's government; what matters most to establish Protestant England is not legitimacy but the capacity of the monarch to unify the nation. As a fiction, therefore, the Bastard in the play could have embodied a convenient vehicle to provide the audience with one way of resolving the political anxiety of the English people at the time. Thus, what is most problematic in the fictional figure of the Bastard in this play is that he poses serious questions as to the legitimacy of the patriarchal social order, which endows with great power only the eldest son born within wedlock. Due to these radical elements of the play, Virginia Mason Vaughan calls *King John* 'Shakespeare's postmodern history play' (Vaughan, 2003 380).

About twenty-five years after *King John* was written, Lady Mary Wroth's *Urania* Part I was published. Because of the uproar caused by the romance at the Court, Lady Mary had to ask the Duke of Buckingham to return to her the presentation copy she had given him, promising to get back all the copies in print. It is quite likely that because of this hostile response to her work, the continuation part of this romance, generally called *Urania* Part II, remained a holograph manuscript for nearly four centuries, published in 1999 for the first time. The date of the composition of the second part is open to question, but Margaret P. Hannay in her recent book thinks that it was written after 1624, in the period following the birth of Wroth's illegitimate son and daughter (2010 248–51). What distinguishes the second part from the first part of *Urania* is the frequent appearance of natural sons. What is more remarkable is that these characters are given favourable descriptions in most cases.

Among the natural sons in *Urania* Part II, the most important figure is the Faire Designe, a man 'designed to all worthy actes' (*Urania* II, 327). He is introduced by the author as the 'most gallant and delicate youthe as eyes cowld possibly beeholde' (*Urania* II, 297) and as 'the bravest of younge knights, the true mirroire of perfect knighthood' (*Urania* II, 324–5). And yet this young man was parentless and made his self-introduction to Amphilanthus: 'I knowe noe parents, nor have I a name more then the unknowne' (*Urania* II, 297). The Faire Designe adored Amphilanthus and wanted to be knighted by him. His request being accepted, the Faire Designe attended Amphilanthus on his adventures, demonstrating his marvellous performances in various battles they fought together. Amphilanthus acknowledged his excellent knighthood, but the romance ended suddenly in the middle when the Faire Designe, separated from Amphilanthus, was still fighting in the island to search for Amphilanthus, whom he had resolved never to leave if once found. The final line of *Urania* Part II reads that on hearing about the Faire Designe's courageous acts, 'Amphilanthus wa[s] extreamly', and then the romance ends incompletely. Amphilanthus's exact response to the Faire Designe's military prowess thus remains unknown forever.

Judging from the whole context of *Urania* Part II, the Faire Designe seems to be the natural son of Pamphilia by her first cousin/lover, Amphilanthus. Critics generally agree that the Faire Designe was modelled on a real historic figure, Mary Wroth's natural son William by William Herbert the third Earl of Pembroke. Wroth's portrayal of the Faire Designe as an embodiment of ideal manhood as well as a powerful supporter of Amphilanthus may have come from her strong desire to make William Herbert acknowledge his parenthood of her son, though Herbert never did so. Herbert's acknowledgement would have given Mary's William, as in the case with the fictional figure of the Bastard in *King John*, various political and economic privileges. The greatest one would have been the possibility that William could have inherited some of the enormous estate and wealth of William Herbert, who did not have a legitimate heir after the death of his son.

What Mary Wroth aimed at through her descriptions of the Faire Designe, however, seems not to have been limited to William's financial and political gain. As Josephine A. Roberts states, at the heart of *Urania* lies an ardent desire for the revival of the Holy Roman Empire through Protestantism in Europe (Introduction to *Urania* I, xxxix–liv). Wroth casts her central male character Amphilanthus in the role of an emperor who unified the Western world. In the year 1621, when Wroth published *Urania*, such a representation of Amphilanthus would have been regarded as a sharp critique of King James, who had been unable to take a definite Protestant position, refusing to extend political help to his daughter Queen Elizabeth of Bohemia and her husband Frederick, who were then involved in a political crisis in the face of Catholic powers in Europe.

The significance of the interconnection between the public and private within *Urania* was examined with great insight in pioneering studies by Paul Salzman, Mary Ellen Lamb and Helen Hackett, but in most cases they relate it mainly to the issue of the complex interaction of gender and genre in the work. Yet, in view of the political climate of England in around 1621, we need to think about the work through a new definition of political power, as has been argued by Susan Wiseman, particularly women's exclusion from political involvement in early modern England (Wiseman, 2007).

The Faire Designe met Amphilanthus for the first time while accompanying the King of Bohemia on his trip from Morea, where Pamphilia's parents reigned, back to his own country, Bohemia (*Urania* II, 297). It is not only the Faire Designe who emphasises the importance of Bohemia to the characters in *Urania* Part II. In relation to Bohemia there appears another illegitimate son, Andromarko, who was knighted by the King of Bohemia (*Urania* II, 289). Andromarko was the Prince of Cyprus and a natural son of Polarchos King of Cyprus, who acknowledged him as his son. Andromarko, a counterpart of the Faire Designe, was also portrayed as a handsome, courageous, fine youth as well as a great admirer of Amphilanthus. Amphilanthus appointed him as an attendant to the Faire Designe in fighting various battles against villains. As is always the case with the characters in her works, Mary Wroth projects real historical figures onto various characters in her fictions (Wynne-Davies, '"So Much Worth"', 2000 76–93). Andromarko seems to be another projection of her own natural son, William. As noted above, Polarchos's acknowledgement of him may have been intended to encourage William Herbert to acknowledge his son.

The King of Bohemia, Ollorandus, was the husband of Melasinda, the Queen of Hungary, and a good friend of Pamphilia and Amphilanthus. After attending Pamphilia's wedding to the King of Tartar in Morea, he departed for Prague, his home town (*Urania* II, 278). However, Ollorandus was attacked by villains in the neighbourhood and Queen Melasinda was taken hostage. Informing Amphilanthus that the King of Bohemia was in need of help against villains (*Urania* II, 297), the

Faire Designe joined Amphilanthus to rescue the King and Queen of Bohemia. Amphilanthus was particularly pleased with the Faire Designe's courageous acts in the battle.

When Wroth was writing the second part of *Urania*, the current King and Queen of Bohemia were indeed in need of help, in particular from Protestant England, in the face of their political and religious conflicts with the Habsburgs. While the marriage of Princess Elizabeth, King James's daughter, with the Elector Palatine Frederick, the future King of Bohemia, was under negotiation, William Herbert and Lucy Harington, Countess of Bedford—who was a good friend of the Princess and had Sidney blood—greatly supported the militant Protestant Prince Henry, who advocated the marriage in order to promote the Protestant cause on the Continent (Wynne-Davies, 2007 100–2). Robert Sidney, Mary Wroth's father, also seems to have been influential in the negotiation of the marriage. Most probably, Mary Wroth herself, under the influence of William Herbert and Lucy Harington, was helping to promote the marriage, despite Queen Anne's strong opposition to it. Elizabeth married Frederick in February 1613 and left England for Heidelberg in April 1613. Robert Sidney, with his son William and Lucy Countess of Bedford, accompanied the royal couple to Heidelberg (Hannay et al., 2005 182). Lucy Harington visited Elizabeth in Bohemia in August 1616. Elizabeth and Frederick became the King and Queen of Bohemia in 1619, but soon after they fell into serious conflict with the Habsburgs, which was part of the Thirty Years War. Although the English Protestants continuously petitioned King James to extend his political and financial help to rescue his daughter in Bohemia, the King refused to make explicit his Protestant position and to antagonize the Habsburgs by helping his daughter. The episode in which the Faire Designe strongly supported Amphilanthus in rescuing the King and Queen of Bohemia seems to suggest his capacity, despite his illegitimacy, for providing strong help to Amphilanthus in fighting for Protestantism on the Continent. Amphilanthus is generally identified with William Herbert, and throughout *Urania* he is called the Emperor of the Roman Empire. Thus, by giving birth to Herbert's natural son William, Mary Wroth, albeit indirectly, acquired the power to become involved in contemporary English politics as well as to make clear her Protestant position under the disguise of the literary form of romance in *Urania* II.

The descriptions of the Bastard in *King John* and the Faire Designe in *Urania* II both indicate the significance of the intermingling of fiction and history for the authors to make their points in the face of both conventional historiography and of social realities. What matters most in these works is whether the male characters possess male potency, not the legal authority by which they come to possess such a quality. Women such as Lady Falconbridge or Mary Wroth, and probably also Pamphilia, though she is not clearly identified as the Fair Designe's mother in *Urania* II, can exert great influence on the political state in the fictional worlds through their illicit, private relations with men of great capabilities, and by giving birth to their illegitimate sons. The issue of bastardy represented in these works thus opens up possibilities for women's political involvement through the interconnection between the public and private in early modern England.

Pamphilia's cabinets in *Urania*

In view of the fact that Lady Mary Wroth published *The Countess of Montgomery's Urania* at the time when the issue of female self-assertion was a very controversial topic in society, the role of ladies' cabinets, which are often referred to in both Parts I and II, features importantly at the border between the public and the private domains of women's self-expression.

In *Urania* Mary Wroth uses the term 'cabinet' mainly in three ways. First, a cabinet is a repository or case in which to keep valuable items and documents (*OED*, cabinet, 5). It can be small and light enough for a woman to move from one place to another. Such a seventeenth-century cabinet covered with stump work is displayed in the Queen Elizabeth's Room in Penshurst Place. This box is decorated with the embroidery of Biblical stories on the colourful, rich textile, and has a keyhole in the front centre. The cabinet (see Figure 3.2) is small enough to be portable for a woman[22].

Second, a cabinet can be a closet in which to keep precious things; in this case it is rather large and heavy, not easily movable (*OED*, cabinet 5). In Penshurst Place many such cabinets are on display, some of which came from the Netherlands in the seventeenth century. Furthermore, Wroth uses the term 'cabinet' as a small private chamber (*OED*, cabinet 3). In respect of women's self-expression, it is a cabinet in the first sense that entails the most complicated and important issues. Not only 'a cabinet' but other terms such as 'a cask', 'a desk' or 'a closet' are used in *Urania* to refer to a small repository where a woman keeps her precious items.

It is interesting that there is a difference between Wroth's description of Pamphilia's cabinets and those cabinets owned by other women in *Urania*. Pamphilia keeps her poems or other writings in her cabinets.

Figure 3.2 A seventeenth-century English cabinet covered with stump work
Source: By kind permission of Viscount De L'Isle from his private collection at Penshurst Place, Kent, England.

She often goes to her private space, which is called a cabinet or a chamber or a room, particularly when confronted with repeated betrayals by her beloved, Amphilanthus. She reads books and poetry in solitude, examining her own emotions at her desertion by the man she believes to be 'the strongest and bravest man breathing' (*Urania* I 197). On one such occasion, the narrator describes her as follows:

> Being heavie, she went into her bed, but not with hope of rest, but to get more libertie to express her woe. [. . .][T]aking a little *Cabinet* with her, wherein she had many papers, and setting a light by her, [she] began to reade them, but few of them pleasing her, she took pen and paper, and being excellent in writing, writ these verses following. (*Urania* I 62. Italics are mine.)

It is not clear whether the papers Pamphilia was trying to read were written by herself or by others. However, since in both parts of *Urania* she is often portrayed as reading romance or poetry written by others, she may have here attempted to read works by others but, discontented with them, started her own writing.

When Rodomandro, the King of Tartar, tries to make a marriage proposal to Pamphilia, he finds her in the woods, working on her writing and surrounded by books. Noticing his approach, she first puts them into her cabinet, which is called a 'deske' here, and then greets him in a formal manner:

> Then hee went to her whom hee found alone, onely boockes about her, which she ever extreamly loved and she writing. Butt when she parceaved him, she clapt her papers into her *deske*, and rising told him she was glad to see him waulke soe well abroad. (*Urania* II 270–1. Italics are mine.)

Thus, Wroth describes Pamphilia's cabinets as embodying her creative self itself.[23]

On the other hand, Wroth uses the cabinets belonging to other women for the purpose of offering her critique of gender or society. In Part I there is an interesting episode, in which Wroth employs both terms, 'cabinet' and 'deske', in her description. On one of his visits to Pamphilia, Amphilanthus asked her to show him her poems, the excellence of which he had heard from others but had never seen. Although reacting in her usual modest manner, she accepted his request and said that she was going to her 'Cabinet [her chamber] to fetch them'. But Amphilanthus insisted on accompanying her there and they both went into Pamphilia's 'Cabinet':

> When they were there, she tooke a *deske*, wherein her papers lay, and kissing them, delivered all shee had saved from the fire, being in her owne hand unto him, yet blushing told him, she was ashamed, so much of her folly should present her selfe unto his eyes. (*Urania* I, 320. Italics are mine.)

The passage implies that Pamphilia used to burn her poems if she was not satisfied with them. Probably this was what Wroth had done with those writings of her own that she did not like. In fact, Pamphilia's poems drew great admiration from Amphilanthus: 'the best he had seene made by women' (*Urania* I 320). Yet, remarking that 'he must find fault with' them (*Urania* I 320), he pointed out that in her poems, which seemed to deal with her love, she probably counterfeited her passion. She immediately denied that this was so:

She smild, and blusht, and softly said (fearing that he or her selfe should heare her say so much), 'Alas my Lord, you are deceived in this for I doe love.' (*Urania* I 320)

In the same box Amphilanthus found a portrait of Pamphilia, which she had drawn to send to her sister but forgotten about:

He tooke it up, and looking in it, found her picture curiously drawne by the best hand of that time. (*Urania* I 321)

Amphilanthus liked the portrait so much that he pleaded with her to give it to him, so that he could carry it with him to the field. He said that her sister 'may have others' (*Urania* I 321). In going to the battlefield, knights in romance often carried the portrait or tokens of the ladies they loved. Amphilanthus wanted the portrait to display as his gesture of chivalry following the traditions among the knights in romances. Thus, Pamphilia's cabinet contained her truth, and naturally the access to its contents was strictly limited to her very close family, friends and lover/cousin. The happiness of the lovers described here, however, is deconstructed in the episodes in Part II, in which while staying in Crete, Amphilanthus fell into a trap set by the Queen of Candia, resulting in his marrying the Princess of Slavonia (*Urania* II 132–4), despite the *de praesenti* marriage ceremony he had performed with Pamphilia some time before (*Urania* II 45–6).

In the cases of other women, cabinets are used by Wroth to imply her criticism of gender and society. One of the most impressive episodes in relation to ladies' cabinets is that involving Melasinda, the Queen of Hungary. She was in love with Ollorandus, the young son of the King of Bohemia. However, following a revolt led by Rodolindus, a bastard son of her uncle who ascended to the throne after her father died, she was forced to marry him in order to save the country from destruction. Despite the political power and military prowess of many princes around her, including Amphilanthus, ironically, as Wroth describes it, her forced marriage was the only means to rescue her country from the revolt.

Even after her marriage with Rodolindus, Melasinda secretly continued to love Ollorandus. One day she received a loving letter from Ollorandus, but she decided to burn it:

"[. . .] mine eyes thrice happy that have seene these words written by the best of men, and yet," sigh'd she, "when al is done the fire must consume you, that is *the cabinet* must hold your truths," [. . .] the Queene, whose letter was no sooner ended, but with teares with the same light shee sealed hers, she also gave the death to the other, or rather the safer life, sacrificing it unto their loves, carefully putting the ashes up in a daintie *Cabinet*, and inclosing them within.... (*Urania* I 272. Italics are mine.)

While watching the letter being burned, she wrote a poem about her sorrow. After the letter turned into ashes, she put it in the cabinet, which she locked. But she had memorised the expressions in Ollorandus's letter. Every day she repeated the action of bringing out the ashes from the cabinet, looking at them in tears while reciting his letter from her memory, kissing them, and returning the ashes to the cabinet.

Through this episode Wroth suggests that in the locked cabinet Melasinda kept her private world, which was entirely distinct from her pubic life as the married Queen of Hungary; this was her world into which no one could intrude. Later, after Rodolindus's death, Melasinda and Ollorandus married and became the King and Queen of Bohemia as well as of Hungary. As has been argued above, the representations of the King and Queen of Bohemia in Part II of *Urania* have strong resonances with the King and Queen of Bohemia at Wroth's time; the King and the Queen in *Urania*, after having attended Pamphilia's wedding to Rodomandro in Moria, encountered the rebellion of their countrymen and could not go back to their country. Like the historical King and Queen of Bohemia in the seventeenth century, the King and Queen in *Urania* Part II were confronted with serious political struggles in Bohemia. Though Melasinda could keep her private sphere in her cabinet in Part I of *Urania*, after she became the Queen of Bohemia and Hungary in Part II, the political problems of the world were too large in scale to be contained in her cabinet.

Another problematic episode with regard to ladies' cabinets is the one concerning Sirelius and his wife. Although happily married at first, their marriage having been solemnised by the King's command at the Court, less than two years afterwards, the couple's discord reached a peak. Sirelius suspected that his wife had a lover and forbade the man to come to his house or his wife to see him. However, she refused to obey her husband's command, saying that 'by chance shee might meet him' (*Urania* I 516). Sirelius broke up her cabinets to examine the letters kept there, but found only ones such as those between friends. According to the narrator, the letters 'appeared to jealousie to be amorous' and Sirelius treated his wife badly. Sirelius thought that he would find the truth of his wife in her cabinets, but could not. Thus, the cabinet is described as limited in its capacity to embody female selfhood. Melasinda's cabinet contains the truth of her selfhood, but only as the ashes of her beloved's letter. Nobody could gain access to her self, even if they opened her cabinet, where only the ashes lay. The same can be said about the cabinets of Sirelius's wife; though her husband broke up her cabinets, the letters kept there failed to reveal the truth of her mind.

This episode is often referred to in relation to Lord Edward Denny, a friend of Sir Philip Sidney. Thinking that Wroth portrayed his daughter Honora and her husband James Hay in this episode, Lord Denny fiercely attacked Wroth in his poem for writing and publishing such a 'scandalous' book, calling her 'Hemaphrodite' for breaching the gender code. He wrote that Wroth should model herself upon her aunt Mary, Countess of Pembroke, writing only on religious matters and publishing translations.[24] In this episode, the wife's father, who was furious with his only daughter for damaging their family honour, is drawn satirically:

> her father a phantastical thing, vaine as Courtiers, rash as mad-men, and ignorant as women, would needs (out of folly, ill nature, and waywardnesse, which hee cald care of his honour, and his friends quiet) kill his daughter, and so cut off the blame, or spot, this her offence might lay upon his noble bloud, [. . .] hee held his hand, which with a Dagger was giving her a cruel and untimely end, yet a little scratch he gave her just on her hart, which otherwise had laine open to the disgrace of an unmerciful and unworthy father. She cryd out, the husband held his wife, who poore Lady was ready to fall under the weight of unkindnes and danger. (*Urania* I 516)

Procatus, who used to serve Sirelius but was now disguised as a shepherd, added a sardonic comment:

> It was a strange sight to behold a father incensed for a husbands sake against an onely child, and that husband to be the shield of her defence, from whom, if at al, the wrong was to rise. (*Urania* I 516)

Some other episodes also depict a woman's cabinet as not large enough to hold female selfhood. For instance, Liana, in order to explain to Urania her deep sorrow at her beloved's betrayal, compared her heart to a cabinet: 'so fild with treasure, as though not it self, yet the lock or hinges cannot containe it, but breake open' (*Urania* I, 253). Liana told Urania that like such a cabinet her anger and sorrow grew too strong to be held within herself, so that she came to the woods where she could freely express her emotions (*Urania* I 253).

Despite the suppression of its sale, the published Part I, *The Countess of Montmogery's Urania*, seems to have been read rather widely at the time. In 1640, Judith Man, an Englishwoman living in France, published in London her English translation of the abridged version of Barclay's *Argenis*, written by M. N. Coeffeteau in French. In her preface, she says that while reading in her closet books suitable for young women over the Christmas period, she came across Coeffeteau's version of *Argenis*, which she liked very much and decided to translate into English in order to practise her French. Her translation, entitled *An Epitome of Fair Argenis and Polyarches*, was dedicated to Lady Anne Wentworth, the eldest daughter of William Wentworth, whom Judith's father seems to have served in France and to whom she was introduced by her parents. William Wentworth was a Protestant, and Judith Man changed Barclay's Catholic points of view to Protestant in her translation. In her preface to the readers, she tried to explain her motivation for publishing her translation, emphasising the necessity of making the work more widely available. She locates herself among female writers who published their works, such as a woman who translated Philip Sidney's *Arcadia* into French, and the author of *Urania*. Man somehow seems to have got hold of a copy of *The Countess of Montgomery's Urania*. Moreover, she insists that more esteem should be paid to these female writers:

> because it is not without example, and could produce thee many of my sexe, who have traced me the way, witnesse the translation into French of Sir Philip Sidneys *Arcadia*, the *New Amarantha*, and the *Vrania*, with many others; neither have I done it to be spoken of, knowing very well, that those of, my sexe, who are least spoken of, are the more to bee esteemed: (Man, 1940 sig. A7r-A7v)

In fact, there is a possibility that Wroth's works were not only circulated among her friends in manuscript form but may also have been read by other people by chance. There is an episode in Part I that indicates this possibility. Pamphilia's private chamber seems to have been kept unlocked. Leaving Pamphilia and Amphilanthus in her chamber, some of her friends—Urania, Selarinus and others—happened to enter her other private chamber, or Cabinet:

> they went into the next room, which was a Cabinet of the Queenes, where her bookes and papers lay: so taking some of them, they paused a while in reading them. (*Urania* I, 260)

Female silence and modesty were highly admired virtues in early modern England, as they were in classical and early modern Japan. A cabinet, whether as a repository box or as a private room, played an important role in secretly preserving women's writings in Jacobean England. Around twenty years after Wroth's publication of *The Countess of Montgomerry's Urania*, Judith Man, a woman eighteen years of age, as has been noted above, insisted in the preface to her translation on the necessity of female writers publishing their works, so that they could be read by a wider world. Cabinets seem to have accomplished their most important function for writing women by the time of Man's publication of her translation in 1640.

Mary Wroth and Murasaki Shikibu

To highlight the characteristics of Wroth's representations of the female self in the context of love in *Urania* I and II, it is useful to glance at the representations of women by Murasaki Shikibu in *The Tale of Genji*. With regard to the periods when Lady Wroth and Lady Murasaki wrote their works, there is a gap of nearly six hundred years; *The Tale* was written from around 1005 to 1012, whereas *Urania* I was published in 1621. Despite a huge interval between the dates of their creative works and the great cultural differences between these two pioneering women, there were some common aspects to their lives. The most important points in which they were similar were that they were both from highly educated families and they themselves were also very well educated.

The greatest difference between Mary Wroth and Murasaki Shikibu is that the former frequently uses the pastoral in her descriptions of womanhood. Most of the women in *Urania* are descended from royal or aristocratic families, but they are given opportunities to be entirely free of their lives at the Court, even going on outings on horseback, and to consider their self-identity in the surroundings of nature (Figure 3.3).[25] The first part of *Urania*, for instance, starts with Urania, a shepherdess, together with the sheep she is in charge of, deep in thought about her self. Urania's lamentation at the loss of her self-identity contrasts with the arrival of the lively season of spring and the vivacity of the sheep, ignorant of the predicament of their shepherdess.

Though she is deeply depressed, the power of nature in her surroundings endows Urania with the vitality required to undertake her pursuit of who she is. In fact, soon afterwards, she encounters Perissus, nephew to the King of Sicily, in a cave. He is feeling deep sorrow because he has been forced to leave his beloved Limena in the hands of her cruel and

Figure 3.3 A double portrait of two ladies, (probably) Lady Mary Wroth and Lady Barbara Sidney. With the inscription 'Lady Wroth and Lady Gamage', dated 1612. By Marcus Gheeraerts II
Source: By kind permission of Viscount De L'Isle from his private collection at Penshurst Place, Kent, England.

jealous husband Philargus. Hearing from him about his miseries, Urania reveals her vitality, encouraging him to take action instead of wallowing in despair:

> leave these teares, and woman-like complaints, no way befitting the valiant Perissus, but like a brave Prince, if you know shee bee dead, revenge her death on her murderers; (*Urania* I 15)

In the case of *The Tale of Genji*, women were hardly given any chance to move beyond the boundaries of the Court of the Emperor or of their social circles. This is partly due to the conditions faced by women of the upper class at the time, who had to wear twelve-layered kimonos, called *junihitoe*, with their hair long enough to trail on the floor, which would have prevented their free movement in the woods or the fields. Here, instead of invigorating, nature is often portrayed as daunting to women, embodied in storms or thunderbolts, which actually deprived some women of their lives.

The main themes in the work of both writers concern love, both of them having been fascinated by its power. However, in the case of Lady Mary, what she particularly foregrounded in her works was the force of love and desire felt by women for men, whereas Lady Murasaki placed her focus on the effects of the love that the central character, Hikaru Genji, felt for women. Lady Murasaki's narrative primarily considered how these women succumbed to Hikaru's approaches to them or how they felt about him after having been raped by him; in fact, they usually came to love him, continuing the affair until his affections were diverted to other women. Nevertheless, *The Tale of Genji* presents some exceptional women who did not fit into this pattern. Utsusemi was one of them; she was the beautiful, well-educated wife of a lower-class aristocrat and was raped by Hikaru one evening in her husband's absence. Although she did not love her husband, who was much older than her, she defiantly refused to meet Hikaru again, leaving Kyoto, the capital of Japan at that time, to go to the rural area where her husband served as the governor under the commission of the Emperor (*The Tale of Genji*, tr. Seidensticker, 1980, Vol. 1. 49–56). She tried to demonstrate her integrity by accommodating herself to the ideal image of the wife in society, a wife who should protect her husband's honour. Although the women in *The Tale* were situated in a complicated entanglement of desire, passion and power, none of them, unlike the women created by Mary Wroth, wrote about their own feelings, except for responding to Hikaru's approaches by means of short poetry.

It is generally considered that both writers recreated in their writings some of their experiences at the Courts. Although Lady Murasaki's social rank was not as high as Lady Mary's, and naturally the political influence of her family was not as powerful as that of Lady Mary, she had one advantage over Lady Mary: educated women in eleventh-century Japan did not suffer from a prejudice against women writing creative works. In fact, as has been mentioned in the Introduction, women's writings were sometimes made use of politically by powerful men at the Court. In the case of Lady Murasaki, *The Tale of Genji* was commissioned by a powerful courtier (see Introduction, 5–8).

As was the case with Lady Mary's writings, *The Tale of Genji* was roughly modelled on people Lady Murasaki knew at the Court. Nonetheless, in contrast to the great scandal caused by the publication of *Urania* I in 1621, *The Tale of Genji* was welcomed not only by the Emperor and his wife, Shoshi, but also by the elite aristocracy, whose interest in the tale was sparked in part because they could speculate about the real-life models for the characters in the story.

The creation of characters based upon real people in Lady Mary's writings is much more complicated than that in *The Tale of Genji*. Lady Mary used for her model the Sidney family tradition of writing pastoral romance and poetry, in particular *The Countess of Pembroke's Arcadia* (1590) and *Astrophel and Stella* (1591) by her well-known uncle, Sir Philip Sidney. The former work was written for Philip's sister Mary, Countess of Pembroke, the latter being modelled by Philip Sydney on himself and his beloved, Penelope Rich. As Marion Wynne-Davies has pointed out, Wroth's writing excels in binding together the lives of the Sidney family and in appropriating the private and public identities of men and women in the writings by her family. We cannot, therefore, say clearly which particular Sidney relationship is being represented (Cerasano and Wynne-Davies, *Renaissance Drama by Women*, 1996 92–3). The purpose of Lady Mary's strategy should have been to avoid clear identification with particular individuals, but also to express, in a wider context and complex variety, the passions and desires embodied by people with whom the readers and the audience were familiar.

Double standards were applied to sexual relations in eleventh-century Japan, as they were in seventeenth-century England. Both Lady Mary and Lady Murasaki expressed, in their characteristic ways, their critical views of the conventions governing women's lives in the society in which they lived. In the case of Lady Mary, however, she enjoyed two privileges that Lady Murasaki did not have. First, she had some family houses she could often visit, the most important one being Penshurst

Place. What Penshurst Place offered Lady Mary was not only the security assured by the Sidney family, but its rich world of nature—orchards, meadows, woods and brooks—where she could dissociate herself from the entanglements of her personal life at the Court. Here she had a chance to look at her life from an alternative point of view to the conventional value systems prevalent in society.

The second advantage Lady Mary had over Lady Murasaki was a family tradition of expressing their feelings and views through writing, particularly via pastoral romances and poetry. Even when she wrote the pastoral comedy *Love's Victory*, she had a model provided by her aunt Mary, Countess of Pembroke, who translated Italian and French plays into English. As has been pointed out by critics, the title of *Love's Victory* seems to have been drawn from Mary Sidney's translation of *The Triumph of Death* by Petrarch.

In contrast, the women created by Lady Murasaki could be freed from men and the Court only by becoming nuns. In traditional Japanese society of the time, once women had become nuns, men of even the highest social rank, such as Hikaru Genji, were forbidden to make sexual approaches to them. What is amazing is that Murasaki's female characters, in becoming nuns, came to possess a strong sense of self, refusing to meet Hikaru with a dignity that they had never before displayed. Before they formally became nuns, Hikaru was allowed to speak to them, but only from behind a curtain. He was portrayed as being overwhelmed by their dignified manners, as in the case of Lady Rokujo, the widow of the former Crown Prince, who had been passionately in love with Hikaru, though she was much older than him; she was deeply jealous of the women he loved, and her curses even killed some of them, such as Yugao and Aoinoue. Yet, in the face of Hikaru's fickle affections, Lady Rokujo despaired of life and decided to serve Buddha as a nun (*The Tale of Genji*, Vol. 1. 57–83, 158–214). Hikaru, however, deprives some women even of the chance to enter the religious life. Wakamurasaki (later, Murasakinoue), Hikaru's second-ranked wife, who had been brought up by Hikaru to fit into his ideal image of womanhood, wanted to become a nun when Hikaru was forced to marry a daughter of the Emperor Sujaku after twenty years of marriage with Murasakinoue. Hikaru loved Murasakinoue so much that he never allowed her to enter religious life. She suffered from profound depression and died, much to Hikaru's deep sorrow (*The Tale of Genji*, Vol. 2. 537–635).

One technique that the two writers shared in expressing their criticisms of the social conditions of their respective periods is the use of irony. Lady Mary often describes the double standards in society ironically. For instance, when Pamphilia, an alter-ego of the author, was depressed by the change of affection of Amphilanthus, she often went to the woods, where she thought about her life or read a romance. On one such occasion, she ironically explained the changes in the mind of a lover in the story she was reading:

> the subject was Love, and the story she then was reading, the affection of a Lady to a brave Gentleman, who equally loved, but being a man, it was necessary for him to exceede a woman in all things, so much as inconstancie was found fit for him to excell her in, hee left her for a new. (*Urania* I, 317)

Lady Murasaki also used irony to criticise the social condition of women in eleventh-century Japan. She wrote, for instance, about the way that Hikaru took good care of his former wives and mistresses even after their affairs were over. In this period, most men simply deserted women once they had lost interest in these women, so that their financial situations were extremely precarious. By describing Hikaru's conscientious actions in contrast to such social customs, Lady Murasaki ironically presented her criticism of the cruel social conditions in which women were placed in her day.

As has been discussed, Lady Wroth often assigned to women the roles of agents and initiators of action, which Lady Murasaki never did. Moreover, Lady Mary made not only the narrator of the story but also her female characters themselves express their critique of society by means of irony, as Pamphilia did in the forest. On the other hand, Lady Murasaki demonstrated her criticism of the social situation in eleventh-century Japan not through the discourse of her female characters but through an ironical development of the stories. For instance, Hikaru himself had to deal with the problem of an illegitimate son when he became older, following his first-ranked wife's adultery with one of the young courtiers he knew very well (*The Tale of Genji*, Vol. 2, 636–56).

Although the ages and circumstances in which these two extraordinary women wrote their works are widely different, they courageously challenged social mores in their own ways, questioning the norms that women were expected to accept. For both of them, their education and creative writings were extremely important in helping them to represent a sense of female selfhood. However, a comparison of their works makes it clear the that the chief characteristic of Lady Mary Wroth's work derives from the significance to her of Penshurst Place and of the literary traditions of the Sidney family.

4
Representing Elizabeth I in Jacobean England

As King James's reign continued, people's disappointment with the monarch increased, especially because of his peace-oriented policy towards foreign countries, his favouritism for his Scottish subjects and his negative attitude towards women. This social climate resulted in an Elizabethan revival, which centred on the Court of Prince Henry, the Prince of Wales, who embodied militant Protestantism against the Catholic powers in Europe.[1]

Although the writers engaged in this revival were both male and female, there seems to be a gender difference in their ways of admiring the late Queen. Whereas the male writers' admiration for Elizabeth I was mostly directed towards her political ingenuity in dealing with the repeated threats by the Catholic powers and her dedication to Protestant England, female writers, especially poets such as Emilia Lanyer or Puritan women such as Rachel Speght, praised the Queen particularly for her great achievements in learning and her female virtues.[2] For these women, Elizabeth I was a role model of the monarch, a model that could invalidate the denigration and dislike towards women displayed by King James. This revival was transformed into an expectation that England might become the ruling power for Protestants in Europe, especially when the Protestant union of Princess Elizabeth, King James's daughter and the late Queen's god-daughter, with the Palatine Frederick, who was the Protestant leader in Europe, was realised in 1613. Numerous works were written to compare Princess Elizabeth to Elizabeth I on the occasion of the royal wedding.[3]

In 1619 Frederick accepted the crown of Bohemia without waiting to hear King James's opinion, and consequently Princess Elizabeth became the Queen of Bohemia. Lady Mary Wroth demonstrated an interesting way of invoking two queens, Elizabeth I and Queen Elizabeth of

Bohemia, in *The Countess of Montgomery's Urania*, which was published two years after the event.

Mary Wroth's representations of the two queens in *Urania*

On the East Wall of the State Dining Room, generally called the Solar, in Penshurst Place, there hangs an impressive painting (see Figure 4.1). However unlike many other paintings in this room, including the one of Lady Mary Wroth with an archlute, it has not yet drawn much attention from critics. It is the painting of a young man with a sweet but dignified appearance, together with a handsome young black man in a gorgeous yellowish African garment, who obviously looks like this youth's servant, standing a step behind him. The guidebook of the house used to explain that the model of this man was unknown, though sometimes it was said to be Prince Rupert; on the pillar on the left side of the painting there remained an identifying description: 'Prince Rupert Aetassus 13.4.8 Anno Dom 1626'.[4] More recently, however, the sitter has been identified as Charles Louis Stuart, later Elector Palatine (1617–80), the second son of Queen Elizabeth of Bohemia. Charles Louis went to England for the first time in 1635, when his father was already dead and his mother was in exile in The Hague after their loss of the Palatine in 1620. The purpose of his trip could have been to ask Charles I, his uncle, for financial and/ or military aid so as to raise a troupe to restore the Palatinate against the Habsburgs. He stayed in England until the summer of 1637, though it is not known whether he actually visited or stayed at Penshurst Place during his visit. However, the possibility cannot be denied in view of the close relationship between the Sidney/Herbert group and Queen Elizabeth of Bohemia, which had lasted for many years. On Frederick's return trip from England to Bohemia in April 1613, Robert Sidney and William Sidney, Mary Wroth's father and brother, together with Lucy Harington, Countess of Bedford, who had Sidney blood through her paternal grandmother, had accompanied the newly married Elizabeth to Heidelberg.

In particular, Lucy Harington and William Herbert, the third Earl of Pembroke, kept close contact with Princess Elizabeth after her marriage. It was Prince Henry who earnestly promoted the Protestant union between his sister Elizabeth and Frederick of the Palatine, who was regarded as representing Protestant power in the Continent. Until the Prince's untimely death in 1612, they were both powerful members of the Court of Prince Henry, who was regarded as the embodiment of militant Protestantism in England. Lucy, Countess of Bedford, continued to try to intercede for Elizabeth and Frederick with King James, who was

Figure 4.1 The portrait of Charles Louis Stuart with his black page
Source: By kind permission of Viscount De L'Isle from his private collection at Penshurst Place, Kent, England.

indignant when Frederick accepted the crown of Bohemia in November 1619 without waiting to hear his advice. Lucy visited Elizabeth in The Hague in July and August 1621. The first visit of Charles Louis to England took place long afterwards, but the fact that this precious portrait of him exists in Penshurst Place is worth noting, since it indicates the possibility that the Sidneys had been in close contact with Queen Elizabeth of Bohemia for all these years. After Queen Elizabeth finally returned to England in 1662, she stayed, though briefly, at a flat in Leicester House, the Sidney residence in London, and died there.[5]

Elizabeth Stuart had constantly been seen as the reincarnation of her godmother, Queen Elizabeth I. After the sudden death of her brother, Prince Henry, in November 1612, she came to be regarded as representing Protestantism by English militant Protestants, and seemed to fashion herself as an embodiment of English Protestantism by following the public image of Elizabeth I. In many poems and pageants celebrating Princess Elizabeth's marriage with Frederick, which took place on St Valentine Day in 1613, she was represented as a revival of the Protestant champion of England in the past, Queen Elizabeth I (Ziegler, *Resurrecting Elizabeth I*, 2007 111–31). Leigh William, for instance, describes her close relation to the late Queen in his collection of sermons dedicated to Princess Elizabeth; one of these was entitled *Queene Elizabeth, Paraleld in Her Princely Virtues, David, Josua, Hazekia* (1612).

Lady Mary Wroth published *The Countess of Mountgomeries Urania* in 1621, at a time when the King and Queen of Bohemia were desperately struggling against the Habsburgs. This chapter aims to explore the possibility of reading *Urania* as Mary Wroth's critique of the political situation at the English Court in Jacobean England as seen from a female perspective. The focus will be on the representations of Elizabeth I in *Urania* Part I in relation to Elizabeth of Bohemia and the Sidney/Herbert group, which continually extended their Protestant sympathy towards the unfortunate Winter Queen and her husband. As has been argued in Chapter 3, Murasaki Shikibu in *The Tale of Genji* ambiguously expressed her critique of the gender system in eleventh-century Japanese society, and her literary creativity was made use of by a powerful man in politics. In contrast, Mary Wroth articulated her views not only on gender issues but on political matters in late Jacobean England by writing and publishing her own original romance.

Pamphilia and two Queen Elizabeths

As Josephine A. Roberts stated in the introduction to her modern edition of *Urania* Part I, at the heart of this romance there lies a strong desire for the revival of the Holy Roman Empire through Protestantism in Europe (xxxix–liv). Wroth casts her central male character Amphilanthus, the King of Naples, in the role of the Holy Roman Emperor who successfully unifies the Western world through a policy of religious and political toleration. In 1621, the year of Wroth's publication of *Urania*, such a representation of Amphilanthus could have been regarded as a sharp critique of King James, whose foreign policy looked too weak for militant Protestants in England; the King had declared his intention of maintaining his position of non-involvement and, despite ardent petitions by Protestants at the Court as well as by the general public, kept refusing to extend military and financial help to his daughter and her husband, who were in the midst of a political and religious crisis.[6]

Critics have generally agreed that Amphilanthus was based roughly on William Herbert, Mary Wroth's cousin and long-standing lover. Certainly the characteristics of Amphilanthus as portrayed in *Urania*, including his love for Pamphilia, a heroine who has been considered as Lady Mary's self-projection, recall many qualities observed in Herbert by his contemporaries, such as military prowess, vulnerability to female charms, a melancholic disposition, poetic creativity and, above all, love for his cousin.

Nevertheless, it is Wroth's usual strategy to project onto each of her characters a number of people from real life (Wynne-Davies, 'For Worth', 2000 164–83) and thus to stress the indeterminancy of the 'intertextual' relationship (Clarke, 2001 239–52). Hence, it is possible to consider the possibility that Frederick, the King of Bohemia, is also projected onto the characterisation of Amphilanthus. In particular, in around 1621, the time when *Urania* Part I was published, the reading of Amphilanthus as representing some aspects of Frederick would certainly have been possible. Elector Frederick V of the Palatinate had long been looked to as a Protestant champion in Europe, and was elected King of Bohemia in 1619. Frederick was renowned for his military valour; moreover, like the fictional Amphilanthus, he was frequently away fighting against the Catholic forces, and was well known for suffering from melancholia, which became increasingly worse in his late years. Of course, the King and Queen of Bohemia in real life were different from Amphilanthus and Pamphilia in many respects; above all, they were married and continued to be a loving couple until Frederick's death in 1632. And yet, it is significant that, as Pamphilia's constancy is frequently contrasted with Amphilanthus's inconstancy in *Urania* Part I, so was Elizabeth's persistence in her thinking and attitudes often compared by contemporary people with Frederick's vacillation in the face of political turmoil.[7]

At the same time, in other aspects Pamphilia can also be identified with Elizabeth I, particularly in her firm political commitment to her country. She was the female monarch of the kingdom of Pamphilia and, like Elizabeth I, was often exposed to marriage proposals by kings and princes who wanted to dominate her country as well as to threats of military invasion by male rulers in the neighbourhood. Interestingly, this was also the case with Queen Elizabeth of Bohemia. She had been the object of marriage negotiations since she was an infant, and after her marriage with Frederick she was often praised for her courage and commitment to the Palatine despite the political difficulties she was confronted with. She seems to have been deeply conscious of Elizabeth I in taking her Protestant position amidst the troubles with Catholic forces. For instance, in one of her letters to the Countess of Bedford, thanking the Countess for her continuing support, she referred to her enemies in the English Court who advised King James not to support her cause, by using the rhetoric of Queen Elizabeth's supposedly well-known Armada speech at Tilbury: 'though they have English bodies they have Spanish hartes' (Qut. from Lewalski, 1993 62).[8]

In the case of Pamphilia, in some places in *Urania* Part I she uses expressions believed to be employed in Queen Elizabeth's speeches to Parliament. For example, she uses the term 'blabb' while articulating her own sorrow for Amphilanthus's unfaithfulness as well as her sympathy with the betrayed lady depicted in the romance she was reading alone in the woods in Book II of Part I: 'shall I turne blabb?' (*Urania* I, 318).

Queen Elizabeth used the same word 'blabb' in her speech to Parliament in reference to Mary, Queen of Scotland in 1586-7.

> For now I will play *the blab*—I secretly wrote her a letter upon the discovery of sundry treasons. (Qut. from Neale, 1957 117. Italics are mine.)

The most conspicuous case is when Pamphilia refused the marriage proposal of Leandrus, Prince of Achaya, a marriage proposal endorsed not only by her own father, the King of Morea, but by 'her mother, her brothers, and most of her friends' (*Urania* I, 264). In her speech to her father, she echoed Queen Elizabeth's well-known speech before the House of Commons in 1559, recorded by William Camden:

> "I am already bound unto an husband, which is the kingdom of England, and that may suffice you. And this," quoth she, "makes me wonder that you forget, yourselves, the pledge of this alliance which

I made with my kingdom." And therewith, stretching out her hand, she showed them the ring with which she was given in marriage and inaugurated to her kingdom in express and solemn terms. (*Elizabeth I: Collected Works*, 2000 59)

Pleading with her father not to proceed with the marriage negotiation with Leandrus, Pamphilia said:

> his Majestie had once married her before, which was to the Kingdome of Pamphilia, from which Husband shee could not bee divorced, nor ever would have other, if it might please him to give her leave to enjoy that happinesse; and besides, besought his permission, 'for my Lord,' said shee, 'my people looke for me, and I must needs bee with them. (*Urania* I 262)

According to Amphilanthus, who was, ironically, asked by Leandrus to help to promote this marriage, 'she said, shee was already bestowed upon her people, and had married her selfe to them' (*Urania* I 264). Moreover, she also told him that even if she should die unmarried and without leaving children, she would have no regret: 'her friends (she hop'd) would keepe her memory, and that should be enough for her' (*Urania* I, 264). This speech also refers to a well-known speech of Queen Elizabeth that demonstrates her devotion to her country:

> And to me it shall be a full satisfactions, both for the memorial of my Name, and for my Glory also, if when I shall let my last breath, it be ingraven upon my Marble Table, '*Here lies Elizabeth*, which Reigned *a Virgin, and did a Virgin*'. (Qut. from MacCaffrey, 1970 29–30)

Pamphilia's use of expressions attributed to Elizabeth I has strong Protestant resonances; while in the first speech Queen Elizabeth asserts her Protestant position in the face of the imminent execution of her Catholic rival, Mary Queen of Scots, in the other two speeches, she declares her position on her total commitment to protect Protestant England.

What should also be noted here is that Pamphilia's use of Queen Elizabeth's expressions motivated by political strategy was to pursue her private desire; in other words, there is a disparity between Pamphilia's assumption of the role of queen and her real intention. In employing Queen Elizabeth's expression 'blabb' when pleading with her father, Pamphilia's purpose is not simply to display her commitment to her country and people. She appropriates Queen Elizabeth's powerful speech in order to avoid marrying a man other than Amphilanthus. Thus, she is well aware of the impact of Queen Elizabeth's speech both on her father and on the public, and uses it in order to fulfil her private desire while maintaining her respectable appearance as monarch. In other words, this strategy helps her to successfully perform her theatrical self as queen, while discreetly maintaining her selfhood as a loving woman.

Moreover, since Pamphilia knew that Leandrus's real reason for wanting to marry her was not what he claimed—that is, his ardent love for her—but rather his political ambition for her territory and his interest in her social standing, she voiced her protest to her father, the King of Morea, by saying, 'nor can I believe he loves in me ought besides my kingdome, and my honour in being your daughter' (*Urania* I 262). Having received numerous marriage proposals from foreign kings and princes in Europe, Elizabeth I, like Pamphilia, must have been well aware that the real motive of these rulers was to take England into their territory. Keeping her public stance as monarch, however, she never referred, at least in her public speeches, to these men's real intentions as plainly as Pamphilia does. Thus, the way in which Pamphilia uses Queen Elizabeth's expressions shows her deliberately pointing out the relation of the public sphere of politics to the private sphere of desire, particularly with regard to the discourse that the body politic and the body natural must be clearly separated from each other. Pamphilia's interrelating of two key concepts imposed upon the monarch poses a challenge to the commonly accepted political discourse of the time, that is, 'The Queen's Two Bodies'.

The Tudor political ideology had claimed that in order to successfully rule the country, the monarch was obliged to separate his/her two bodies, giving greater precedence to the body politic than to the body natural (Axton 11–17). In the case of the female monarch, it was feared that the traditionally assumed weakness inherent in any woman would make this division impossible. Notably, having gone through the troublesome reign of Mary Tudor, John Knox vehemently attacked the female monarch by publishing the treatise, *The First Blast of the Trumpet against the Monstrous Regiment of Women* in 1558, a year before Elizabeth ascended to the throne. The contemporary reports of the Court as well as the biographies of Queen Elizabeth[9] show, however, that although in public she had successfully represented her body politic, in her private life she had gone through various emotional upheavals stemming from her body natural. Queen Pamphilia's use of Queen Elizabeth's speeches makes clear that there actually exists a division between the female monarch's two bodies, though emphasising their interrelatedness, instead of their separation. Pamphilia's manipulative employment of Queen Elizabeth's expressions underlines the point that keeping both parts of the queen's body, without subjugating the body natural to the body politic, does not necessarily ruin her rule as monarch, and therefore does not deprive a woman of legitimacy as a ruler.

'The Queen's Two Bodies'

Josephine A. Roberts argues that in comparison to the representations of the Queen's two bodies in John Knox's *First Blast*, Edmund Spenser manages through the description of Britomart in *The Faerie Queen*, to offer the possibility of the female ruler's maintenance of the two bodies in balance, though with great difficulty. On the other hand, Roberts thinks that by underlining the burdens imposed upon the woman ruler situated amidst the struggles for male power, Wroth places even stronger emphasis on the pessimistic view of its impossibility through the portrayal of Pamphilia, who is described frequently as subjugated to her private feelings for her ever-changing lover, Amphilanthus (1990 187–207). In particular, in one place in *Urania* Part I, Pamphilia's sense of self is so dependent upon Amphilanthus's love for her that during his absence she regards herself as 'a poore weake shadow of my selfe' (*Urania* I 318). There are also in *Urania*, as Roberts points out, many queens, such as Nereana, Princess of Stalamine, who were overruled by their private desires, ignoring their responsibilities to the body politic. However, *Urania* presents not only incompetent female monarchs, but also many decadent male rulers. In particular, it is interesting to note that in *Urania* Part I some portrayals of kings who failed to separate the king's two bodies recall King James. For instance, Veralinda, a good friend of Pamphilia, went back to her own country and found her father, the King of Frigia, being tortured by a group of angry women who had been sexually abused by the king (*Urania* I 562–3). As already mentioned, the way in which these women tortured the king—by binding and whipping him with great rods—resembles the way in which the female characters torture Swetnam, a notorious woman-hater at the time, in *Swetnam the Woman-hater Araigned by Women*, an anonymous play published a year before the publication of *Urania*. Towards the end of this play, a band of angry women torture Swetnam for abusing women in his pamphlet *The Araignment of Lewd, Idle, Froward, and vnconstant women*. As has been pointed out by some critics, the image of Swetnam on the title page of the first edition of the play published in 1620 might recall King James. Wroth also offers an episode of a duke of Morea, whose homosexual passion for a lovely young man destroyed both his dukedom and family (*Urania* I 34–7). Thus, she shows that even in the case of the male monarch, the body natural can threaten the body politic, as in the case of King James.[10]

Pamphilia, though privately, constantly suffered emotional struggles, but never ignored her responsibility as a sovereign, maintaining the queen's two bodies. In public, like Elizabeth I, Pamphilia successfully maintained her posture of her body politic: 'for her government continued just and brave, like that Lady she was, wherein she shewed her heart was not to be stirr'd, though her private fortunes shooke round about her' (*Urania* I 484). It is true that she sometimes fell into despair because of Amphilanthus's betrayals, and that Urania, Amphilanthus's sister and Pamphilia's good friend, criticized Pamphilia for giving precedence to her private feelings over her public duty: 'you that have been admired for a Masculine spirit, will you descend below the poorest Feminine in love?' (*Urania* I 468). And yet, Pamphilia soon recovered her public stance, presiding over her country despite the despair and sorrow she was privately feeling. The portrayal of Pamphilia as maintaining, not separating, the queen's two bodies in balance, offers innovation in treating the concept of the nature of female monarchy.

Wroth's description of the female ruler provides a sharply contrasted portrayal to that of Elizabeth I in John Barclay's *Argenis*, an extremely popular romance written in Latin and published in Paris in the same year as *Urania*. The first English translation was published by Kingesmill Long in 1625; a second translation was published by 'his Majesties Command' by Sir Robert Le Grys in 1628 and there were subsequently numerous translations in the following years. Even in the eighteenth century two translations were published, one in 1734 and the other in 1772 (Salzman, 2002 76). Barclay's romance was so exceedingly popular in Europe that it was difficult to get hold of a copy. John Chamberlain wrote to Dudley Carlton about the book on 30 May 1622:

> I had borrowed for a set time Barclaies Argenis (a booke somwhat rare yet, and hard to come by) I was so taken and caried away with yt that I could not geve over, (as indeed yt is the most delightfull fable that ever I met with). (Vol. II. 427–8)

On 11 May 1622, Chamberlain wrote about its popularity and the difficulty of obtaining the book in England, responding to Carlton's problem in getting a copy in the Netherlands.

I am sory you cannot meet with Barclayes Argenis which indeed are somwhat rare here beeing printed at Paris, and risen from five shillings they were sold at first to fowreteen, but I have taken order to have one yf there were any to be had at Franckford mart: I heare the King hath geven order to Ben: Johnson to translate yt, and that yt is in goode forwardnes, but I am deceved yf he can reach the language in the originall, or expresse himself in that manner, whatsoever he doth in the matter: besides there be many covert names shadowed sometimes in Anagrams and sometimes otherwise, wherein I had the fortune to discifer three or fower by meere chaunce, though I be nothing goode at riddles, nor love not to trouble myself about that is hard to finde. (Vol. II. 435–6)

King James first ordered Ben Jonson to translate the book, and his translation was entered in the Stationer's Register on 2 October 1623. Unfortunately, though, it was among his works burned in the fire in Jonson's lodgings in November 1623.[11]

In this romance written about the reign of Henry III and Henry IV with Catholic sympathy, as Paul Salzman pointed out, Hyanisbe, modelled on Queen Elizabeth, is portrayed as completely subject to her female passion for Poliarchus, a poet. She describes herself as 'Wretched Woman, that I am' (Barclay, 1636 634), and 'even forgetting all Majestie' (Barclay, 1636 637), she threw herself at one character's feet. Entirely dependent upon Poliarchus, she is never allowed to demonstrate her body politic independently of male power.[12]

The concept of constancy

As has been mentioned, constancy and persistence were also the characteristics that contemporaries saw in Elizabeth of Bohemia. While she was Princess, she held to her constant passion for Frederick despite King James's reluctance for, and Queen Anne's strong opposition to, their union. After she became Queen of Bohemia, she remained constant in her affection for her husband despite Frederick's frequent mental depression and the difficulties of maintaining her political position of representing militant Protestantism while confronted with the overwhelmingly mighty Catholic power in Europe.

In *Urania* Pamphilia is represented as the embodiment of constancy. Urania thinks that a changeable man such as Amphilanthus is not worthy of such devotion:

"'Tis pittie," said Urania, "that ever that fruitlesse thing Constancy was taught you as a vertue, since for vertues sake you will love it, as having true possession of your soule, but understand, this vertue hath limits to hold it in, being a vertue, but thus that it is a vice in them that breake it, but those with whom it is broken, are by the breach free to leave or choose againe where more staidnes may be found; besides tis a dangerous thing to hold that opinion, which in time will prove flat heresie. (*Urania* I 470).

And yet, as has been argued earlier, Pamphilia remains constant, at least in Part I, declaring that her constancy is to prove her autonomy independent of Amphilanthus's vacillating self (*Urania* I 470).

Although Pamphilia's constancy is more frequently illustrated in terms of her private passion for Amphilanthus, it is shown in political terms as well. Despite the problems in her private life, like both Queen Elizabeth I and Queen Elizabeth of Bohemia, she constantly shows her commitment to her country and remains popular with the people. While her contemporary male writers emphasise the difficulty for the female monarch of dissociating her two bodies from each other, Wroth shows that the female ruler who keeps the body natural can still embody the body politic. Thus, Wroth challenges the contemporary assumption about the nature of the female monarch by invoking Queen Elizabeth in the past as well as Queen Elizabeth of Bohemia in her own time.

In fact, despite Pamphilia's great admiration and respect for Amphilanthus's manhood, severe criticism of patriarchy runs throughout *Urania*, which is often articulated using irony. For instance, as has already been argued, while alone in a wood reading a romance, the story of which is very similar to her own experience with Amphilanthus, Pamphilia throws the book away and eventually says that 'being a man, it was necessary for him to exceede a woman in all things, so much as inconstancie was found fit for him to excel her in, hee left her for a new' (*Urania* I 317).

Conscious of the unstable mentality of her contemporary male rulers, King James and the King of Bohemia, which stands in sharp contrast to the mental state of Elizabeth I and Elizabeth of Bohemia, Wroth presents her view in *Urania* I that despite the claims of political orthodoxy at the time, men were not necessarily endowed with more legitimacy as the sovereign than women. Also, being a relative of the Earls of Leicester and Essex, Wroth must have heard about Queen Elizabeth's emotional involvements with them, and was conscious of the fictitious nature of the political discourse of the queen's two bodies.

Male writers, such as Sir Philip Sidney, Samuel Daniel and Edmund Spenser, used the genre of romance to write their views on the political issues from the late 1580s to the 1590s. As Paul Salzman argued

(Salzman, 2002 80–1), although the vogue for chivalric romance was over by the time Wroth wrote *Urania*, the genre of political romance, which presents a political critique under the guise of chivalric elements, became popular again in around the year 1620. Being well aware of King James's intolerance of any criticism of his policy, Wroth probably thought that the guise of romance would be the only way in which she could present her audacious challenge to the contemporary political discourse on the queen's two bodies as well as to the increasing exclusion of women from the public arena. In view of the uproar caused by the publication of *The Countess of Montgomery's Urania*, Wroth's assuming the guise of romance turned out not to be so effectual after all. What she makes clear in her prose romance is her critique not only of politics in the Jacobean Court but also of the conventional discourse of the female monarch's two bodies. The most dominant theme throughout both parts of *Urania* is a pursuit of the construction of female selfhood and of freedom for female self-expression in a male-dominated society. It is of great significance that by addressing these issues under the guise of romance, Wroth demonstrates the possibility of women's engagement with politics at this early stage in the history of woman and politics.

5
Women and Publishing Their Works in the Late Jacobean Years

During the English Renaissance, male authors of high social rank tended to refrain from publishing their works due to an informal social code of the 'Stigma of Print'.[1] Female writers of the aristocracy had to overcome an even higher barrier: that of contemporary prejudice against women writing their original works, let alone publishing them. In the case of translations, this social code was not so strict, particularly if the works had classic or religious themes. Mary Sidney Herbert, Countess of Pembroke, published her translations with her name on the title page. As far as writing about matters in the private domain was concerned, women apparently did not feel any self-restraint. Partly because of the increase of female literacy, writing letters and diaries had been popular among elite women since Tudor times.[2] Lady Margaret Hoby (1577–1633), for instance, kept a diary from 1599 to 1605. It mainly consists of a daily record of her religious practice and of details of the management of her house and household. In the Jacobean years, Lady Anne Clifford, as previously mentioned, kept a diary between 1616 and 1619, and Lady Cornwallis kept her correspondence with her friends and family between 1613 and 1644. These were not published until later, but provide important information about the cultural climate of women's writing, and particularly about their ways of thinking at the time. In seventeenth-century England, however, some women took up authorial positions, circulating their manuscripts among their friends or even publishing their poetry, romances and plays as well as religious tracts. This chapter examines the significance of women's entry into the field of authorship and publication in relation to the print culture of the time.

Mary Wroth and publishing *Urania* I

As mentioned in Chapter 3, it can be said that Mary Wroth gave up her own performance of her theatrical self when she published *The Countess of Montgomery's Urania* in 1621, exposing to the public what she felt inwardly. The genre of pastoral romance was started in England by her uncle, Sir Philip Sidney, and was employed by many contemporary male writers, particularly those who were close to the Sidneys.[3] *Urania* was the first original literary work in the genre written by a woman, not only in the Sidney family but also in England.

On the title page of *Urania*, Wroth identified herself as the niece of both Sir Philip Sidney and of Mary, Countess of Pembroke; she dedicated her book to another woman within the family, the Countess's daughter-in-law, Susan de Vere, Countess of Montgomery, who was a close friend of Wroth. Wroth was presenting herself as belonging to the Sidneys, not to the Wroths, as well as introducing a new voice of the new generation of her family taking up the family's heritage of pastoral romance. Moreover, she emphasised her Sidney origins, giving her romance a title similar to that of her uncle's, *The Countess of Pembroke's Arcadia*.

Although the genre had been linked in popular opinion to 'feminine' frivolousness in the late Elizabethan and early Jacobean years, in the late Jacobean period it was restored to its original function, that is, to present political critique of the state of the Court under the guise of pastoral and romance.[4] It was not only in England that pastoral romance of this kind became popular. As discussed in Chapter 4, in France, John Barclay's *Argenis*, which is a political satire of the French Court of Henry III and Henry IV under the guise of pastoral romance, was published in 1621, the same year as that of the publication of Wroth's *Urania*. Whereas Barclay's *Argenis* was written from a pro-Catholic point of view, Wroth's romance reflects the Protestant viewpoints. Despite the difference in religious perspective, both authors adopted the genre of pastoral romance to articulate their critique of politics at the Courts.

Wroth published her romance, which features the power of love, not of religion, with her name and her family background on the title page, and what is worse—worse from the Jacobean point of view—the work is replete with episodes that recalled courtiers and actual happenings at the Jacobean Court. Not only Lord Edward Denny, but also some other courtiers must have been quite upset, thinking that their families served as models for Wroth's stories. Faced with the uproar she had caused at the Court,[5] Wroth decided to withdraw all copies of her book from the market and wrote a letter to the Duke of Buckingham on 15 December 1621, asking him to return a presentation copy she had sent him. In this letter she used a customary strategy of denying responsibility for publication by asserting that it had been done against her will. However, in view of her obvious intention to place her romance within the writing traditions of the Sidney family, she must certainly have aimed for publication. In publishing *The Tragedy of Mariam* in 1613, Elizabeth Cary also met with vehement criticism, in particular from her husband and family, though her work was not an original work in a strict sense, being drawn heavily from a story in Josephus's Jewish history. Actually, Cary wrote the play in 1603, but did not dare to publish it for ten years. It has been said that her tutor, Sir John Davies, a great admirer of Florio's Montaigne, recommended that she should publish her tragedy. He thought it a pity that some excellent works written by women, including Cary's, were kept in the private sphere because of the gender code in society, and not read in the wider world.[6] Likewise, some male writers may have supported Mary Wroth in publishing her romance; her poetry had already been highly admired by Ben Jonson and Samuel Daniel.[7]

Urania Parts I and II also reflect the great popularity of travel writing in seventeenth-century England; the geographical information in the two parts was mostly derived from George Sandy's *A Relation of a Journey begun: An: Dom: 1610* (1615), one of the most popular books at the time (Roberts ed. 1995 (Introduction) xliv). Despite these possible influences of the Sidney literary traditions[8] as well as of contemporary popular writings, and despite the possibilities that some episodes were modelled on real people and incidents at the Court, Wroth's romance was her original work in a true sense. Whatever the disastrous outcome that followed, the fact that a woman of her social standing published her original work of romance together with the sonnet sequence appended to it, both of which deal with love and not religious matters, marks the culmination of a great change in Jacobean culture in relation to women—a change in attitude towards a woman's desire for self-actualisation, which had been happening since the beginning of the seventeenth century.

Scandalous incidents caused by women at the Court in the late Jacobean years

In considering the significance of Wroth's publication of her romance, it is important to understand the cultural climate in the late Jacobean years, to which the scandals caused by some women of the aristocracy contributed. Probably the most scandalous incidents that took place in the second decade of seventeenth-century England were the downfalls of three men of the highest political position, all of which were attributed to their wives' actions. When the murder of Sir Thomas Overbury leaked out in August 1615, the King immediately ordered Sir Edward Coke, the Chief Justice of the King's Bench, to investigate the case. On 25 May 1616, the Countess of Somerset pleaded guilty and received the sentence of death, while her husband the Earl was tried in Westminster Hall and also sentenced to death. Although the death sentences were later repealed by the king, both the Earl and the Countess remained imprisoned in the Tower of London until January 1622. Thus, the power of the Earl of Somerset, who had been prominent for many years at the Court, came to an end as a result of his wife's involvement in the murder of his secretary.[9] Wroth treated the Overbury affair in one episode about an unnamed lady in *Urania* I (563–5), though the story does not include the murder case of Sir Thomas Overbury.

The second scandalous incident was that Thomas Howard, the first Earl of Suffolk, was accused of corruption as Lord Treasurer and dismissed from office in 1618. The Countess was also indicted for extorting money from people associated with the Treasury. After an eleven-day hearing in the Star Chamber in October–November 1619, the Earl and the Countess were fined, commanded to restore all the money extorted, and sentenced to imprisonment in the Tower. It was a popular rumour that Howard had acted under the influence of his wife.[10]

Moreover, in February 1619, Sir Thomas Lake was dismissed from the office of Secretary of State on account of his involvement in the scandalous Lake–Roos case. His daughter had married Lord Roos, grandson of the first Earl of Exeter. There was a family quarrel about property. Lady Lake not only accused Lord Roos of an incestuous relationship with his step-grandmother, the young Countess of Exeter, but also accused the Countess of having tried to poison her and her daughter Lady Roos.[11] She alleged that, in order to be forgiven by the mother and the daughter, the Countess had even read and signed a confession of her own guilt in a room of her house at Wimbledon, and that this scene had been observed by Lady Lake's maid, Sarah Swardon, from behind the arras. Late in 1618, the Countess of Exeter brought a charge of defamation against Lord Lake, his wife, son and daughter in the Star Chamber, and the witnesses were examined for five days in early February 1619. The whole affair ended unexpectedly when King

James insisted on seeing the room in Wimbledon and discovered that the said arras did not reach within two feet of the floor, so that nothing but an ostrich could have hidden behind it. On 13 February 1619 the King decreed that the defendants should all be fined and imprisoned at his majesty's pleasure. John Chamberlain writes that the 'King spake long and excellently to every point, comparing this to the first judgement, Sir Thomas Lake to Adam, his Lady to Eve and the Lady Roos to the serpent' (13 February 1619, Vol. II, 214). In his later letter, Chamberlain endorses the popular criticism of Lady Lake when she was carried away to the Tower:

> They say she takes this affliction very impatiently, and was faine to be caried as yt were by violence into the coach; a thing usuall to such insolent natures, that can neither beare prosperitie nor adversitie. (20 February 1619, Vol. II. 216)

Lady Roos was said to have been 'cursed horribly' by the people as she went to the Tower (*Calendar of State Papers, Domestic Series, (1619–23)*, 16). She confessed her guilt on 19 June 1619 and was released from the Tower. Lake himself admitted the justice of the sentence on 28 January 1620 and thereupon was set free. But his wife obstinately kept refusing to answer the charge and did not gain her freedom until 2 May 1621; her prolonged imprisonment, due to her obstinacy, was often compared by contemporaries to that of Mary, Countess of Shrewsbury. Anthony Weldon, looking back on Sir Thomas Lake's political career, reveals sympathy for him because he was 'so overawed by his Wife, that if he did not what she commanded, she would beat him, and in truth his Wife was afterward his over-throw'.[12]

To what extent we can trust these contemporary accounts is, of course, difficult to assess. Besides, vicissitudes in great men's lives, as portrayed by Webster in his tragedies, were nothing unusual in Renaissance England. But the downfall of great men had normally been regarded as the outcome of their own actions.[13] It is an extraordinary fact that, in the space of a few years, the overthrow of three powerful men of the highest rank was attributed to their wives. The evil of a wife's dominance over her husband, which had been familiar as a concept since the Middle Ages and which had recently again been denounced emphatically in Swetnam's *Araignment of Lewd, Idle, Froward, and vnconstant women*, became an actuality for Londoners of the time.

That marriages were fraught with various dangers to husbands is also suggested by a series of ballads that depict the actual murders of husbands by their wives.[14] Chamberlain also laments such terrible murders frequently committed by women:

> That morning early there was a joyners wife burnt in Smithfield for killing her husband. [. . .] The same day likewise another woman poisoned her husband about Algate, and divers such like fowle facts are committed dayly, which are yll signes of a very depraved age and that judgements hang over us. (6 July 1616, Vol. II. 15)

Apart from these scandals closely related to women, Londoners at the time also witnessed a notorious lawsuit undertaken by a woman, Lady Hatton, against her husband, Chief Justice Coke. Their quarrel started soon after their marriage in 1598 over Sir Edward Coke's handling of his wife's property. Elizabeth Hatton refused to change her family name to Coke's on her marriage, maintaining her maiden name. Their relationship worsened when they disagreed over the marriage of their daughter, Frances, to Sir John Villiers, who was elder brother of the Duke of Buckingham and suffered from mental illness.

Lady Hatton appealed to the court against Sir Edward's abduction of Frances to enforce the marriage.[15] At the council held in May 1617, Lady Hatton declaimed against Sir Edward Coke so well that, according to Chamberlain, many people present thought that 'Burbage could not have acted better' (24 May 1617, Vol. II. 77). Popular reactions against Lady Hatton's highhanded actions were, however, generally critical, though often tinged with a sense of irresponsible amusement.[16] The possible allusion to the lawsuit in Middleton and Webster's *Anything for a Quiet Life* (1620-1) also reflects sympathy for the husband:[17] 'Have you made him/So miserable, that he must take a Law from his wife?' (V. 1. 227-8)

The social climate against women's self-assertion

These incidents surely must have resulted in increasing antagonism against female power in society, promoting consideration of the traditional concepts of the nature and role of women. Particularly, King James seemed to be quite annoyed by self-asserting women; his annoyance probably related to Queen Anne's independent mindedness and actions.[18] When the King issued a proclamation in April 1617, urging the nobility and gentry to stay in their country homes instead of flocking to London, he ascribed the undesirable custom to women:

One of the greatest causes of all gentlemen's desire, that have no call or errand, to dwell in London is apparently the pride of the women, for if they be wives, then their husbands, if they be maids, then their fathers, must bring them up to London.[19]

However, the King's order seems to have had little effect. Between 1617 and 1623 he issued three proclamations on the matter, the effectiveness of which Chamberlain doubts in his letters (19 April 1617, Vol. II, 70; 5 April, 1623, Vol. II, 487). The flouting by women of the King's command is also described by an anonymous writer as follows:

> You women that do London loue so well,
> whom scarce a proclamation can expell.
> And to be kept in fashion fine and gay
> Care not what fines your honest husbandes pay;
> Who dreame on nought but vissets, maskes & toyes
> And thinke the Country contributes no ioyes.[20]

Much evidence of King James's irritation against self-assertive women is referred to in Chamberlain's letters. Appointing Sir George Calvert to the office of Secretary of State as a successor to Sir Thomas Lake, the King sent for Calvert and 'asked him many questions, most about his wife'. Calvert answered that 'she was a goode woman and had brought him ten children', assuring his Majesty that 'she was not a wife with a witnes'. Chamberlain adds his own comment: 'this and some other passages of this kind, seeme to shew that the King is in great vaine of taking downe highhanded women' (20 February 1619, Vol. II. 216).

King James's exasperation against female self-assertion reached its peak in his order of January 1620, in which he called for men to take action to control the insolence of women. Chamberlain writes to Carlton:

Yesterday the bishop of London called together all his Clergie about this towne, and told them he had express commaundment from the King to will them to inveigh vehemently and bitterly in theyre sermons against the insolencie of our women, and thyre wearing of brode brimd hats, pointed doublets, theyre haire cut short or shorne, and some of them stilletaes or poniards, and such other trinckets of like moment, adding withall that yf pulpit admonitions will not reforme them he wold proceed by anothr course; the truth is the world is very far out of order, but whether this will mend yt God knowes. (25 January 1620, Vol. II. 286–7)

Priests, playwrights and ballad-writers seem to have responded immediately. Less than three weeks later, Chamberlain describes the results:

> our pulpits ring continually of the insolence and impudence of women: and to helpe the matter forward the players have likewise taken them to taske, and so to the ballades and ballad-singers, so that they can come no where but theyre eares tingle: and yf all this will not serve the King threatens to fall upon theyre husbands, parents, or frends that have or shold have powre over them and make them pay for yt. (12 February 1620, Vol. II. 289)

Unfortunately, it remains uncertain which plays and ballads Chamberlain refers to here, though F. L. Lucas thinks that 'the Ballet' alluded to by Ariosto in *Anything for a Quiet Life* (IV. 1. 33–4) was one of 'the ballades' created in response to the royal command.[21]

Hic Mulier: Or, the Man-Woman, published in 1620, may also have been designed to capitalise on the King's proclamation. The anonymous author of this pamphlet thinks that 'since the daies of *Adam* women were neuer so Masculine' (1620 sig. A3r). He attacks the recent fashion of women's masculinity (by which he means women's discarding 'bashfull shamefastnesse' (1620 sig. B3r)) 'in attire, in speech, in manners [. . .] in the whole courses and stories of their actions' (1620 sig. B1r), especially women's fondness for copying men's clothes. The pamphlet goes little beyond conventional diatribes against women, but has special significance in having been accompanied by an interesting anonymous pamphlet, *Haec-Vir: Or The Womanish-Man*, a pamphlet in which a female central figure, Hic-Mulier attempts to justify her breach of propriety in wearing mannish clothes. The appearance of these documents around the year 1621 makes it clear that when Mary Wroth's *The Countess of Montgomery's Urania* was published, the wave of antagonism to female self-assertion was at its height in England.

The controversy over Swetnam's anti-women pamphlet

One of the characteristic social phenomena in late Jacobean England was that the climate of anti-female power in society invited protests from the defenders of women at the time, thus reviving the *querelle des dames* in a Jacobean form. A series of pamphlets appeared in answer to Swetnam's pamphlet *The Araignment of Lewd, Idle, Froward, and unconstant women* of 1615, written under the pseudonym of Thomas Teltroth. They started with Daniel Tuvil's *Asylum Veneris, Or A Sanctuary for Ladies*, published in 1616.²² As Joad Raymond rightly said, the 'years 1615 to 1620 saw a series of pamphlets arguing over the merits and demerits of womankind, and discussing transgressive behaviour by men and women that seemed to challenge the gender hierarchy' (*Pamphlets and Pamphleteering*, 2003 283–34). Responses to Swetnam's pamphlet by three writers, all claiming to be women, followed: Rachel Speght's *A MOVZELL FOR MELASTOMVS, The Cynicall Bayter of, and foule mouthed Barker against EVAHS SEX*, entered into the Stationer's Register on 14 November 1616, and published in 1617; Ester Sowernam's *Ester hath hang'd Haman: OR AN ANSWER TO a lewd Pamphlet, entituled, The Arraignment of Women*, published in 1617; Constantia Munda's *The WORMING of a Mad Dogge: OR, A SOPPE FOR CERBERVS THE Iaylor of Hell*, entered on 29 April 1617, published in the same year. The controversy over Swetnam's pamphlet led to the appearance of an anonymous play, *SWETNAM, The Woman-hater, ARRAIGNED BY WOMEN* (Queen Anne's, 1617–9), licensed on 17 October 1619, and published in 1620.²³ Although the exact date of its first performance is unknown, it has been generally accepted that the play was written after the publication of these answers and before Queen Anne's death. The year 1620, a year before the publication of Mary Wroth's *Urania* I, also witnessed three pamphlets by anonymous writers on cross-dressing. Joad Raymond thinks that, taken together, these pamphlets offer 'a useful window on the gendering of pamphlet authorship [. . .] and women in print before the civil wars' (*Pamphlets and Pamphleteering*, 2003 285).²⁴

Meanwhile, Eva Griffith suggests that Ester Sowernam might have been a pseudonym used by Frances, Countess of Hertford (*A Jacobean Company and its Playhouse*, 2013 128–35). That Sowernam and Lady Hertford were the same person is an interesting claim. The Countess of Hertford was one of Queen Anne's two chambermaids, the other being Lucy, Countess of Bedford. Although the Countess of Hertford was kept in the country by her husband until 1621, she must have known the Countess of Bedford as well as Anne Clifford, Countess of Pembroke, Dorset and Montgomery, who visited Penshurst Place often, and saw Mary Wroth there. By associating with these members of Queen Anne's female circle, Mary Wroth, who had already left London by then, must have been well aware that these women were printing their views against Swetnam's pamphlet. (I will come back to Rachel Speght in the section on Puritan women later in this chapter.)

In these responses, the defence of woman is conducted mainly from conventional Christian viewpoints; the pamphleteers all assume orthodox Christian female virtues as the sole female virtues, and all affirm women's worth through Biblical references. Even Ester Sowernam, who took the most aggressive attitude among these writers, defends only those who are 'most zealous, faithfull and deuout women' (1617 14), condemning all those who failed to live up to these ideals. The play, *Swetnam the Woman-Hater* begins with a note which sounds like feminism in the twentieth century, the prologue telling that the play's purpose is to rectify anti-feminine views in society, by castigating a detractor against women. Misogynos (Swetnam) is presented as a comic object of scorn, and the satire on him reaches a climax in his arraignment by misogynous women. The popularity of this scene is indicated by the fact that it is referred to in both its prologue and epilogue and that a woodcut of the scene is printed on the title page of the first edition.[25] Despite these feminist elements, though, the play, unlike Webster's plays, does not place traditional assumptions about the nature of woman in any different light, treating the man-woman controversy only with a somewhat amused detachment.[26]

As has already been discussed in Chapter 3, *Urania* I includes an episode that recalls the scene in the play where Swetnam/Mysogynos is bound and attacked by angry women with pins and rods. Veralinda, a daughter of the King of Frigia, happened to encounter this scene, in which her father, the King, had been physically attacked by a group of women who wanted to take revenge for the sexual abuse they had suffered from the King (*Urania* I 562–63). At the same time, Eva Griffith thinks that *Swetnam the Woman-Hater* is not only a play centring on the gender debate, but it can also be seen as an attempt to replicate real court proceedings. Griffith argues that the play was relevant both to the context of Queen Anne's circle, in which a few women, including Lady Anne Clifford, were involved in legal problems of their own, and to the Red Bull's interest in court drama in the later repertoire (2013 140–4). Griffith goes on to propose that the Queen's Men's device of cross-dressing in the play—men-playing-men-disguised as women—was intended to invoke a similar device in Sir Philip Sidney's *Arcadia*. If Griffith's proposition is correct, the play would surely have stirred the interest of Mary Wroth. There is a possibility, therefore, that Wroth was conscious of this scene in the play in writing the episode about the torture inflicted on the King of Frigia by furious women in *Urania* I.

On the other hand, *Haec-Vir*, which appeared as a companion piece to *Hic Mulier*, presents an attitude towards women's self-assertion similar to that in Webster's plays. As has been argued above, like Vittoria, Hic-Mulier in the pamphlet attempts to justify women's defiance of conventional images of womanhood from an existential viewpoint, saying 'we are as free-borne as Men, haue as free election, and as free spirits' (1620 sig. B3r).

Among the numerous treatises upon women published in this period, *Haec-Vir* is the only pamphlet that draws attention to contemporary women's awakening sense of independence. Greatly impressed by its modernity, Louis B. Wright once called it the '*Areopagitica* of the London woman' (1964 497). Yet the author of the pamphlet seemed to feel uneasy in adopting this attitude, since Hic Mulier agrees to return to traditional femininity on condition that Haec-Vir re-affirms his own masculinity.

Puritan women's religious activities in late Jacobean England

With regard to publications by women in this period, another important factor concerns the activities of Puritan women. Compared with many other religions, Christian doctrine in general seems to give women more recognition; it certainly seems so to a person like myself, who was brought up in the religious climate of Buddhism and Shintoism, the doctrines of which make no specific reference to the existence of women. For all the emphasis on the necessity of woman's self-effacement in Pauline doctrine, the creation story in Genesis at least offers an explanation of the creation of woman as well as that of man. It also gives a definition not just of man, but also of woman, though it identifies woman merely as a helpmate for man, not as an independent being. Feminists in the twentieth century found these explanations deficient or problematic, but still, the fact that women's existence was recognised by Biblical authority was of great significance in the process of constructing female selfhood in earlier periods of history.

As has been mentioned, the Biblical explanations of the relationship between man and woman contain some ambiguities and contradictions. Although the concept of male superiority and female inferiority is explicitly established in the Scriptures, the creation story in Genesis identifies the material from which God formed Eve as Adam's rib, a material that may justify women's refusal of subjection to men. Detractors of women had insisted since medieval times that the rib being crooked, women were intractable by nature. On the other hand, the fact that the rib is located in the central part of the body may indicate the spiritual equality of the two sexes; indeed, some writers, including women such as Rachel Speght, took up this point, as we read in her argument (1617 sig. D1v). Furthermore, the whole episode may be understood as implying female superiority; as defenders of women often pointed out, woman was made from a part of Adam's body, the Divine creation, whereas man was made from dust. It is interesting to note how differently people in seventeenth-century England interpreted these ambiguities and contradictions implicit in the Scriptures, as well as to examine what impact these different interpretations made upon society.

This impact can be seen most clearly in the relationship between women and Puritanism in early seventeenth-century England. Returning to the anecdote of 'the rib', for instance, we may observe direct contradictions in the interpretation of this Biblical episode among Puritan men and women at that time. For instance, Thomas Adams, a formidable Puritan preacher, inveighed against contemporary women's fondness for fine ornaments in his sermon 'Mystical Bedlam', asserting that the cause of their offence originated in the material from which they were made, Adam's rib, which was less substantial and authentic than the dust from which man was made.[27] On the other hand, Rachel Speght, a Puritan woman, tried to vindicate, as will be discussed later in this chapter, her belief that 'the rib' signified the integrity of women.

As the Reformation introduced a new perspective on marriage into England, by proposing the ideal of chastity in marriage, matrimony came to be regarded as a divinely ordained unity, 'an hie, holye and blessed order of life',[28] instead of the necessary evil required for the production of posterity or the release of sexual frustration. In this new view of marriage, love and affection are emphasised and partnership is considered the cornerstone of the relationship between husband and wife. From the 1580s to the 1630s, this view was disseminated throughout England in Puritan preachers' sermons and writings. However, the Puritan emphasis on mutual affection between spouses also contains a contradiction: this 'blessed order of life' is actually maintained only through wives' submission to their husbands' authority, based on the sanction for man's controlling power over his wife from Biblical authority:

> Wives, submit yourselves unto your own husbands, as unto the Lord. For the husband is the head of the wife, even as Christ is the head of the church: and he is the saviour of the body. (Ephesians 5: 22–3)

What Puritan divines advocated, therefore, was a patriarchal form of marriage based on wives' willing subjection to their husbands' authority. Drawing on Biblical examples, Puritan preachers developed a role model for women in which they fulfilled their function, as wives, through voluntary submission to their husbands' will. William Gouge, one of the most influential Puritan preachers at the time, delivers a typical view: 'though husband and wife may mutually serve one another through love: yet the Apostle suffereth not a woman to rule over the man' (1622 272). As R. Valerie Lucas argued, Puritan preachers' sermons and writings in fact created the illusion of partnership by proposing male authority and female submission as duties to God in marriage (1990 228–31). Thus, the Puritan notion of partnership actually concealed the repressive aspect of the power relations in marriage. Through ingenious rhetorical strategies, Puritan divines persuaded females in congregations to accept their subjection in the household.

Because of the stress on the necessity of wives' submission to their husbands' authority, the Puritan view of marriage denied women selfhood in a true sense. In consequence, language—as a means of expressing their individual thoughts—was not attributed to women. A basis for male authority and female silence is firmly established in the Scriptures:

> Let your women keep silence in the churches: for it is not permitted unto them to speak; but they are commanded to be under obedience, as also saith the law. And if they will learn anything, let them ask their husbands at home: for it is a shame for women to speak in the church. (1 Corinthians 14: 34–5)

John Dod and Robert Cleaver in *A Godlie Forme of Householde Government* (1612) elaborate on this doctrine:

> Now silence is the best ornament of a woman, and therefore the law was given to the man, rather then to the woman, to shew that he should be the teacher, and she the hearer; and therefore shee is commanded to learne of her husband. (1612 104)

Yet, some Puritan women in the late Elizabethan and Jacobean periods interpreted this seemingly obvious injunction to female silence in ways that were incompatible with the orthodox view.[29] Already in the early years of the Jacobean period, long before the 1640s, it seems that there were some Puritan women who had not only been teaching their husbands and children but had also been preaching in public. Their activities are visible in the criticism and complaints of contemporary writers, which was also the case with the female preachers of the later seventeenth century. William Heale, for instance, expresses his disapproval of these Puritan women in *An Apology for Women* (1609), a tract intended to defend women, commissioned by an unidentified noble lady:

> I could never approue those too too holy women-gospellers, who weare their testament at their apron-strings, and wil weekely catechize their husbands, citing places, clearing difficulties, & preaching holy sermons too, if the spirit of their devotion moue them. For sure I am, antiquity helde silence to be a womans chiefest eloquence, & thought it their part to heare more then to speake, to learne rather then to teach. (1609 35–6)

The presence of these assertive Puritan women indicates that some women, having found alternative ways to understand the meanings of the Scriptures, were already putting these interpretations into practice in the early Jacobean period. On the other hand, as has been discussed, it was the doctrine of Puritanism itself that contained a contradiction concerning women's independence of thought and freedom of expression. Coexisting with teachings on the necessity of women's silence and their obedience to male authority was the stress in Puritan thought on the dictates of individual conscience, which fostered in women the habit of building selfhood in relation to God. Even though they were not officially allowed to speak in church, large numbers of women flocked to sermons and lectures (Lucas, 1990 226–33);[30] for not only men, but also women and 'even' servants were taught to strive to understand the Bible for themselves. The seriousness of women who attended sermons was noted by their contemporaries; some preachers were annoyed by women taking notes or transcribing sermons in shorthand (Lucas, 1990 224–30). In religious meetings, women were encouraged to express their views during discussions of the meanings of the Scriptures (Collinson, 1967 378–82).

In these circumstances, the Puritan emphasis on the exposition of God's Word through preaching and lecturing must have greatly assisted the development of rational thinking and clear expression in women. Moreover, Puritans agreed that it was women's responsibility to instruct their families in religious matters. Wives' responsibilities for the spiritual life of the family must have made them, as well as the members of their families, very conscious of the importance of their language. Thus, while persuading women to conform to the ideal of female silence and obedience, Puritan doctrine paradoxically encouraged them to form habits of independent thinking and self-expression.

Puritan women's construction of a sense of self, thus started in the private sphere—that is, in their personal efforts to examine their selfhood in relation to God. The division between the private and public spheres easily disappeared, however, especially when women had ideological support for their activities in public. Considering it also their duty to enable others to understand God's Word, some Puritan women stepped over the boundary of the private into the public sphere, and started to preach openly. Furthermore, society's overreaction to this changing consciousness in Puritan women made that change even more publicly conspicuous. In particular, contemporary plays drew public attention to Puritan women's unconventional attitudes through dramatising the various impacts of their activities.

Society's fears about the liberating aspects of Puritan thought are reflected in the stereotypical portrayals of Puritan women in early Jacobean plays. Stock features of the female Puritans in these plays are lustfulness and volubility. Simon Shepherd, in his examination of representations of lechery in Puritan women in drama, argues that such a portrayal represents a common reaction against the Puritan emphasis on love and affection, especially as found among the radical Puritan sects like the Family of Love. Such attitudes could lead to the celebration of love and sex and, more dangerously, to the concept of gender equality, which might pose a serious threat to male authority (Shepherd, 1981 55–62). The stereotypical feature of volubility in female Puritans on stage in this period also seems to suggest a common reaction against the freedom of expression and independence of thought that Puritan women were developing at the time. In earlier plays, such as Middleton's *The Family of Love* (Admiral's (?), 1603) or *The Puritan, or The Widow of Watling Street* (Paul's, 1606), Puritan women are shown to hold independent points of view and to engage in free speech, thus contradicting Jacobean assumptions about the female virtues of silence and modesty. In these plays the Puritan women's speeches are presented only in terms of their hypocrisy; that is, as being merely a strategy designed to conceal their sexual drives or material greed.

Although sympathetic treatment of Puritans is rare in literature of the period (Shepherd, 1981 65), in some later plays such as Thomas Drue's *The Duchess of Suffolk* (Palsgraves, 1624), the speeches of women who show Puritan inclinations are treated in a positive light.[31] Even though the women violate the ideal of female silence, they are presented as having integrity. Self-assertive speeches by Puritan women are designed to represent the Puritan principle itself, such as the levelling attitudes of Puritan Parliamentarians in later years, or the Puritan concept of marriage. This phenomenon became particularly clear among plays of the later period, particularly of the 1630s when Puritan opposition leaders were increasing in power, and some City magnates were trying to use the stage as a means of propaganda in their conflict with the Crown (Heinemann, 1980 200–36). In most cases, the speeches of Puritan women in the plays do not function to construct their selfhood. Nonetheless, the fact that they show no hesitation in speaking out in these plays, frequently at length, in order to express their refusal to accept a female virtue of silence, deserves attention.

Rachel Speght represented Puritan women who believed in the necessity of expressing and publishing their views. She was the first female author to launch a counter-attack upon Swetnam's publication of his mysogynist pamphlet. The daughter of James Speght, the rector of more than one London church, she was twenty in 1617 when she published her pamphlet, *A Movzell for Melastomvs*.

Speght's Puritan stance is clear from her argument against Swetnam; she responds to his attack on women through the Puritan defence of marriage. She discredits his references to Biblical examples of women's inferiority by pointing out his misreadings of the Scriptures and offering what she thinks are their correct meanings. The method she employs in her argument recalls the one used by male Puritans in their preachings and lectures. Speght's Puritan position became even stronger in her poem published four years later, *Mortalities Memorandum, with a Dreame Prefixed imaginarie in manner; reall in matter*, for which she appears to have used the Geneva Bible as her scriptural source.[32] Ester Sowernam, the writer who next attacked Swetnam, refers to Speght as 'a Ministers daughter' (1617 sig. A2v). At the beginning of the pamphlet, Ester writes that she had heard about Swetnam's outrageous pamphlet while having supper with some friends, and that later she was told about Speght's forthcoming response (1617 sig. A2r-A2v). Therefore it seems to have been fairly well known at the time that the first criticism of Swetnam came from a Puritan woman. It is probable that like Ester, Mary Wroth discovered this pamphlet debate against Swetnam during some casual occasions, such as those at Penshurst Place. Alternatively, it is possible that she came to know about Speght through criticism by Ester Sowernam, whom, if she really was the Countess of Hertford as Griffith suggests, Wroth must have known.

Speght uses the tactic of presenting herself as a woman who embodies the Puritan ideal of modesty. Adopting a meek, modest, mild pose, she apologises for venturing on the immodest, unfeminine act of publishing her writing, especially because of her 'insufficiency in literature and tenderness in yeares' (1617 sig. A4v); she is 'vnworthiest of thousands' (sig. A3r), for she has *'not as yet seene twenty yeares,/Though in her carriage older she appeares'* (sig. B4v). Speght's self-deprecating pose seems to have irritated Ester Sowernam so much that she decided to launch her own attack on Swetnam. Yet Speght's tone is in fact quite misleading; from the beginning, her criticism of Swetnam is conducted with great self-confidence. She starts by accusing him of blasphemy for condemning women—the 'excellent worke of Gods hands' (1617 sig. B2v)—as a curse upon men. Throughout the pamphlet her argument is eloquently delivered and well structured, lucidly pinpointing the logical flaws in Swetnam's pamphlet.

Moreover, as Ann Jones pointed out (1990 52), Speght extends the Puritan concepts of marriage and womanhood to present her own views on gender equality. Using a method often employed in contemporary tracts on matrimony, she returns to the creation story in Genesis, but her purpose is to assert the equality of man and woman by making use of ambiguities in the text:

> man was created of the dust of the earth, but woman was made of a part of man, after that he was a liuing soule: yet was shee not produced from *Adams* foote, to be his too low inferiour; nor from his head to be his superiour, but from his side, neare his heart, to be his equal; that where he is Lord, she may be Lady [. . .] (Speght, 1617 sig. D1v)

Because Eve was created as a respectable helpmate to Adam, men and women were promised equal authority: 'he makes their authority equall, and all creatures to be in subjection vnto them both' (1617 sig. D1v). Speght's view of marriage is typically the one of Puritans in that she acknowledges the authority of husbands over wives and the importance of their mutual assistance, and accepts the common analogy of the role of husband in the family with Christ's role as head of the Church. And yet, her emphasis is actually upon the husband's responsibility as the head for creating a harmonious relationship between spouses.

In spite of her apologetic tone, Speght's pamphlet consistently demonstrates her firm belief in the necessity for women to speak out against injustice in society and to use their capacity for rational thinking. Her argument stands in sharp contrast to contemporary stereotypical views of women as silent and lacking rationality. Speght's belief is demonstrated again in her next published work, *Mortalities Memorandum* (1621). As in her pamphlet, while assuming a modest, meek pose, she forcefully advocates gender equality and the rights of women to make the most of the intellectual capacities with which they are endowed by God:

> Both man and woman of three parts consist,
> Which *Paul* doth bodie, soule, and spirit call:
> And from the soule three faculties arise,
> The mind, the will, the power; when wherefore shall
> A woman have her intellect in vaine,
> Or not endeavor *Knowledge* to attaine.
>
> The talent, God doth give, must be imploy'd,
> His owne with vantage he must have againe:
> All parts and faculties were made for use;
> The God of *Knowledge* nothing gave in vaine. (*A Dreame*, lines 127–36, *Polemics and Poems* ed. Lewalski, 1996, 53)[33]

In the dedication of her poem Speght wrote about her irritation at the hostility directed against her unwomanly act of writing and publishing her pamphlet four years earlier, and especially at the accusation that it was her father who wrote the pamphlet. In spite of these reactions to her work, she at least publicly exhibited the right of women to use their ability of speech and learning in publishing her pamphlet and poem.

Some women's dissatisfaction with the passive, subordinate roles assigned by society in late Jacobean England can be observed in the examples of female insubordination examined in this chapter. This can also be understood by the fact that a great number of the Quakers and sectarians of later years were women, who were attracted to religious groups that offered gender equality and the opportunity to preach or even hold priestly office. Despite constant attack from men with orthodox views, women preached and prophesied in England in the 1640s and 1650s. During these decades some women even turned to activism, presenting petitions to Parliament and organising demonstrations.[34] The change in Puritan women's attitudes towards themselves had by then moved beyond the private world, and they manifested their beliefs in the public sphere.

Puritanism could serve to provide ideological support for women's cultivation of their sense of self and desire for self-expression in prerevolutionary England. These Puritan women's belief in speaking and publishing their views was justified, since the purpose of such expression was to worship God and to enhance others' faith. Yet the bounds of such justification could easily be extended to non-religious spheres such as creative writing in which women could invest their language with meaning and integrity.

Although the Sidneys/Herberts were the prominent Protestant families and Mary Wroth took a Protestant position, she never mentioned religion in her works. However, she would have taken great interest in Rachel Speght, who, despite her young age, courageously published her tract against Swetnam and her original work of poetry, in which she eloquently argued from a Protestant point of view on mistakes in conventional assumptions about womanhood in society.

Mary Wroth decided to expose her romance to the public through publication, though Pamphilia, her heroine, kept her works in her cabinets. Her true motivation for this action will probably never be known. Wroth may have simply intended to join the self-assertive tendency among women at the time, making public her views on gender and society. Like Liana's broken cabinet in *Urania*, Wroth may have felt her mind 'so fild with treasure' of her creativity that she took 'the lock' off her speech to let it 'flie abroad', and as a result published her romance. Alternatively, publication may have been related to the financial predicament she was suffering at the time (Hannay, 2010 248–51). In view of her high social standing, however, people's reactions to her publication were exceedingly severe. As she promised the Duke of Buckingham, she may actually have withdrawn copies from the market. Nevertheless, what is most important is that, despite the hostile response she had received from the public, she continued to write the second part, the manuscript of which must have been kept in various cabinets before it reached the Newberry Library in Chicago. Although its publication was delayed for nearly four centuries, *The Second Part of The Countess of Montgomery's Urania* was published in 1999. Both parts of *Urania* have continued to provide great inspiration and interest for students and scholars of both genders, raising important issues concerning the female desire for self-expression in the English Renaissance.

In contrast, few Japanese women had engaged in any form of *the querelle des dames* or challenged the social norms of womanhood so defiantly as the women in Jacobean England described in this book. This difference seems to have been deeply related to the fact that, compared with British women, Japanese women since the twelfth century have had little chance to participate in substantial ways in forming new modes of their country's culture until recent years.

Conclusion

The growing recognition of women's desire for self-expression and self-actualisation in Jacobean England was closely related to many facets of culture in the English Renaissance. This book has examined its process, by focusing on plays and prose writings written by authors of both genders in the period, placing special emphasis on works by Lady Mary Wroth. In terms of women's pursuit of self-actualisation, it is an historical fact that many more constraints were imposed upon women than men in Jacobean society. Yet it was not my intention to divide literary and theatrical activities by gender, far less to present the victimisation of women by male authority. As has been demonstrated in this book, the works by some male writers, particularly playwrights, helped to create understanding and sympathy for non-conforming women both in fiction and in actual society. Their new perspectives concerning the realities that confronted women as well as women's defiance of conventional concepts of womanhood helped the emergence of a new kind of view of women in the late Jacobean years. In this sense some male playwrights in the period were active agents in forming and altering contemporary culture, not simply reflecting on or commenting on the social changes of the time. The purpose of this book has been to investigate the interactions between women's desire for self-actualisation and the construction of female selfhood as represented by both male and female writers in Jacobean England.

Space has prevented me from discussing many important related issues. Choosing to concentrate on women's dramatic communication with other characters in Jacobean plays and prose writings, I had to exclude from my argument the exceedingly fruitful area of women's poetry as well as many of their diaries and letters. Only two female playwrights in Jacobean England, Elizabeth Cary and Mary Sidney Wroth, turned out to fit my chosen category. Cary's *The Tragedy of Mariam* was probably the first tragedy written by an Englishwoman, though she later wrote in other genres, such as her historical account of Edward II as well as the translation of a religious tract written in French by Cardinal Perron. Although it has been said that Cary's play was probably not intended for actual performance, Mariam's dramatic exchange with other characters, in particular with her husband Herod and the Chorus, who articulate conventional concepts of wifely duties, are, as was argued in this book, illuminating. It shows not only the heroine's but also the author's struggle in a society that denied a woman her own sense of self. As Cary seemed to be fond of theatre-going in her early years, she might have been influenced by her contemporary playwrights in constructing the dramatic structure of her play.

In the case of Mary Wroth, her pastoral comedy *Love's Victory* was most likely intended for performance on the occasion of the marriage of her sister Barbara in September 1619. The play's dramatic possibilities in an actual performance were fully exhibited in the production by Read Not Dead of Shakespeare's Globe, held in the Baron's Hall of Penshurst Place on 8 June 2014. Her romance *The Countess of Montgomery's Urania* and its continuation part are mostly written in prose, though interspersed with songs and poetry. Wroth's *Urania* differs from other romances in the period in that the stories are mostly developed through the dramatic communication between the characters. As has been said, this is why the two parts of her romance are included in this book.

Wroth seems to have engaged in writing poetry since her childhood, following in the Sidney tradition. Although excluded from the discussion in this book, her sonnet sequence, 'Pamphilia to Amphilanthus', was appended to *The Countess of Montgomery's Urania*, the published part of her romance. Her poems, both published ones and those left in manuscript form,[1] provide material that reveals how Wroth tried to construct her selfhood as a poet. This theme has been widely studied, and important books and articles have been published to help explain the place of Wroth in the history of poetry in early modern England.[2]

Another important matter this book could not fully investigate is the place of Lady Mary Wroth in Stuart political history. She was distinguished as a woman at the time in terms of her international experience and knowledge. She was half-Welsh, with an English father, Robert Sidney, Earl of Leicester, and a Welsh mother, Barbara Gamage, who was a wealthy heiress and the first cousin of Sir Water Raleigh. In Wroth's childhood Robert Sidney was the Governor of Flushing in the Low Countries, and she visited him there with her family. Furthermore, it has been said that she was even sent to The Hague to learn the French language. The Hague was one of the international centres in Europe at the time, and a family friend of the Sidneys, Sir John Dudley Carlton, was the English ambassador there. She must have had a lot of experiences that she could never have enjoyed if she had lived only in England. In Flushing or in The Hague, as I mentioned in the book, she may have had a chance to get to know intelligent, attractive black people, like her character Rodomandro or the black page in the portrait in Penshurst Place, who were possibly brought over from the Dutch colonies. Even though she had probably never met Sir Philip Sidney, she was raised amidst the family and cultural memories of this Protestant champion. Her first cousin and lover William Herbert, Earl of Pembroke, and her distant relative Lucy, Countess of Bedford were good friends of Prince Henry, the embodiment of militant Protestantism in Jacobean England, whose untimely death in 1612 changed history not only for England but also, in hindsight, for Europe. While the man Mary Wroth married, Sir Robert Wroth, came from the family of an Essex landowner, many of her Sidney relatives were deeply engaged in international politics. Her interest in international affairs was fostered by the climate of her family as well as by her own experiences abroad. In other words, she is one of the unusual women in Jacobean England who knows, to borrow Innogen's words in *Cymbeline*, 'I' th' world's volume/Our Britain seems as of it, but not in 't' (3. 4. 151–2). As has been mentioned in the book, her wide knowledge of international affairs was noted by Anne, the second Countess of Montgomery, on her visit to Penshurst Place.[3]

Her role, for instance, in the Protestants' intercession between Queen Elizabeth of Bohemia and King James during the years of the crisis in Bohemia, has not yet been examined deeply. Julie Crawford explored in her recent book Wroth's role in the political sphere in terms of her inner relationship with the Sidney/Herbert family, in particular with William Herbert and Robert Sidney. In her thorough examination of Robert Sidney's letters and documents kept in the Sidney archives, Crawford found much affinity between Wroth's *Urania* and her father's writings (*Mediatrix*, 2014 160–216).

However, Wroth may have had her own purpose in her writings, which was independent from her family interests. The manuscript of *Urania* Part II, kept in the Newberry library, suggests this possibility. Some pages of this holograph manuscript were written in such a disorderly manner that they are difficult to read. They seem to reveal some emotional upset on the part of their author. This manuscript is very different from the Penshurst manuscript of *Love's Victory*, which has been kept in the Sidney archive. The latter, written in an orderly Italian hand, can certainly be regarded as a 'manuscript publication', which was, as Crawford argues, more highly regarded than publication in print (2014 25–9). In the light of the difference in these manuscripts, it is hard to think that Wroth had intended to write the continuation part to stand as a 'manuscript publication'. Rather, it seems that despite the uproar after the publication of *Urania* I, she herself had something she wanted to express, which was related to the society and politics of her contemporary world.

Although women in the later periods also met with various constraints in publishing their original works, British culture in general came to take it as granted that women, like men, could have a desire for self-actualisation, in particular for self-expression. This change in culture originated in the English Renaissance. As this book has demonstrated, the interaction between self-asserting women and their surrounding world can most clearly be observed in the plays and polemical writings written by authors of both genders in Jacobean England.

Although the scope of the examination of Jacobean culture conducted in this book is by no means thorough, the significance of these women's assertions of themselves and the publication of their dramatic creations and polemical writings is made clear in both literary and historical terms. Comparative studies of how female and male writers treated the same issues are useful in this respect. In view of the strictly patriarchal structure of the society in which these writers lived and of the fact that they did not have our post-modern cultural or psychoanalytical theories to resort to, their courage in struggling against social norms and in attempting to rewrite the position of women in their works is not only remarkable but also very important in the history of women. These writers were in many ways 'governed' by conventional ideologies, but made a breakthrough by enabling women's voices to be heard or to be published. Regardless of gender, these writers in Jacobean England were forerunners of the emerging female discourses, which were to be developed in different cultural contexts in the following years.

In contrast, even though a culture of female writings, including poetry, romance and essays, flourished among ladies at the Courts from the tenth to the eleventh century in Japan, there was a long hiatus afterwards. There were constant civil wars not only in Kyoto but throughout the country, and when the Tokugawa government came to rule the country in Edo (Tokyo) in 1603, it established a society with a powerful feudal system. Moreover, in order to prevent the influence of Christianity, in 1616 they limited their commerce with European countries to Hirato, a small island in Kyushu, and officially closed the country to almost all Western countries from 1639 for more than two hundred years. These circumstances made it difficult for early modern Japanese women to engage in creative writing and to make space for themselves in the warrior culture or the culture under strict feudalism. There were, though, some exceptional cases. For instance, Lady Tama Gracia Hosokawa (1562–1600), wife of Lord Tadaoki Hosokawa, who ruled the Kumamoto area in Kyushu Island, left quite an impressive farewell poem at her death.[4] She had become one of the 'Clandestine Catholic Converts', despite Christianity having been virtually banned in sixteenth-century Japan. She, like Shakespeare's Cleopatra, chose to commit suicide instead of being captured by the enemies of her husband. Although Lady Gracia's courageous act has been much admired in Japan—even today—it did not make a significant impact on the culture as a whole at the time. It was only in the late nineteenth century that Japanese women began to participate in shaping a new culture in significant ways, particularly after the country was re-opened, first to North America in 1854 and then to European countries.

Meanwhile, Kabuki retained its tradition and popularity, especially among people of the merchant class; women flocked to the Kabuki theatres in Edo and Kyoto in eighteenth-and nineteenth-century Japan, in order to see their favourite actors. In many Kabuki plays, the roles of women are exceedingly important. However, partly because men play the female roles, the greatest emphasis has been placed on the aesthetic aspects or conventional female virtues. In Kabuki plays, as demonstrated in this book, when women are aggressive in insisting on their will, they are usually represented as monsters or ghosts in pursuit of revenge. Although women in these plays indirectly question the social system of that time, in performance they invoke only fear or pity from the audience without investigating the heart of the matter.

After the early modern period, English culture became multicultural. It is interesting to examine how multicultural elements were interacted with women's desire for self-actualisation, which was recognised in Jacobean England. British culture is unique in that women's ardour for both self-actualisation and self-construction came to be acknowledged in such an early period. This change in Jacobean England seems to have been deeply related to British women's continual and active participation in creating new modes of culture in the following periods.

Notes

Introduction: Concepts of Womanhood in Early Modern England

1. I hope this current situation will change owing to the recent publication of two important books on Wroth: *Mary Wroth and Shakespeare*, ed. Paul Salzman and Marion Wynne-Davies (New York and London: Routledge, 2015); *Re-Reading Mary Wroth*, ed. Katherine R. Larson, Naomi Miller and Andrew Strycharski (New York: Palgrave Macmillan, 2015).
2. For the discussion of the issue of the self in the Renaissance and early modern period, see, for instance, Jonathan Sawday, 'Self and Selfhood in the Seventeenth Century', in *Rewriting the Self: Histories from the Renaissance to the Present*, ed. Roy Porter (London and New York: Routledge, 1997), 17–57; Phippa Kelly and L. E. Semler ed., *Word and Self Estranged in English Texts, 1550–1660* (Farnham: Ashgate, 2010); Michael Mascuch, *Origins of the Individualist Self: Autobiography and Self-Identity in England, 1591–1791* (Cambridge: Polity Press, 1997); Jerrold Seigel, *The Idea of the Self: Thought and Experience in Western Europe since the Seventeenth Century* (Cambridge: Cambridge University Press, 2005).
3. For the authorship of these Characters, see F. L. Lucas, *The Complete Works of John Webster* (1927) (New York: Gordian Press, 1966), 4 vols., Vol.4, 6–10; David Gunby, Introduction to New Characters, *The Works of John Webster: An Old-Spelling Critical Edition*, ed. David Gunby, David Carnegie and MacDonald P. Jackson et al. (Cambridge: Cambridge University Press, 1995–2007), 3 vols., Vol. 3, 440–51. All citations from Webster's works in this book are taken from this edition.
4. All citations from Overbury's *A Wife* in this book are taken from the second impression of the text published in 1614.
5. For the concepts of marriage in early modern England, see Martin Ingram, *Church Courts, Sex and Marriage in England, 1570–1640* (Cambridge: Cambridge University Press, 1987); Lawrence Stone, *The Family, Sex, and Marriage in England, 1500–1800* (London: Weidenfeld and Nicolson, 1977).
6. The dates of the plays and the names of the companies that first performed these plays are according to the *Annals of English Drama 975–1700* (1964), ed. Alfred Harbage, revised by S. Schoenbaum, the Third Edition, revised by Sylvia Stoler Wagonheim (London and New York: Routledge, 1989).
7. For a different view of the effect of chaste marriage on men, see, for instance, Bernard Capp, 'The Double Standard Revisited: Plebeian Women and Male Sexual Reputation in Early Modern England', *Past and Present* 162 (1999): 70–100. For a brief review of the issue of the double standard, see Jennifer Jordan, 'Her-story Untold: The Absence of Women's Agency in Constructing Concepts of Early Modern Manhood', *Cultural and Social History* 4 (2007): 575–83.

8. William Shakespeare, *William Shakespeare The RSC Shakespeare Complete Works*, ed. Jonathan Bate and Eric Rasmussen (Basingstoke: Macmillan, 2007). All citations from Shakespeare's plays in this book are taken from this edition.
9. Edward G. Seidensticker tr., *The Tale of Genji* (Vermont and Tokyo: Charles E. Tuttle, 1980), 2 vols, Introduction xii–xv. All references to *The Tale of Genji* in this book are to this edition.
10. For Jacobean learned ladies' activities at the Court of Queen Anne, see Leeds Barroll, *Anna of Denmark of England: A Cultural Biography* (Philadelphia: University of Pennsylvania Press, 2001); Curtis Perry, *The Making of Jacobean Court Culture* (Cambridge: Cambridge University Press, 1997).
11. For instance, Ben Jonson's *Epistles* to the Countess of Rutland and the Countess of Bedford; Barnaby Rich in *The Excellency of Good Women* (1613), 2–3.
12. Ben Jonson, *The Works of Ben Jonson*, ed. C. H. Herford, Percy Simpson and Evelyn Simpson, 11 vols (Oxford: Clarendon Press, 1925–52). All citations from Jonson's works in this book are taken from this edition.
13. John Marston, *The Plays of John Marston*, ed. Harvey Wood (London: Oliver and Boyd, 1934–9), 3 vols. All citations from Marston's plays in this book are taken from this edition. As Wood used the numbers of act, scene and page, the citations in this book are indicated in the same way.
14. This issue was much discussed recently. Particularly important studies include, Stephen Orgel, *Impersonations: The Performance of Gender in Shakespeare's England* (Cambridge: Cambridge University Press, 1996); Michael Shapiro, *Gender in Play on the Shakespearean Stage: Boy Heroines and Female Pages* (Ann Arbor: University of Michigan Press, 1994); David Mann, *Shakespeare's Women: Performance and Conception* (Cambridge: Cambridge University Press, 2008).
15. For the song 'Tomorrow is St. Valentine's Day' in *Hamlet* 4.4, see Ross W. Duffin, *Shakespeare's Songbook* (New York and London: W. W. Norton & Company, 2004), 407–8; for 'Bonny Sweet Robin' in *Hamlet* 4.4, 72–4. For music in Shakespeare's plays, see David Lindley, *Shakespeare and Music* (London: Thomson Learning, 2006); Christopher R. Wilson and Michela Calore ed., *Music in Shakespeare: A Dictionary* (London: Continuum, 2007).
16. For the dramatic function of these qualities of their languages, see also Inga-Stina Ewbank. '"My name is Marina": The Language of Recognition', in *Shakespeare's Styles*, ed. Philip Edwards, Inga-Stina Ewbank, and G. K. Hunter (Cambridge: Cambridge University Press, 1980), 111–30.
17. Sir Thomas Overbury. John Considine, 'Overbury, Sir Thomas (*bap.* 1581, *d.* 1613)'. *The Oxford Dictionary of National Biography* (*DNB*), online edn. Jan 2008 [http://0-www.oxforddnb.com.catalogue.ulrls.lon.ac.uk/view/article/20966, accessed 15 Feb 2015].

1 Emerging New Attitudes towards Women in Early Jacobean England

1. Florio's translation, though, seems to have some misreadings. For this issue, see David Pascoe, 'The Dutch Courtesan and the Profits of Translation', in *The Drama of John Marston*, ed. T. F. Wharton (Cambridge: Cambridge

University Press, 2000), 162–80. For the characteristics of Marston's use of *a double entendre* in his courtesan plays, see Richard Scarr, 'Insatiate Punning in Marston's Courtesan Plays' in this volume, 82–99. See also William M. Hamlin, *Montaigne's English Journey: Reading the Essays in Shakespeare's Days* (Oxford: Oxford University Press, 2013).

2. The Great Picture in the Appleby Castle shows books that Lady Anne possessed. Among them are Montaigne's *Essays* and Ben Jonson's *Works*.
3. William M. Hamlin, in *Montaigne's English Journey*, includes Elizabeth Cary among the writers in seventeenth-century England who most frequently borrowed expressions from Florio's Montaigne (11). Her private tutor, Sir John Davies, who has been said to have advised Cary to publish her tragedy, was one of the great admirers of Florio's Montaigne.
4. Michael Montaigne, *The Essays of Michael Lord of Montaigne*, tr. John Florio, Everyman (London: Dent, 1910), 3 vols. All citations from the *Essays* in this book are taken from this edition.
5. Mary Sidney Wroth, *The First Part of the Countess of Montgomery's Urania*, ed. Josephine A. Roberts (Binghamton, NY: Medieval and Renaissance Texts and Studies, 1995); *The Second Part of the Countess of Montgomery's Urania*, ed. Josephine A. Roberts, completed by Suzanne Gossett and Janet Mueller (Tempe, AZ: Renaissance English Text Society/Arizona Center for Medieval and Renaissance Studies, 1990). All citations from *Urania* I and II in this book are taken from these editions.
6. The author of the play has been a matter of discussion. In *Thomas Middleton: The Collected Works*, ed. Gary Taylor and John Lavagnino (Oxford: Clarendon Press, 2007), the author is presented as Middleton. All references to Middleton's works in this book, except for *The Roaring Girl*, are taken from this edition.
7. For the main plot, see John J. O'Connor, 'The Chief Source of Marston's *Dutch Courtesan*', *Studies of Philology* 54 (1957): 509–15; for the subplot, see James J. Jackson, 'Sources of the Subplot of Marston's *The Dutch Courtesan*', *Philological Quarterly* 31 (1952): 223–4.
8. Philip J. Finkelpearl, *John Marston of the Middle Temple: An Elizabethan Dramatist in His Social Setting* (Cambridge, MA: Harvard University Press, 1969), 200–1, discusses Montaigne's influence on Marston's attitude towards male sexuality, although his discussion is not concerned with female sexuality.
9. Gustav Cross, 'Marston, Montaigne, and Morality: *The Dutch Courtesan* Reconsidered', *English Literary History* 27 (1960): 30–43, calls Freevill 'Montaigne's Natural Man', and discusses the parallels between Montaigne's naturalism and Marston's characterization of Freevill. For Freevill's departure from Montaigne in his attitude towards marriage and love, see also Finkelpearl, *John Marston of the Middle Temple*, 200–1.
10. The idea and some of the phrasing of Sophonisba's speeches draw on 'Upon Some Verses of Virgil'.
11. For the Stoicism in the play, see Peter Ure, 'John Marston's *Sophonisba*: A Reconsideration', in *Elizabethan and Jacobean Drama: Critical Essays by Peter Ure*, ed. J.C.Maxwell (Liverpool: Liverpool University Press, 1974), 75–92. See also William Hamlin, 'What Did Montaigne's Scepticism Mean to Shakespeare and His Contemporaries?', *Montaigne Studies* 17 (2005), 1–2: 195–210.

12. Although some scholars have traced Webster's hand in the revision of the play, the evidence is inconclusive. See Lucas, Vol. 3, 298.
13. For the functions of the images of serpents and flies in the play, see Maurice Charney, *Shakespeare's Roman Plays: The Function of Imagery in the Drama* (Cambridge, MA: Harvard University Press, 1961), 97–100.
14. For Shakespeare's use of the Hercules-Omphale myth, see Anne Barton, '"Nature's Piece 'gainst Fancy": The Divided Catastrophe in *Antony and Cleopatra*' (1974/1992), in *Essays, Mainly Shakespearean* (Cambridge: Cambridge University Press, 2006), 113–35.
15. Contemporary moralists frequently refer to Antony in pointing out the disastrous consequence of women's domination over men. See Franklin M. Dickey, *Not Wisely But Too Well: Shakespeare's Love Tragedies* (San Marino, CA: Huntington Library, 1966), 144–60.
16. For instance, Thomas Coryat, *Coryat's Crudities* (1611) (Glasgow: James MacLehose and Sons, 1950), 405.
17. Dickey, *Not Wisely But Too Well*, 159–60, after discussing the treatment of Cleopatra by Shakespeare's predecessors, concludes that Chaucer's *Legend of Good Women* alone gives a sympathetic picture of her as one of love's martyrs.
18. For the imagery of Isis and Venus, see Michael Lloyd, 'Cleopatra as Isis', *Shakespeare Survey* 12 (1959): 88–94; Raymond B. Waddington, 'What Venus Did to Mars', *Shakespeare Studies* II (1966): 210–27.
19. G. L. Taylor, *Shakespeare's Debt to Montaigne* (Cambridge, MA: Harvard University Press, 1925), 24–5, cites seven Montaigne passages echoed in the play and 98 words not used by Shakespeare before the Florio-Montaigne work; Hamlin, in *Montaigne's English Journey*, recognizes the strong influence of Florio's Montaigne on Shakespeare's play, 110–28, in particular 123.
20. See Geoffrey Bullough ed., *Narrative and Dramatic Sources of Shakespeare* (London: Routledge and Kegan Paul; New York: Columbia University Press, 1957–75), 8 vols, Vol. 5, 282.
21. See J. E. Neale, *Queen Elizabeth I* (1934) (London: Penguin books, 1990), 302. For the historical accuracy of this episode, see Susan Flye, *Elizabeth I: The Competition for Representation* (Oxford: Oxford University Press, 1993), 3–5.
22. Joseph Swetnam, *The Araignment of Lewd, Idle, Froward, and vnconstant women* (London, 1615). All citations from Swetnam's pamphlet in this book are taken from this edition.
23. For the date of *The White Devil*, see also John Webster, *The Works of John Webster: An Old-Spelling Critical Edition*, ed. David Gunby, David Carnegie and Antony Hammond (Cambridge: Cambridge University Press, 1995–2007), 3 vols, Vol. 1. 55–56. All citations from the play in this book are taken from this edition.
24. Webster, *The Works of John Webster*, 1995–2007, Vol. 1, 140.
25. Qut. in *The Works of John Webster* ed. David Gunby, David Carnegie and Antony Hammond (Cambridge: Cambridge University Press, 1995-2007) 3 vols. Vol.1, 140.
26. A number of writers have made the point that, although some sixteenth-century humanists admired learning in elite women, they were at the same time concerned to limit its scope, such as learning in religious matters and classics. See, for instance, Randall Martin, *Women Writers in Renaissance England* (London and New York: Longman, 1997), 311; Gemma Allen, *Cooke Sisters: Education, Piety and Politics* (Manchester: Manchester University Press, 2013), 20–1. This issue will be discussed in the final chapter of this book.

27. For an overview of James's reign, see also Pauline Croft, *King James* (Basingstoke: Palgrave Macmillan, 2003). At the same time, for his attempts to create the intellectual climate in the Jacobean Court, together with Queen Anne, see Leeds Barrol, *Anna of Denmark Queen of England: A Cultural Biography* (Philadelphia: University of Pennsylvania Press, 2001), 8–13.
28. In *Polyhymnia*, written for the occasion of the tilt on Accession Day in 1590, George Peele described Charles Blount playing with the name Rich. See also C. B. Falls, *Mountioy: Elizabethan General* (London: Obhama Press, 1954), 62–3.
29. For the issues concerning marriage and annulment in early modern England, see Martin Ingram, *Church Courts, Sex and Marriage in England, 1570–1640* (Cambridge: Cambridge University Press, 1987), 125–292; Lawrence Stone, *The Family, Sex, and Marriage in England, 1500–1800* (London: Weidenfeld and Nicolson, 1977); *Road to Divorce: England, 1530–1987* (Oxford: Clarendon Press, 1998), 51–120.
30. On the life of Lady Rich and her relationship with Charles Blount, see Maud Stepney Rawson, *Penelope Rich and Her Circle* (London: Hutchinson, 1911); Sylvia Freeman, *Poor Penelope: Lady Penelope Rich, an Elizabethan Woman* (Abbostbrook, Bourne End: Kensall Press, 1983); Sally Varlow, *The Lady Penelope: The Lost Tale of Love and Politics in the Elizabeth I* (London: Andre Deutsch, 2007); Johanna Rickman, *Love, Lust, and License in Early Modern England: Illicit Sex and the Nobility* (Aldershot: Ashgate, 2008), 111–40.
31. 'Aulicus Coquinariae', *Secret History of the Court of James the First*, ed. Sir Walter Scott (Edinburgh: J. Ballantyne, 1811), 2 vols, Vol. II, 200–1.
32. The Earl's funeral was performed with great pomp, but the herald declined to impale the Countess's arms with the Earl's. Christopher Maginn, 'Blount, Charles, Eighth Baron Mountjoy and Earl of Devonshire (1563–1606)', *DNB*, online edn. Jan 2008 [http://0-www.oxforddnb.com.catalogue.ulrls.lon.ac.uk/view/article/2683, accessed 15 Feb 2015].
33. Currently she is also called Arbella.
34. On the life of Lady Arabella, see Elizabeth Cooper, *The Life and Letters of Lady Arabella Stuart, Including Numerous Original and Unpublished Documents* (London: Hurst and Blackett, 1866); Ian McInnes, *Arabella: The Life and Times of Lady Arabella Seymour, 1575–1615* (London: W. H. Allen, 1968); David N. Durant, *Arabella Stuart: A Rival to the Queen* (London: Weidenfeld and Nicolson, 1978); Sarah Gristwood, *Arbella: England's Lost Queen* (London: Bantam, 2003); Rosalind K. Marshall, 'Stuart, Lady Arabella (1575–1615)', *DNB*, online edn. [http://0-www.oxforddnb.com.catalogue.ulrls.lon.ac.uk/view/article/601, accessed 15 Feb 2015].
35. William Seymour was a grandson of Catherine Grey, a stepdaughter of the Duchess of Suffolk, whose life also seems to have inspired Webster in his characterisation of the Duchess of Malfi. Catherine Grey was sister to Lady Jane Grey, on whose life Webster's earlier collaborative work, *Lady Jane*, had been based.
36. For rumours of Lord Seymour's death, see Chamberlain's letters of 11 March 1613 (Vol. I. 437); 9 September 1613 (Vol. I. 476); 7 July 1614 (Vol. I. 546–7). For those of Lady Arabella's distraction, see Chamberlain's letters of 29 April 1613 (Vol. I. 443); 9 September 1613 (Vol. I. 476); 7 July 1614 (Vol. I. 546–7).
37. Chamberlain writes in his letter of 12 February 1612: 'The Lady Shrewsberie is still in the Towre rather upon wilfulnes, then upon any great matter she is

charged with all: only the King is resolute that she shall aunswer to certain interrogatories, and she is as obstinate to make none, nor to be examined' (Vol. I. 334). See also Chamberlain's letter of 12 July 1612 (Vol. I. 364).

38. For her fight against her husband and uncle over the estates in this period, see Anne Clifford, *The Diary of Anne Clifford, 1616–1619: A Critical Edition*, ed. Katherine O. Acheson (New York: Garland, 1995), 65–6.

39. For the murder case of Sir Thomas Overbury, see William McElwee, *The Murder of Sir Thomas Overbury* (London: Faber, 1952); Beatrice White, *Cast of Ravens: The Strange Case of Sir Thomas Overbury* (London: Murray, 1965); David Lindlay, *The Trial of Frances Howard: Fact and Fiction at the Court of King James* (New York: Routledge, 1993); Anne Somerset, *Unnatural Murder: Poison at the Court of James I* (London: Weidenfeld and Nicolson, 1997); Rickman, *Love, Lust, and License in Early Modern England*, 83–5.

40. In April 1613, on refusing to accept the King's diplomatic appointment, Sir Thomas Overbury had been committed to the Tower, where he was poisoned and died on 15 September 1613. The official procedure to obtain the annulment of the Countess's marriage did not start until May 1613.

41. In *The Narrative History of King James, for the First Fourteen Years* (1651), the scandal is described as follows: 'almost all men spake of the looseness of her carriage, and wonders that the *Earle* will suffer these courses in her' (10); 'since it was so that the world took notice of their loosenesse, now to make some satisfaction, they would consummate a *Wedding* between them' (31). Anthony Weldon also writes in *The Court and Character of King James* (1650) that 'the world took notice they two long had lived in Adultery' (79–80).

42. M. C. Bradbrook, *John Webster: Citizen and Dramatist* (London: Weidenfeld and Nicolson, 1980), 9–28.

43. Webster's interest in Robert Carr was shown by him dedicating *Monumental Column* (1612), an elegy on Prince Henry, to this courtier.

44. Some of Swetnam's sayings correspond with those in *The Schole House of Women*. For instance, Swetnam's view that women 'haue two faults, that is, they can neither say well, nor yet doe well' (sig. E2v) is found in *The Schole House of Women*, while women's ability to weep at will, which Swetnam harps on, is also attacked there.

45. It went into ten editions between 1615 and 1637, and there was one each in 1690, 1702, 1707, 1733 and 1877; the Dutch translation appeared in 1641 and again in 1645.

46. The actual character referred to in the title, however, is open to question. See R. W. Dent, 'The White Devil, or Vittoria Corombona?', *Renaissance Drama* IX (1966): 179–203; H. Bruce Franklin, 'The Trial Scene of Webster's *The White Devil* Examined in Terms of Renaissance Rhetoric', *Studies in English Literature* 1500–1900, 1 (1961): 35–51.

47. John Webster, *The White Devil* (1612) (Menston: Scholar Press, 1970).

48. Shakespeare dramatized this episode in *Henry VIII*, which was probably not staged until 1613, but the episode had already been in Holinshed.

49. If Webster studied at the Middle Temple, as M. C. Bradbrook thought in *John Webster*, he must have been fully aware of these dangers. Another reference to the absurdity of the legal procedure is in III. ii. 89–91, which may have alluded to Raleigh's loss of Sherborne in 1608 due to a minute legal

technicality. See R. W. Dent, *John Webster's Borrowing* (Berkeley: University of California Press, 1960), 105.
50. This kind of stage direction, in which Webster describes the character's state of mind, is rare in his plays.
51. Swetnam writes: 'There are three waies to know a whore: by her wanton looks, by her speech, and by her gate' (sig. D1v). Kay Stanton, *Shakespeare's 'Whores': Erotics, Politics, and Poetics* (Houndsmills: Palgrave Macmillan, 2014), makes a thorough examination of the use of the term 'whore' in early modern England.
52. For instance, to describe woman's deceitfulness, Swetnam, like Monticelso, uses the image of the sea: women are 'like vnto the Sea, which at some times is so calm, that a cockbote may safely endure her might, but anon againe with outrage she is so growne, that it ouerwhelmeth the tallest ship that is' (sig. D4r).
53. For instance, see Garvis Markham, *The Famovs Whore, or Noble Curtizan* (London, 1609), sig. D4v-E1r.
54. This homiletic concept is traced by Dent, *John Webster's Borrowing*, 105–6 to Dekker's *If It Be Not Good, the Devil Is in It*, II. iii. 63–4, and Samuel Hieron's sermon.
55. For instance, Swetnam repeats a well-known saying about woman's cunningness: 'if all the world were paper, and all the sea inke, and all the trees and plants were pens, and euery man in the world were a writer, yet were they not able with all their labour and cunning, to set downe all the crafty deceits of women' (sig.F1r).
56. *The Oxford English Dictionary* lists Fynes Moryson's *Itinerary* (1617) as the first use of 'masculine' as a female attribute (*Oxford English Dictionary* Second Edition on CD-ROM (v. 4.0), Oxford University Press 2009). Shakespeare uses 'mannish' as a bad female attribute in *Troilus and Cressida*: 'a woman impudent and mannish grown' (3. 2. 217).
57. Nicolas de Montreux, *Honovrs Academie*, tr. R. Tofte (1610), part 2, sig. Ee2r: 'O you blinde and frantike Louers, who always make your Mistresses the motius of all your misfortunes.' Swetnam writes: 'women haue deuices and inuentions to allure men into their loue' (sig. F2r). This male attitude is also severely criticized in the pamphlets by a woman in answer to Swetnam, Rachel Speght's *A Mouzell for Melastomus* (1617); also those written allegedly by women, Ester Sowernam's *Ester hath hang'd Haman* (1617), sig. F2v-F3r; Constantia Munda's *The Worming of a mad Dogge* (1617), sig. D4v-F1r.
58. For instance, Swetnam attacks woman's tongue as follows: 'Is not strange of what kinde of mettall a womans tongue is made of? that neither correction can chastise, not faire meanes quiet: for there is a kinde of venome in it, that neither by faire meanes nor foule they are to be ruled' (sig. F4v). Swetnam also mentions 'womans revenge with tongue' (sig. G3r). The male fear of woman's tongue is satirized in Ben Jonson's *Epicoene, or The Silent Woman*.
59. Swetnam says that 'there is nothing more dangerous then a woman in her fury', and that all these are nothing so terrible as the fury of a woman' (sig. B1v).
60. Women's tears are often described in contemporary diatribes against women: 'wash away your black sin with the cristall teares of true sorrow and repentance' (Swetnam, Sig. E2r); 'the weapon of a virtuous woman was her teares, which euery good man pitied, and euery valiant man honoured' (*Hic Mulier* (1620), sig. B3r).

61. In the Consistory Court in 1605, she was charged with wearing manly apparel as well as practising bawdry, but she denied these charges. W. X. Fincham, 'Notes from the Ecclesiastical Court Records at Somerset House', *Transactions of the Royal Historical Society*, 4th series, IV(1921): 111–3. Moll's pseudo-autobiography *The Life and Death of Mrs Mary Frith, Commonly Called Mol Cutpurse* was written by an anonymous writer and published in 1662.
62. All citations from the play in this book are taken from *The Works of Beaumont and Fletcher*, ed. Arnold Glover and A. R. Waller (New York: Octagon Books, 1969), 10 vols, Vol. 8. As in the text the references are given by the numbers of act, scene and page, my citation of the play follows this style.

2   Female Selfhood and Ideologies of Marriage in Early Jacobean Drama: *The Duchess of Malfi* and *The Tragedy of Mariam*

1. Johanah Rickman argues in *Love, Lust and License* (2008) that the sexual abberation of noblewomen at the Court in the period derived from the opposition of two different gender ideals: one a primarily religious and conventional one, and the other more secular ideals, which encouraged the women to be responsive to courtly love. I would rather consider that their rebellion was chiefly caused by their sense of injustice done to their selfhood, as on the occasions of their enforced marriages, particularly in the case of the highly intelligent women described in this book.
2. See, for instance, Laura Gowing, *Domestic Dangers: Women, Words and Sex in Early Modern London* (Oxford: Clarendon Press, 1996); Eleanor Hubbard, *City Women: Money, Sex, and the Social Order in Early Modern London* (Oxford: Oxford University Press, 2012); Duncan Salkeld, *Shakespeare among the Courtesans: Prostitution, Literature, and Drama, 1500–1650* (Farnham: Ashgate, 2012).
3. For details of the relationship between Frances Villiers and Robert Howard, see Rickman, *Love, Lust, and License*, 174–200.
4. Many detailed examinations have been made of the illicit relationship between Mary Wroth and William Herbert, the third Earl of Pembroke. Particularly useful ones are Margaret Hannay, *Mary Sidney, Lady Wroth* (Farnham: Ashgate); Rickman, *Love, Lust and License*, 141–72.
5. For this, see Wynne-Davies, '"For *Worth*, Not Weakness, Makes in Use but One"', 164–84. See also Robyn Bolam, 'The Heart of the Labyrinth: Mary Wroth's *Pamphilia to Amphilanthus*', in *The Cambridge Companion to English Renaissance Literature and Culture*, ed. Michael Hattaway (Cambridge: Cambridge University Press, 2000), 257–66.
6. For Cary's life and the construction of the female sense of identity in *The Tragedy of Mariam*, see Barbara Kiefer Lewalski, *Writing Women in Jacobean England* (Cambridge, MA: Harvard University Press), 178–211; Heather Wolfe ed., *Elizabeth Cary, Lady Falkland: Life and Letters* (Tempe: Arizona Center for Medieval and Renaissance Studies, 2001), 1–64.
7. For a discussion of the authorship of *The History of the Life, Reign, and Death of Edward II*, see Lewalski, *Writing Women in Jacobean England*, 317–20.
8. The terms 'grotesque' and 'grotesqueness' are used here in the senses defined by the *OED* [s. vv. grotesque B. 2. a. and 3; grotesqueness]; that is, as referring

to things or events or artistic works characterized by distortion or unnatural combinations, or by incongruous absurdity. *The Oxford English Dictionary* Second Edition on CD-ROM (v. 4.0). Oxford University Press, 2009.
9. My understanding of Wroth's theatrical vision of female selfhood is indebted to Heather Weidemann's chapter, 'Theatricality and Female Identity in Mary Wroth's *Urania*', in *Reading Mary Wroth*, ed. Naomi Miller and Gary Waller (1991), Knoxville: University of Tennessee, 191–209.
10. Kabuki was originated by a female dancer called Okuni in early seventeenth century Kyoto. Her productions were prohibited by the government for the reason of licentiousness. Kabuki came to be played by young men, but this style was also forbidden for fear of provoking homosexual desire among men. Thus, mature men came to play the female roles, and since then Kabuki has kept its tradition of an all-male cast for over three hundred years. It has been extremely popular among female audiences since the eighteenth century.
11. Joannus Ludovicus Vives, *The Instructions of a Christian Woman*, tr. R. Herde (1530?), Book III, Chapter VII.
12. A series of ballads, though of a slightly later period, also satirize widows' readiness to remarry: 'A Proverb Old, Yet Ne'er Forgot'; ''Tis Good to Strike While Iron's Hot'; 'The Wiving Age'; and 'The Cunning Age', in *A Pepysian Garland*, ed. Hyder E. Rollins (Cambridge: Cambridge University Press, 1922), 229–43. The sentiments against widows' remarriage are also expressed in some tracts on women; see, for example, Alexander Niccholes, *A Discourse of Marriage and Wiving* (London, 1620) 27–30; Joseph Swetnam, *The Araignment of Lewd, Idle, Froward, and vnconstant women* (London, 1615).
13. For the contemporary situation of widows' marriage, see Lu Emily Pearson, 'Elizabethan Widows', *Stanford Studies in Language and Literature* (Stanford: Stanford University Press, 1941), 124–42; Carroll Camden, *The Elizabethan Woman* (1951) (New York: Mamaroneck, 1975), 78–105; Frank W. Wadsworth, 'Webster's *Duchess of Malfi* in the Light of Some Contemporary Ideas on Marriage and Remarriage', *Philological Quarterly* 35 (1956), 394–407; Lawrence Stone, *The Family, Sex and Marriage in England, 1500–1800* (London: Weidenfeld and Nicolson, 1977), 627–32.
14. Inga-Stina Ekeblad (Ewbank), in 'The "Impure Art" of John Webster', in *Twentieth Century Interpretations of 'The Duchess of Malfi'*, ed. Norman Rabkin (Englewood Cliffs, NJ: Prentice Hall, 1968), 49–65, argues the significance of the madmen's scene as a form of public censure, relating the scene to the folk tradition of the 'charivari', which was directed at unpopular or unequal matches.
15. John Chamberlain writes to Carleton in his letter of 22 November 1598: 'The seventh of this moneth the Quenes atturney married the Lady Hatton to the great admiration of all men that after so many large and likely offers she shold decline to a man of his qualitie, and the world will not beleeve that yt was without a miserie'. *The Letters of John Chamberlain*, Vol. I, 54.
16. On contemporary marriage practices, see Henry Swinburne, *A Treatise of Spousals or Matrimonial Contracts* (written around 1620, published in 1686); Stone, *The Family, Sex and Marriage*; Martin Ingram, *Church Courts, Sex and Marriage in England*; Ernest Schanzer, 'The Marriage-Contracts in *Measure for Measure*', *Shakespeare Survey* 13 (1960): 81–9. On clandestine marriage, see

Alison D. Wall, 'For Love, Money, or Politics? A Clandestine Marriage and the Elizabethan Court of Arches', *Historical Journal* 38 (1995): 511–33; R. B. Outhwaite, *Clandestine Marriage in England, 1500–1850* (London and Rio Grande: Hambledon Press, 1995).

17. See Violet Wilson, *Queen Elizabeth's Maids of Honour and Ladies of Privy Chambers* (London: John Lane, 1922).
18. According to an Act of 1536, it was treason for one of royal blood to marry without the consent of his sovereign.
19. For sexual scandals in the Courts of Elizabeth and James, see Rickman, *Love, Lust and License*, 27–110.
20. *The Palace of Pleasure*, quoted from John Webster, *The Duchess of Malfi. The Revels Plays*, ed. John Russell Brown (Manchester: Manchester University Press, 1964), 175–209.
21. Ferdinand's lycanthropia and the Cardinal's story of the ghost of the old woman are drawn from Goulart's account. See Simon Goulart, *Admirable and Memorable Histories: Containing the Wonders of Our Time*, tr. Edward Grimeston (London, 1607), 386–7.
22. For these rumours, see John Chamberlain's letters of 11 March and 29 April 1613, Vol. I, 437: 443.
23. Thomas Becon, a popular divine, exclaims: 'How light, vain, triffling unhonest, unhousewifelike young widows have been in all ages, and are also at this present day, experience doth sufficiently declare' (*Works* CCCCXXIX (the Catechism), 1564). Alexander Niccholes thought that, though a widow might have a fairer face than a man's, she had a heart more deformed than the devil's (Niccholes, *A Discourse of Marriage and Wiving*, 27–8). In *Overbury's Characters* 'an ordinarie Widdow' is described as the one whose 'chiefest pride is in the multitude of her Suitors; and by them shee gaines; for one serues to drawe on another, and with one at last shee shootes out another, as Boies do Pellets in Elderne Gunnes' (sig. M1R).
24. Vives would have a widow cease the 'trimming and arraying of her body' advising a widow to avoid the Courts and other resorts of men or any gatherings of people (*The Instructions of a Christian Woman* (1530?), Book III, Chapter IV, 133).
25. F. L. Lucas thinks that Antonio is such a weakling that it was an error for the Duchess to fall in love with him (22). An even more severe attack is mounted by Robert Ornstein, who regards Antonio as an ignoble coward (*The Moral Vision of Jacobean Tragedy* (Madison: University of Wisconsin Press, 1960), 142). The opposite assessment is expressed by Peter Murray, who admires him as 'the model courtier in his poetical ideals, in the honesty of his motives, in his candid and intelligent assessment of the life around him, and in his versatility as an excellent horseman and lancer on the one hand and a manager of affairs on the other' (*A Study of John Webster* (The Hague: Mouton, 1969), 147). Between these polarities stand views that regard him as mediocre. Gunnar Boklund, in *The Duchess of Malfi: Sources, Themes and Characters* (Cambridge, MA: Harvard University Press), 140, sees him as 'an indubitably virtuous man of average personal ability, who is overwhelmed by events with which he is not equipped to cope'. D. C. Gunby, in '*The Duchess of Malfi*: A Theological Approach', in *John Webster*. Mermaid Critical Commentaries, ed. Brian Morris (London: Ernest Benn, 1970), 200, similarly defines him as 'a character of thoroughgoing ordinariness'.

26. The suggestion of Antonio's versatile talents seems to come from Painter. While condemning his ambition, Painter describes Antonio as a versatile Renaissance man.
27. Goulart's account of Antonio's son is entirely different from Webster's treatment: 'As for his Sonne who was not with him, hee was forced to flie out of *Milan*, to change his name, and to retire himselfe farre off, where he died vnknowne' (367).
28. See, for example, Gunby, *The Duchess of Malfi*, 179–204.
29. For the contemporary state of these frustrated men of intellect, see Mark H. Curtis, 'The Alienated Intellectuals of Early Stuart England', *Past and Present* 23 (1962): 25–43.
30. In Bosola's case, unlike Flamineo's, his financial difficulties are not stressed in the play, except by use of general terms such as neglected scholars and soldiers.
31. See also Morris P. Tilley ed., *A Dictionary of the Proverbs in England in the Sixteenth and Seventeenth Centuries* (Ann Arbor: Michigan, 1950), V 81, 699.
32. In the candle-lit production of the play in the Sam Wanamaker's Playhouse in March 2014, however, the grotesque quality of the scene seems to have been modified through the effect of darkness. Most of the audience, like the Duchess, thought that the corpses were genuine.
33. For the interpretation of the madmen's scene, see Inga-Stina Ekeblad (Ewbank), *Shakespeare's Styles: Essays in Honour of Kenneth Muir*, ed. Philip Edwards, Inga-Stina Ewbank and G. K. Hunter (Cambridge: Cambridge University Press, 1980), 49–64.
34. For the translations of Kabuki plays, see *Traditional Japanese Theater: An Anthology of Plays (Translations from the Asian Classics)*, ed. Karen Brazell (New York: Columbia University Press, 1999). On the *Dojoji*, see also Mae Smethurst, 'The Japanese Presence in Ninagawa's *Medea*', in *Medea in Performance 1500–2000*, ed. Edith Hall *et al.* (Oxford: European Humanities Research Centre, 2000), 191–216, esp. 200–1, 208–9.
35. *The Lady Falkland: Her Life*, ed. R.(ichard) S.(impson) (London: Catholic Publishing and Bookselling Company, 1861), 8. For Cary's biography, see Georgiana Fullerton, *The Life of Elizabeth, Lady Falkland 1585–1639* (London: Burns and Oates, 1861); Wolfe, *Elizabeth Cary, Lady Falkland*; Elizabeth Cary, 'Introduction', in *The Tragedy of Mariam: The Fair Queen of Jewry* (1613), ed. Ramona Wray. Arden Early Modern Drama (London: Methuen, 2012), 3–8.
36. R. S., *The Lady Falkland*.
37. For instance, Travitsky, 184–96.
38. Sandra K. Fischer, in 'Elizabeth Cary and Tyranny, Domestic and Religious', in *Silent But for the Word: Tudor Women as Patrons, Translations, and Writers of Religious Works*, ed. Margaret Patterson Hannay (Ohio: The Kent University Press, 1985), 235–7, also takes this view.
39. Margaret W. Ferguson, in *Rewriting the Renaissance: The Discourse of Sexual Difference in Early Modern Europe*, ed. Margaret W. Ferguson, Maureen Quilligan and Nancy J. Vickers (Chicago: University of Chicago Press, 1986), 27, also takes this view.
40. Elizabeth Cary, *The Tragedy of Mariam 1613* (1914), ed. A. C. Dunstan, The Malone Society Reprints (Oxford: Oxford University Press, 1914, reprint, 1992). All citations from the play in this book are taken from this edition.

41. For instance, Jacques Lacan, *Feminine Sexuality: Jacques Lacan and the École Freudienne*, ed. Juliete Mitchell and Jacqueline Rose, tr. Jacqueline Rose (London: Macmillan, 1982); Michel Foucault, *The Order of Things*, tr. Alan Sheridan-Smith (New York: Pantheon, 1971).
42. For the parallel between Mariam and Salome, see also Ferguson, *Rewriting the Renaissance*, 32–5.
43. For the annulment suit of the marriage by Frances Howard see, David Lindley, *The Trial of Frances Howard: Fact and Fiction at the Court of King James* (New York: Routledge, 1993); Anne Somerset, *Unnatural Murder: Poison at the Court of James I* (London: Weidenfeld & Nicolson, 1997); Rickman, *Love, Lust and License*, 74–5, 84–5. On annulment of marriage in early modern England or judicial operation, see Ingram, *Church Courts, Sex and Marriage in England, 1570–1640*, 171–88; Lawrence Stone, *Road to Divorce: England, 1530–1987* (Oxford: Clarendon Press, 1990), 51–95.
44. This analogy, repeatedly asserted by authorities, is based on *Ephesians*, 5: 20–30.
45. The typical case is seen in William Shakespeare, *The Taming of the Shrew*, Act 2 Scene 2, 219.
46. Philip Massinger, *The Duke of Milan*, in *The Plays and Poems of Philip Massinger*, ed. Philip Edwards and Colin Gibson (Oxford: The Clarendon Press, 1976), 5 vols, Vol. I. The citation from the play in this book is taken from this edition.
47. For the relationship between the text of the play and Cary's biographies, see Wray's Introduction to Cray, *The Tragedy of Mariam*, 3–16.

3 Lady Mary Wroth and Ideologies of Marriage in Late Jacobean England

1. Ben Jonson's *Cythia's Revels* (Chapel Royal, 1600, 1601) also has this dramatic structure. For this Wroth may have been influenced by Jonson, with whom she had close contact. For Jonson's literary influence on Wroth, see Michael G. Brennan, 'Creating Female Authorship in Early Seventeenth Century: Jonson and Lady Mary Wroth', in *Women's Writing and the Circulation of Ideas: Manuscript Publication in England, 1550–1800*, ed. George L. Justice and Nathan Tinker (Cambridge: Cambridge University Press, 2002), 73–93. She played in Jonson's masque at the Court, *The Mask of Blackness* (1605), and his masterpiece *The Alchemist* (King's, 1610) was dedicated to her. On Jonson's relationship to Lady Mary, see also Introduction in *The Poems of Lady Mary Wroth*, ed. Josephine A. Roberts (Baton Rouge, LA: Louisiana State University Press, 1983), 15–22. According to the *Conversations* written by William Drummond, Jonson gave a part to Lady Mary in his pastoral, *The May Lord*, which was lost (*Works of Ben Jonson*, Vol. I. 143).
2. Mary Wroth, *Lady Mary Wroth's Loves Victory*, The Penshurst Manuscript, ed. Michael G. Brennan (London: The Roxburghe Club, 1988), Act 3, 192. All citations from the play in this book are taken from this edition.
3. For the argument of Louis Adrian Montrose, see Louis Adrian Montrose, '"Eliza, Queene of Shepheardes," and the Pastoral of Power', *English Literary Renaissance* 10 (1980): 153–82; 'Of Gentlemen and Shepherds: The Politics of Elizabethan Pastoral Form', *English Literary History* 50 (1983): 415–59.

4. For Wroth's employment of courtly games and a fortune-telling in the play, see Katherine R. Larson, *Early Modern Women in Conversation* (Basingstoke: Palgrave Macmillan, 2011), 89–109. For the songs of Mary Wroth, see Katherine R. Larson, 'Voicing Lyric: The Songs of Mary Wroth', in *Re-Reading Mary Wroth* (New York: Palgrave Macmillan, 2015), 119–36.
5. Montaigne in the *Essays*, in particular in 'Upon Some Verses of *Virgil*', especially 3: 77–95, argues that sexuality is part of human nature and criticizes men for imposing the norm of chastity upon women (see Chapter 1 in this book). As also mentioned in Chapter 1, it is remarkable how popular Florio's Montaigne was among educated women at the time. The three books of his translation of the *Essayes* are all dedicated to highly educated women, many of whom were closely related to the Sidney family. The lists of the books possessed by Lady Elizabeth Cary and by Lady Anne Clifford include the *Essayes*. Book I was dedicated to the Countess of Bedford, a distant relative of the Sidneys, who seems to have instigated Florio to translate the *Essays*. The Countess of Bedford's copy has been kept at the Bodleian Library in Oxford (William M. Hamlin, *Montaigne's English Journey: Reading the Essays in Shakespeare's Days* (Oxford: Oxford University Press, 2013, 13). Through the Sidney connection it is most likely that Wroth also read Florio's Montaigne. William Herbert, the third Earl of Pembroke, who was a long-standing lover of Wroth, was one of Florio's pupils and when Florio died in 1625, his French and Italian books were bequeathed to him (Hamlin, *Montaigne's English Journey*,13). For Wroth's response to a dialogue between William Herbert and Benjamin Rudyard about love and reason in *Poems*, see Mary Ellen Lamb, '"Can You Suspect a Change in Me?": Poems by Mary Wroth and William Herbert, Third Earl of Pembroke', in *Re-Reading Mary Wroth* (2015), 53–68.
6. For the life of Lady Mary Wroth, see Wroth, *The Poems of Lady Mary Wroth*, Introduction, 3–40; Wroth, *The First Part of the Countess*, xc–civ; Hannay, *Mary Sidney, Lady Wroth*.
7. For the important topic of death/miraculous recovery in *Love's Victory* in relation to Wroth's contemporary writers, see Marion Wynne-Davies, *Women Writers and Familial Discourses in the English Renaissance: Relative Values* (Basingstoke: Palgrave Macmillan, 2007), 90–8. For a comparative study of *Love's Victory* and *Romeo and Juliet*, see Akiko Kusunoki, 'Wroth's *Love's Victory* as a Response to Shakespeare's Representations of Gender Distinctions', in *Mary Wroth and Shakespeare*, ed. Paul Salzman and Marion Wynne-Davies (New York and London: Routledge, 2014), 73–83.
8. The first public performance of *Love's Victory* was given by Read Not Dead of the Shakespeare's Globe in the Baron's Hall in Penshurst Place in June 2014. The vitality and power of the female characters, played by actresses, were overwhelming in this production. The image of Musella (played by Bech Park) on the cover of this book is taken from this production. For the circumstance of the original performance of the play, see Beverly M. Van Note, 'Performing "fitter means": Marriage and Authorship of *Love's Victory*', *Re-Reading Mary Wroth* (2015), 69–81.
9. It may be said, however, that Wroth herself gave up her performance of theatricality when she published the first part of *Urania* in 1621.
10. For the concept of Wroth's theatrical self, I am indebted to Heather L. Weidemann, 'Theatricality and Female Identity,' in *Reading Mary Wroth* (1991), 191–209.

11. For the significance of Wroth's representation of Philargus's sadistic torture of Limena's body, see also Helen Hackett, 'The Torture of Limena: Sex and Violence in Lady Mary Wroth's *Urania*', in *Voicing Women: Gender and Sexuality in Early Modern Writing*, ed. Kate Chedgzoy, Melanie Harsen and Susanne Trill (Edinburgh: Edinburgh University Press, 1998), 93–110.
12. For discussions of Wroth's autobiographical narratives in her work, see Wynne-Davies, '"So Much Worth": Autobiographical Narratives in the Work of Lady Mary Wroth', in *Betraying Ourselves: Forms of Self-Representation in Early Modern English Texts*, ed. Henk Dragstra, Sheila Ottway and Helen Wilcox (New York: St. Martins, 2000), 76–93.
13. Leonard Tennenhouse discusses this issue in *Power on Display: Politics of Shakespeare's Genre* (New York and London: Methuen, 1986), 115: 'Mutilation assumes a more central place in Jacobean tragedy. It is almost as if all the prominent playwrights of the day suddenly felt obliged to torture, smother, strangle, stab, or poison an aristocratic woman when assembling the materials for a tragedy.'
14. In the Royal Shakespeare Company's production of the play in 1987, directed by Deborah Warner, the grotesque elements in this scene were particularly emphasised.
15. For this issue, see also Maureen Quilligan, 'The Constant Subject: Instability and Authority in Wroth's *Urania* Poems', in *Soliciting Interpretation: Literary Theory and Seventeenth-Century English Poetry*, ed. Elizabeth D. Harvey and Katherine Eisaman Maus (Chicago, IL: University of Chicago Press), 307–35.
16. For Wroth's representations of selfhood in her poems, see Ilone Bell, 'Joy's Sports: The Unexpurgated Text of Wroth's Pamphilia to Amphilanthus', *Modern Philology* 111 (2013): 231–52; 'Sugared Sonnets Among Their Private Friends: Mary Wroth and William Shakespeare', in *Mary Wroth and Shakespeare*, 9–24.
17. Gary Waller, 'Struggling into Discourse: The Emergence of Renaissance Women's Writing', in *Silent but for the World*, ed. Margaret Hannay (Kent, OH: Kent State University Press, 1985), 238–56, for instance, took this position, one that has been challenged by scholars such as Barbara Kiefer Lewalski, *Writing Women in Jacobean England* (Cambridge, MA: Harvard University Press, 1993), 243–307; Naomi J. Miller, 'Engendering Discourse: Women's Voices in Wroth's *Urania* and Shakespeare's Plays', in *Reading Mary Wroth* (Knoxville: The University of Tennessee Press, 1991), 154–72.
18. For emergence of companionship marriage, Martin Ingram, *Church Courts, Sex and Marriage*, 125–67; Lawrence Stone, *The Family, Sex, and Marriage in England*, 361–74.
19. On Wroth's representation of women's sorrow, see also Akiko Kusunoki, '"To Sorrow I'll Wed": Resolution of Women's Sadness in Mary Wroth's *Urania* and Shakespeare's *Twelfth Night*', *Sidney Journal* 31 (2013): 117–30.
20. In her childhood Wroth visited her father in Flushing, together with her family, and stayed there for some months (Hannay, *Mary Sidney, Lady Wroth*, 63–5). She may have encountered there attractive black people, who were probably brought from the Dutch colonies. If so, Wroth's experience of international encounters might have affected her attitude to black people. For a different view of Rodomandro, see Sheila T. Cavanagh, '"The Great Cham": East Meets West in Lady Mary Wroth's *Urania*', in *Mary Wroth, Ashgate*

Critical Essays on Women Writers in England, 1550–1700, ed. Clare R. Kinney (Farnham: Ashgate, 2009), 7 vols, Vol. 4, 136–51.
21. Concerning the increasing hostility to begetting and giving birth to bastards in late Tudor and early Stuart England, see also Eleanor Fox and Martin Ingram, 'Bridewell, Bawdy Courts and Bastardy in Early Seventeenth-Century London', in *Cohabitation and Non-Marital Births in England and Wales, 1600–2012*, ed. Rebecca Probert (Basingstoke: Palgrave Macmillan, 2014), 10–32. For a more positive view of the roles that the illegitimate offspring of the elite might play in some parts of England, see Katharine Carlton and Tim Thornton, 'Illegitimacy and Authority in the North of England, c.1450–1640', *Northern History* 48 (2011), 23–40.
22. Some people, though, think that this Box was a lady's seventeenth-century English sewing-box.
23. However, in a sense, the published version of *Urania* I did not actually embody Pamphilia's Cabinet, to which her romance is often compared. Ilona Bell demonstrated that the published version of the sonnet sequence of *Pamphilia and Amphilanthus*, which was attached to *Urania* I, was the 'expurgated version' and the manuscript version in the Folger Library is the 'unexpurgated text.' On this issue, see Bell, 'Joy's Sports', 231–52.
24. For the letters written by Lord Denny to Wroth and her reply, see Hannay, *Mary Sidney, Lady Wroth*, 235–42; Josephine A. Roberts, 'An Unpublished Literary Quarrel Concerning the Suppression of Mary Wroth's *Urania* (1621)', *Notes and Queries* 222 (1977): 532–5; Wroth, *The Poems of Lady Mary Wroth*, Introduction, 31–5; Paul Salzman, 'Contemporary References in Mary Wroth's *Urania*', *Renaissance English Studies* 29 (1978): 178–81.
25. In relation to this issue, there is an interesting double portrait hanging on the wall in the State Dining Room of Penshurst Place (Figure 3.3). The sitters were most probably Lady Mary Wroth and her mother, the Countess of Leicester. The landscape seen through the window shows some women. They came to the field apparently on an outing as some horses can be observed, though Margaret Hannay regards them as 'Haymakers' (Hannay, *Mary Sidney, Lady Wroth*, Jacket illustration). It has been said that this part of the portrait used to be sheer black but when the painting was cleaned for the sake of conservation, female figures, horses and the landscape became visible. With regard to the absence of the father in this portrait, see Marion Wynne-Davies, 'Absent Fathers: Mary Wroth's *Love's Victory* and William Shakespeare's *King Lear*', in *Shakespeare and Mary Wroth*, ed. Marion Wynne-Davies and Paul Saltzman (New York and London: Routledge, 2015), 61–72.

4 Representing Elizabeth I in Jacobean England

1. For the Elizabethan revival, see Frances A. Yates, *The Rosicrucian Enlightenment* (London, New York: Routledge and Kegan Paul, 1972); Graham Parry, *The Golden Age Restor'd: The Culture of the Stuart Court, 1603–42* (1981) (Manchester: Manchester University Press, 1985); Perry, *The Making of Jacobean Culture*; John Watkins, *Representing Elizabeth in Stuart England: Literature, History, Sovereignty* (Cambridge: Cambridge University Press, 2002); Elizabeth H. Hageman and Katherine Cornway ed., *Resurrecting Elizabeth*

184 Notes

   I in Seventeenth-Century England (Madison and Teaneck: Fairleigh Dickinson University Press, 2007).
2. See, for instance, Aemilia Lanyer, *The Poems of Aemilia Lanyer: Salve Deus Rex Judæorum*, ed. Susanne Woods (New York, Oxford: Oxford University Press, 1993); Rachel Speght, *The Polemics and Poems of Rachel Speght*, ed. Barbara Kiefer Lewalski (New York, Oxford: Oxford University Press, 1996).
3. For these works, see *Resurrecting Elizabeth I in Seventeenth-Century England*, ed. Elizabeth H. Hageman and Katherine Conway (Madison and Teaneck: Fairleigh Dickinson University Press); Watkins, *Representing Elizabeth in Stuart England*, 14–86.
4. This description no longer exists in the room.
5. For the biography of Queen Elizabeth of Bohemia, see Carola Oman, *The Winter Queen: Elizabeth of Bohemia* (London: Phoenix Press, 1938); M. Everett Green, *Elizabeth, Electress Palatine and Queen of Bohemia* (London: Methuen, 1909); Kiefer Lewalski, *Writing Women in Jacobean England*, 45–66.
6. For King James's policy on the conflicts in Bohemia, see, for instance, Jonathan Goldberg, *James 1 and the Politics of Literature: The Politics of Literature: Jonson, Shakespeare, Donne, and Their Contemporaries* (Baltimore and London: The Johns Hopkins University Press, 1983); Croft, *King James*, 100–16.
7. For this contrast, see, for example, C. V. Wedgewood, *The Thirty Years War* (1938) (New York: New York Review Books, 2005), 97–145.
8. As previously mentioned, with regard to the historical accuracy of this speech, see Susan Frye, *Elizabeth I: The Competition for Representation* (New York and Oxford: Oxford University Press, 1993), 3–6.
9. See for instance, J. E. Neale, *Queen Elizabeth I* (1934) (London: Penguin, 1990); Frye, *Elizabeth I*.
10. For a more positive view of the reign of King James, see, for instance, Croft, *King James*.
11. See also Ian Donaldson, *Ben Jonson, a Life* (Oxford: Oxford University Press, 2011), 369–70, 503 note 57.
12. For the examination of the significance of Barclay's rewriting of historical events during the reign of Elizabeth I through Catholic viewpoints, see Paul Salzman, *Literary Culture in Jacobean England: Reading 1621* (Basingstoke: Palgrave Macmillan, 2002), 75–80; Amelia A. Zurcher, *Seventeenth-Century English Romance: Allegory, Ethics, and Politics* (New York: Palgrave Macmillan, 2007), 81–8.

5 Women and Publishing Their Works in the Late Jacobean Years

1. The Stigma of print is an informal social convention that restricted the literary works of aristocrats in the Elizabethan and Jacobean age to private and courtly audiences, in opposition to commercial endeavours, at the risk of social disgrace if violated.
2. For letter-writers in Tudor England, see, for instance, James Daybell, *Women Letter-Writers in Tudor England* (Oxford: Oxford University Press, 2006); Allen, *The Cooke Sisters*. For letter-writing and diaries in Jacobean England,

see Lewalski, *Writing Women in Jacobean England*, 1–11, 67–92, 309–15; Jane Cornwallis Bacon, *The Private Correspondence of Jane Lady Cornwallis Bacon, 1613–1644*, ed. Joanna Moody (Cranberry, NJ: Associated University Press, 2003), 15–47. As has been pointed out earlier, Gemma Allen, in *The Cook Sisters* (2013, 20–1), made the important point that although some sixteenth-century humanists admired learning in elite women, they tried at the same time to limit its scope, disapproving of women reading certain subjects and leading the creative energies of learned women into translation, in particular that of works on religion and classics. Letter-writing must also have provided learned women with some outlet for their creative energy.

3. For the discussion of these writers, see Wynne-Davies, *Women Writers in the English Renaissance*, 90–6.
4. For this change in the role of pastoral romance in the Jacobean period, see Paul Salzman, *English Prose Fiction 1558–1700: A Critical History* (Oxford: Clarendon Press, 1986); Wynne-Davies, *Women Writers in the English Renaissance*, 90–103; Helen Hacket, *Women and Romance Fiction in the English Renaissance* (Cambridge: Cambridge University Press, 2000); Nandini Das, *Renaissance Romance: The Transformation of English Prose Fiction, 1570–1620* (Farnham: Ashgate, 2011), 163–93; Zurcher, *Seventeenth-Century English Romance*.
5. Even Dudley Carlton, who was a good friend of the Sidney family, criticized her daring act in his letter.
6. Elizabeth Cary, Viscountess Falkland. Stephanie Hodgson-Wright, 'Cary, Elizabeth, Viscountess Falkland (1585–1639)', *DNB*, online edn., May 2014 [http://0-www.oxforddnb.com.catalogue.ulrls.lon.ac.uk/view/article/4835, accessed 22 Feb 2015].
7. Ben Jonson, *The Vnder-Wood*, xxviii, 1. 4, in *The Works of Ben Jonson*, Vol. 8, 182. As has been mentioned, Wroth performed in Jonson's courtly masque, *Masque of Blackness* (1605). It has been said that she was also cast in Jonson's lost masque, *The May Lord*. Jonson dedicated his masterpiece *The Alchemist* (King's, 1610) to Mary Wroth. She was the only woman that Jonson ever dedicated his work to. Regarding the intellectual relationship between Jonson and Wroth, see Michael G. Brennan, 'Creating Female Authorship in Early Seventeenth Century: Jonson and Mary Wroth', in *Women's Writing and the Circulation of Ideas: Manuscript Publication in England, 1550–1800*, ed. George L. Justice and Nathan Tinker (Cambridge: Cambridge University Press, 2002), 73–93.
8. As to the similarities between Wroth's romance and the writings by her father Robert Sidney, see Julie Crawford, *Mediatrix: Women, Politics, and Literary Production in Early Modern England* (Oxford: Oxford University Press, 2014), 206–16.
9. For the fall of the Earl and Countess of Somerset, see, for instance, White, *Cast of Ravens*; William McElwee, *The Murder of Sir Thomas Overbury*; David Lindley, *The Trial of Francis Howard*; Ann Somerset, *Unnatural Murder*.
10. She was said to have had a great ascendancy over her husband and to have used his office to enrich herself. Bacon, speaking against the Earl in the Star Chamber, compared the Countess to an exchange woman; while she kept her shop, her creature, Sir John Bingley, remembrancer of the Exchequer, cried 'What d'ye lack?' See *Calendar of State Papers, Domestic Series, of the Reign of James I (1619–23)*, ed. Mary Anne Everett Green (Longman:

London, 1858), 93–4; Pauline Croft, 'Howard, Thomas, First Earl of Suffolk (1561–1626)'. *DNB*, online edn. [http://0-www.oxforddnb.com.catalogue.ulrls.lon.ac.uk/view/article/13942, accessed 22 Feb 2015].

11. Lady Lake was originally a citizen woman, daughter and co-heiress of Sir William Ryder, alderman of London. *DNB*, online edn. Roger Lockyer, 'Lake, Sir Thomas (bap. 1561, d. 1630)' [http://0-www.oxforddnb.com.catalogue.ulrls.lon.ac.uk/view/article/15903, accessed 22 Feb 2015].
12. Anthony Weldon, *The Court and Character of King James* (London: 1650), 56.
13. One of the few exceptions is the downfall of the Duke of Gloucester ascribed to the Duchess of Gloucester's practice of witchcraft in Holinshed and in Shakespeare's *Henry VI*, Part II.
14. For instance, 'The Unnatural Wife', 'A Warning for All Desperate Women', 'A Warning to Wives' in *A Pepysian Garland* (Cambridge: Cambridge University Press, 1922), 283–304. See also Sandra Clark, 'Shrews, Marriage and Murder', in *Gender and Power in Shrew-Taming Narratives, 1500–1700*, ed. David Wootton and Graham Holderness (Basingstoke: Palgrave Macmillan, 2010), 29–47.
15. See Laura Norsworthy, *The Lady of Bleeding Heart: Lady Elizabeth Hatton 1579–1646* (London: John Murray, 1935), 30–72.
16. Such reactions are reflected in Chamberlain's letters: 'she has caried herselfe very straungely, and indeed neither like a wife nor a wise woman', 9 August 1617 (Vol. II 92); 'men speak diversly of her maner of proceding, and thincke her rather bent to pull down her husband then to use her power or favor either for her owne goode or her frends', 29 November 1617 (119).
17. Lucas, *The Complete Works of John Webster*, ed. F. L. Lucas, 4 vols. (New York: Gordian Press, 1966), Vol. IV, 139.
18. For Queen Anne's independent-minded actions, see Lewalski, *Writing Women in Jacobean England*, 15–43; Barroll, *Anna of Denmark Queen of England*, 74–161.
19. Quoted in Lucas ed., *The Complete Works of John Webster*, Vol. II, 325.
20. 'An Elegy wherein is contenied good & honest counsell for Ladies & gentlewomen to dep't ye citty according to his Matie's p'clamation', in *The Dr Farmer Chetham MS.*, ed. Alexander B. Grosart (Manchester: Chetham Society, 1873), part II, 153. The King's proclamation on women is also referred to by William Lorte, *'In Praise of the Worke'* prefixed to Alexander Niccholes, *A Discourse of Marriage and Wiving* (London, 1620), sig. B4r.
21. Lucas, *The Complete Works of John* Webster, Vol. II, 216. He thinks that *Anything for a Quiet Life* was also intended to support the King's order.
22. Although generally taken as such, there is no concrete evidence that this pamphlet was written in answer to Swetnam. Tuvil says in his introduction that he is publishing his work, which he wrote earlier, only because there is danger that 'some imperfect copies' may be published. See Louis B. Wright, *Middle-Class Culture in Elizabethan England* (1958) (Ithaca: Cornell University Press, 1964), 488.
23. Alexander B. Grosart's attribution to Thomas Heywood or Thomas Dekker, *'Swetnam the Woman-Hater': Manchester Occasional Issues* XIV (Manchester, 1880), xxiv, has been generally accepted.
24. For Joseph Swetnam and the Jacobean revival of the *querelle des dames*, see also Anna Bayman, 'Female Voices in Early Seventeenth-Century Pamphlet

Literature', in *Women and Writing, c.1340–c.1650: Domestication of Print Culture*, ed. Anne Lawrence-Mathers and Phillipa Hardman (Woodbridge: York Medieval Press, 2010), 196–210; Anna Bayman and George Southcombe, 'Shrews in Pamphlets and Plays', in *Gender and Power in Shrew-Taming Narrative, 1500–1700*, ed. David Wooton and Graham Golderness (Basingstoke: Palgrave Macmillan, 2011), 11–28; Linda Woodbridge, *Women and the English Renaissance* (Urbana and Chicago: University of Illinois Press), 81–104, 300–21; Lewalski, *Writing Women in Jacobean England*, 153–75; Megan Matchinske, 'Legislating "Middle Class" Morality in the Marriage Market: Ester Sowernam's *Ester hath hang'd Haman*', *English Literary Renaissance* 24 (1994): 154–83.

25. Eva Griffith argues that this woodcut represents the arraignment scene performed at the Red Bull, with Queen Aurelia as the judge who recalled Queen Elizabeth I (*A Jacobean Company and its Playhouse: The Queen's Servants at the Red Bull Theatre* (c.1605–1619) (New York: Cambridge University Press, 2013), 135–45.

26. Barbara Matulka, in *The Novels of Juan De Flores and Their European Diffusion: A Study in Comparative Literature* (New York: Publications of the Institute of French Studies, 1931), 220, thinks that the play 'serves as a strong feminist document, while at the same time it attacks one of the most notorious woman-haters of the period in England'. However, I agree with Coryl Crandall's view (*Swetnam the Woman-Hater: The Controversy and the Play*, a critical edition with introduction and notes by Coryl Crandall (Lafyett: Purdue University Studies, 1969), 12) that she overestimates the play's feminist inclination.

27. Thomas Adams, 'Mystical Bedlam; or, The World of Madmen', with a memoir by Joseph Angus, in *The Works of Thomas Adams* (Edinburgh: James Nichol, 1861–62), 3 vols, Vol. 1, 278.

28. Thomas Becon, *The Golden Boke of Holy Matrimony* (London, 1560), quoted in William and Malleville Haller, 'The Puritan Art of Love', *Huntington Library Quarterly*, 5 (1942): 244–5. For the Puritan doctrines of marriage; see also Kathleen M. Davies, 'The Sacred Condition of Equality: How Original Were Puritan Doctrine of Marriage?', *Social History* 5 (1977): 563–80; Margo Todd, *Christian Humanism and the Puritan Social Order* (Cambridge: Cambridge University Press, 1987); Anthony Fletcher, 'The Protestant Idea of Marriage in Early Modern England', in *Religion, Culture and Society in Early Modern England: Essays in Honour of Patrick Colins*, ed. Anthony Fletcher and Peter Roberts (Cambridge: Cambridge University Press, 1994), 161–81; Alison D. Wall, *Power and Protest in England, 1525–1640* (London: Arnold, 2000), 81–96.

29. See also Femke Molekamp, *Women and the Bible in Early Modern England: Religious Reading and Writing* (Oxford: Oxford University Press, 2013), particularly 51–150; Patricia Crawford, *Women and Religion in England, 1500–1720* (London and New York: Routledge, 1993), 122, 135, 145–6.

30. See also Christopher Hill, *Society and Puritanism in Pre-Revolutionary England* (Harmondsworth: Penguin, 1986), 65–7; Patrick Collinson, *The Elizabethan Puritan Movement* (London: Methuen, 1967), 85.

31. For these later plays, see Akiko Kusunoki, '"Their Testament at Their Apron-Springs": The Representation of Puritan Women in Early Seventeenth-Century England', in *Gloriana's Face: Women, Public and Private, in the English*

Renaissance, ed. S. P. Cerasano and Marion Wynne-Davies (New York and London: Harvester, 1992), 185–204.
32. *Female Replies to Swetnam the Woman-Hater*, with a new Introduction by Charles Butler (London: Thomas Press, 1995), 76.
33. Rachel Speght, *The Polemics and Poems of Rachel Speght*, ed. Barbara Kiefer Lewalski (New York and Oxford: Oxford University Press, 1996). The citations from *Moralities* in this book are taken from this edition.
34. For these women's activities of later years, see Christine Berg and Philippa Berry, '"Spiritual Whoredom"': An Essay on Female Prophets in the Seventeenth Century', in *1642: Literature and Power in the Seventeenth Century*, ed. Francis Barker et al. (Colchester: University of Essex, 1981), 37–54; Patricia Higgins, 'The Reactions of Women, with Special Reference to Women Petitioners', in *Politics, Religion and the English Civil War*, ed. Brian Manning (London: Edward Arnold, 1973), 177–222; Phyllis Mack, 'The Prophet and Her Audience: Gender and Knowledge in the World Turned Upside Down', in *Reviving the English Revolution: Reflections and Elaborations on the Work of Christopher Hill*, ed. Geoff Eley and William Hunt (London and New York: Verso, 1988), 139–52; Christopher Hill, *The World Upside Down: Radical Ideas during the English Revolution* (Harmondsworth: Penguin, 1978), especially 306–23; Hilary Hinds, *God's Englishwomen: Seventeenth-Century Radical Secretarian Writing and Feminist Criticism* (Manchester: Manchester University Press, 1996).

Conclusion

1. Wroth's autograph manuscript containing 'Pamphilia to Amphilanthus' and other poems are in the archive of the Folger Shakespeare Library (MS Va. 104). Regarding the comparison of the Folger manuscript with the published version of the sonnet sequence, see Bell, 'Joy's Sports', 231–52; 'The Autograph Manuscript of Mary Wroth's *Pamphilia to Amphilanthus*', in *Re-Reading Mary Wroth* (2015), 171–81.
2. For instance, Ilona Bell, *Elizabethan Women and the Poetry of Courtship* (Cambridge: Cambridge University Press, 1998); 'Joy's Sports', 231–52; 'Sugared Sonnets Among Their Private Friends', in *Mary Wroth and Shakespeare*, 9–24; The Autograph Manuscript of Mary Wroth's *Pamphilia to Amphilanthus*, 171–81; Clare R. Kinney, 'Escaping the Void: Isolation, Mutuality and Community in the Sonnets of Wroth and Shakespeare', in *Mary Wroth and Shakespeare*, 25–36; 'Turn and Counterturn: Reappraising Mary Wroth's Poetic Labyrinths', in *Re-Reading Mary Wroth*, 85–102. See also Clare R. Kinney ed., *Mary Wroth. Ashgate Critical Essays on Women Writers in England, 1550–1700* (Farnham: Ashgate, 2009), 7 vols, Vol. 4.
3. In her diary in August 1617, Lady Anne wrote: 'There was *Lady Worth* who told me a great news from beyond sea'. (Anne Clifford, *The Diary of the Lady Anne Clifford*, ed. V. Sackville-West (London: William Heinemann, 1923), 77.
4. Lady Gracia's farewell poem reads: A flower can be a flower as knowing the time to die,/So should be a human. (Translation is mine.) For her life, see Haruko Nawata Ward, *Women Religious Leaders in Japan's Christian Century, 1549–1650* (Farnham: Ashgate, 2009), 199–220.

Bibliography

Primary sources

Manuscript sources
Wroth, Mary. De L'Isle Manuscript. *Love's Victory*. The Penshurst Manuscript.
Wroth, Mary. *Urania* 2. MS Case MS f.Y 1565 W95. The Newberry Library.

Books and articles
Adams, Thomas. 1861–62. *The Works of Thomas Adams*. Ed. Joseph Angus. 3 vols. Edinburgh: James Nichol.
Anger, Jane. 1589. *Jane Anger her Protection of Women*. London.
(anonymous), *The Narrative History of King James for the First Fourteen Years* (London: 1651).
'Aulicus Coquinariae'. 1811. *Secret History of the Court of James the First*. Ed. Sir Walter Scott. 2 vols. Edinburgh: J. Ballantyne. Vol. II.
Bacon, Jane Cornwallis. 2003. *The Private Correspondence of Jane Lady Cornwallis Bacon, 1613–1644*. Ed. Joanna Moody. Cranbury, NJ: Associated University Press.
Barclay, John. 1636. *Barclay His Argenis* (1621). Tr. Kingesmill Long. 2nd edition. London.
Beard, Thomas. 1597. *The Theatre of Gods Iudgements*. London.
Beaumont, Francis and John Fletcher. 1969. *The Works of Francis Beaumont and John Fletcher* (1910). Ed. Arnold Clover and A.R. Waller. 10 vols. New York: Octagon Books.
Becon, Thomas. 1564. *The Workes of Thomas Becon*. 3 vols. London.
Becon, Thomas. 1942. *The Golden Boke of Holy Matrimony*. London, 1560. Qut. William and Malleville Haller, 'The Puritan Art of Love', *Huntington Library Quarterly*, 5 (1942). 244–5.
Blount, Henry. 1638. *A Voyage into the Levant*. 2nd edition. London.
Bullough, Geoffrey ed. 1957–75. *Narrative and Dramatic Sources of Shakespeare*. London: Routledge & Kegan Paul; New York: Columbia University Press. 8 vols.
Calendar of State Papers, Domestic Series, of the Reign of James I (1619–23). 1858. Ed. Mary Anne Everett Green. Longman: London.
Cary, Elizabeth. 1680. *The History of the Life, Reign, and Death of Edward II* (c. 1627, published in 1680). London: J. C. for Charles Harper.
Cary, Elizabeth. 1861. *The Lady Falkland, her Life*. Ed. R.S. [Richard Simpson]. London: Catholic Publishing & Bookselling Co.
Cary, Elizabeth. 1992. *The Tragedy of Mariam 1613* (1914). Ed. A.C. Dunstan. The Malone Society Reprints. Oxford: Oxford University Press.
Cary, Elizabeth. 2001. *Elizabeth Cary, Lady Falkland, Life and Letters*. Ed. Heather Wolfe. Texts from Manuscript No.4. Cambridge: Renaissance Texts from Manuscript.

Cary, Elizabeth. 2012. *The Tragedy of Mariam: The Fair Queen of Jewry* (1613). Ed. Ramona Wray. Arden Early Modern Drama. London: Methuen.

Cerasano, S.P. and Marion Wynne-Davies, ed. 1996. *Renaissance Drama by Women: Texts and Documents*. London and New York: Routledge.

Certain Sermons, Appointed by the Queen's Majesty to Be . . . Read by All Parsons, Vicars, and Curates . . . in Their Church of England. 1850. Ed. John W. Parker. Cambridge: Cambridge University Press.

Chamberlain, John. 1939. *The Letters of John Chamberlain*. Ed. N.E. McClure, 2 vols. Philadelphia: The American Historical Society.

Chapman, George. 1975. *The Widow's Tears* (1613). The Revels Plays. Ed. Akihiro Yamada. Manchester: Methuen.

Chapman, George. 1987. *Bussy D'Ambois*. In *The Plays of George Chapman, the Tragedies: A Critical Edition*. Ed. John H. Smith. Cambridge: D. S. Brewer. 7–264.

Chaucer, Geoffrey. 1994. *Legend of Good Women*. Ed. Sheila Delany. Berkeley and London: University of California Press.

Clifford, Anne. 1922. *Lady Anne Clifford, Countess of Dorset, Pembroke & Montgomery, 1590–1670: Her Life, Letters, and Work*. Ed. George C. Williamson. Kendal: Tites Wilson and Son.

Clifford, Anne. 1923. *The Diary of the Lady Anne Clifford*. Ed. and with an Introductory and Note, V. Sackville-West. London: William Heinemann.

Clifford, Anne. 1990. *The Diaries of Lady Anne Clifford*. Ed. D.J.H. Clifford. Stroud: Sutton, 1990.

Clifford, Anne. 1995. *The Diary of Anne Clifford, 1616–1619: A Critical Edition*. Ed. Katherine O. Acheson. New York: Garland.

Coryat, Thomas. 1950. *Coryat's Crudities* (1611). Glasgow: James MacLehose and Sons.

Daniel, Samuel. 1601. *The Works of Samuel Daniel newly argumented*. London: Simon Waterson.

Dekker, Thomas. 1603. *The Bachelor's Banquet*. London.

Dod, John and Robert Cleaver. 1612. *A Godlie Forme of Householde Government*. London.

Donne, John. 1955. *The Sermons of John Donne*. Ed. George R. Potter and Evelyn M. Simpson. 10 vols. Berkeley and Los Angeles: University of California Press. Vol. II.

Duffin, Ross W. 2004. *Shakespeare's Songbook*. New York and London: W. W. Norton & Company.

Eliot, T.S. 1934. *Selected Essays on Elizabethan Dramatists*. London: Faber & Faber.

Elizabeth I: Collected Works. 2000. Ed. Leah S. Marcus, Janet Mueller and Mary Beth Rose. Chicago and London: The University of Chicago Press.

Female Replies to Swetnam the Woman-Hater. 1995. With a new Introduction by Charles Butler. Bristol: Thoemmes Press.

Ford, John. 1606. *Fames Memoriall, or the Earl of Devonshire Deceased*. London.

Ford, John. 1965. *The Works of John Ford*. Ed. Alexander Dycle. 3 vols. New York: Russel & Russel.

Foucault, Michel. 1971. *The Order of Things*. Tr. Alan Smith. New York: Pantheon.

Gosynhyll, Edward (?). 1541. *Here begynneth a lytle boke named the Schole house of women*. London.

Gouge, William. 1621. *A Short Catechisme*. London.

Gouge, William. 1622. *Of domesticall duties eight treatises*. London.

Goulart, Simon. 1607. *Admirable and Memorable Histories, containing the wonders of our time*. Tr. Edward Grimeston. London.
Greene, Robert. 1579. *The Forest of Fancy*. London.
Greene, Robert. 1584. *The Carde of Fancie*. London.
Grosart, Alexander B. ed. 1873. *The Dr Farmer Chetham MS*. Manchester: Chetham Society.
Haec-Vir: Or The Womanish-Man. 1620. London.
Heale, William. 1609. *An Apologie for Women*. Oxford.
Herbert, Mary Sidney, Countess of Pembroke. *The Collected Works of Mary Sidney Herbert*. Ed. Margaret P. Hannay, Noel J. Kinnamon and Michael G. Brennan. 2 vols. Oxford: Clarendon Press.
Herbert, William and Benjamin Rudyard. 1660. *Poems Written by the Right Honourable William Earl of Pembroke*. Ed. John Donne the Younger. London.
Heywood, Thomas. 1607. *A Woman Killed with Kindness*. London.
Hic Mulier: Or, the Man-Woman. 1620. London.
Hic Mulier: Or, the Man Woman and Haec-Vir: Or the Womanish Man (1620). 1973. The Rota at the University of Exeter: The Scholar Press.
Hieron, Samuel. 1620. *The Sermons of Master Samuel Hieron*. London.
Hoby, Lady Margaret. 2001. *The Private Life of an Elizabethan Lady: The Diary of Margaret Hoby, 1599–1605* (1998 rpr.). Ed. Joanna Moody. Stroud: Sutton.
Jonson, Ben. 1923. *Ben Jonson's Conversation with William Drummond of Hawthornden*. Ed. with introduction and notes by R.F. Patterson. London: Blackie & Son, 20–1.
Jonson, Ben. 1925–52. *The Works of Ben Jonson*. Ed. C.H. Herford, P. Simpson and E.M. Simpson. 11 vols. Oxford: Clarendon Press.
Knox, John. 1558. *The First Blast of the Trumpet against the Monstrous Regiment of Women*. Geneva: J. Crespin.
Lacan, Jacques. 1982. *Feminine Sexuality: Jacques Lacan an the École Freudienne*. Ed. Juliet Mitchell and Jacquline Rose. Tr. Jacquline Rose. London: Macmillan.
Lanyer, Emilia. 1991. *The Poems of Aemilia Lanyer: Salve Deus Rex Judæorum*. Ed. Susanne Woods. New York, Oxford: Oxford University Press.
Lodge, Thomas tr. 1620. *Famovs and Memorable Works of Josephus* (1602). London.
Man, Judith tr. 1640. *An Epitome of the History of Fair Argenis and Polyarchus*. London.
Man, Judith tr. 2003. *An Epitome of the History of Fair Argenis and Polyarchus* (1640). The Early Modern Englishwoman: A Facsimile Library of Essential Works Series I. Printed Writings, 1500–1640: Part 3. Vol. 2. Selected and Introduced by Amelia A. Zurcher. Aldershot: Ashgate.
Markham, Garvis. 1609. *The Famovs Whore, or Noble Curtizan* (1609). London.
Marston, John. 1934–39. *The Plays of John Marston*. Ed. H. Harvey Wood. 3 vols. Edinburgh and London: Oliver and Boyd.
Marston, John. 1961. *The Poems of John Marston*. Ed. Arnold Davenport. Liverpool: Liverpool University Press.
Massinger, Philip. 1976. *The Duke of Milan* in *The Plays and Poems of Philip Massinger*. Ed. Philip Edwards and Colin Gibson. 5 vols. Oxford: The Clarendon Press.
Middleton, Thomas. 2007. *Thomas Middleton: The Collected Works*. Ed. Gary Taylor and John Lavagnino. Oxford: Clarendon Press.
Middleton, Thomas and Thomas Dekker. 1987. *The Roaring Girl*. Ed. Paul A. Mulholland. Manchester: Manchester University Press.

Montaigne, Michael. 1910. *The Essays of Michael Lord of Montaigne*. Tr. John Florio. Everyman edition: 3 vols. London: Dent.

Montreux, Nicolas de. 1610. *Honovrs Academie*. Tr. R. Tofte (1610). London.

Moryson, Fynes. 1903. *Shakespeare's Europe: Unpublished Chapters of Fynes Moryson's Itinerary*. With an introduction and an account of Fynes Moryson's career by Charles Hughes (1903). London: Sheratt & Hughes.

Munda, Constantia. 1617. *The Worming of a mad Dogge: Or. A SOPPE FOR CERBERVS The Iaylor of Hell*.

Murasaki Shikibu. 1980. *The Tale of Genji*. Tr. Edward G. Seidensticker. 2 vols (1976). Vermont and Tokyo: Charles E. Tuttle.

Niccholes, Alexander. 1620. *A Discourse of Marriage and Wiving*. London.

Overbury, Thomas. 1614. *A Wife: Now The Widow of Sir Thomas Overburye: Wherevnto Are Added many witty Characters, and conceyted Newes*. London.

Overbury, Thomas. 1615. *A Wife: Now The Widow of Sir Thomas Overburye: Wherevnto Are Added many witty Characters, and conceyted Newes*. London.

Painter, William. 1566–67. *The Palace of Pleasure*. 2. vols. London.

Peele, George. 1590. *Polyhymnia*. London.

Rich, Barnayby. 1613. *The Excellency of Good Women*. London.

Rollins, Hyden E. ed. 1922. *A Pepysian Garland*. Cambridge: Cambridge University Press.

Sandys, George. 1615. *A Relation of a Journey begun: An: Dom: 1610*. London.

Secret History of the Court of James the First. 1811. Ed. Sir Walter Scott. 2 vols. Edinburgh: J. Ballantyne.

Shakespeare, William. 2007. *William Shakespeare the RSC Shakespeare Complete Works*. Ed. Jonathan Bate and Eric Rasmussen. Basingstoke: Macmillan.

Sidney, Philip. 1983. *The Countesse Pembroke's Arcadia* (1598). Delmar: Scholar's Facsimiles & Reprints.

Sowernam, Ester. 1617. *Ester hath hang'd Haman: Or ANSWER To a lewd Pamphlet, entituled, the Arraignment of Women*. London.

Speght, Rachel. 1617. *Movzel for Melastomvs, The Cynicall Bayter of, and foule mouthed Barker against EVAHS SEX*. London.

Speght, Rachel. 1621. *Mortalities Memorandum, with a Dreame Prefixed . . . .* London.

Speght, Rachel. 1996. *The Polemics and Poems of Rachel Speght*. Ed. Barbara Kiefer Lewalski. New York, Oxford: Oxford University Press.

Stuart, Arabella. 1866. *The Life and Letters of Lady Arabella Stuart*, including Numerous Original and Unpublished Documents. Ed. Elizabeth Cooper. London: Hurst and Blackett.

Swetnam, Joseph. 1615. *The Araignment of Lewd, Idle, Froward, and vnconstant women*. London.

Swetnam the Woman-Hater Araigned by women. 1620. London.

Swetnam the Woman-Hater: The Controversy and the Play. 1969. Ed. Coryl Crandall. Lafayette: Purdue University Studies.

Swinburne, Henry. 1686. *A Treatise of Spousals or Matrimonial Contracts* (written around 1620, published in 1686).

The Life and Death of Mrs Mary Frith, Commonly called Mol Cutpurse. 1662. London.

The Narrative History of King James, for the first fourteen Years. 1651. London.

Three Pamphlets on the Jacobean Antifeminist Controversy. 1978. With Facsimile Reproductions with an Introduction by Barbara J. Baines. Delmar, New York: Scholars' Facsimiles & Reprints.

Traditional Japanese Theater: An Anthology of Plays (Translations from the Asian Classics). 1999. Ed. Karen Brazell. New York: Columbia University Press.
Tyler, Margaret tr. 1575. *The Mirrour of Princely Deeds and Knighthood*. London.
Vives, Joannes Ludovicus. 1530?. *The Instruction of a Christian Woman*. Tr. R. Hyrde. London.
Webster, John. 1612. *Monumental Column*. London.
Webster, John. 1960. *The White Devil*. Ed. John Russel Brown. The Revels Plays. Cambridge, MA: Harvard University Press.
Webster, John. 1964. *The Duchess of Malfi*. The Revels Plays. Ed. John Russel Brown. Manchester: Manchester University Press.
Webster, John. 1966. *The Complete Works of John Webster*. Ed. F.L. Lucas. 4 vols. New York: Gordian Press.
Webster, John. 1970. *The White Devil* (1612). Menston: Scholar Press.
Webster, John. 1995–2007. *The Works of John Webster: An Old-Spelling Critical Edition*. Ed. David Gunby, David Carnegie, MacDonald P. Jackson et al. 3 vols. Cambridge: Cambridge University Press.
Webster, John. 2009. *The Duchess of Malfi*. Arden Early Modern Drama. Ed. Leah S. Marcus. London: Methuen.
Weldon, Anthony. 1651. *The Court and Character of King James*. London.
Whetstone, George. 1582. *An Heptameron of Ciuill Discourses*. London.
William, Leigh. 1612. *Queen Elizabeth, Paraleld in Her Princely Virtues with David, Josua, and Hazekia*. London.
Wroth, Mary Sidney. 1621. *The Countesse of Mountgomeries Urania*. London.
Wroth, Mary Sidney. 1988. *Lady Mary Wroth's Love's Victory: The Penshurst Manuscript*. Ed. Michael G. Brennan. London: The Roxburghe Club.
Wroth, Mary Sidney. 1992. *The Poems of Lady Mary Wroth*. Ed. Josephine A. Roberts, 2nd edition. Baton Rouge, LA: Louisiana State University Press.
Wroth, Mary Sidney. 1995. *The First Part of The Countess of Montgomery's Urania*. Ed. Josephine A. Roberts. Binghamton, NY: Medieval & Renaissance Texts & Studies.
Wroth, Mary Sidney. 1996. *Love's Victory*. In *Renaissance Drama by Women*. Ed. Susan Cerasano and Marion Wynne-Davies. 91–126.
Wroth, Mary Sidney. 1996. *The Countesse of Mountgomeries Urania*. Facsimile. Ed. Josephine A. Roberts. *Early Modern Englishwoman: Part 1, Printed Writings, 1500–1640*. Vol. 10. Aldershot: Ashgate.
Wroth, Mary Sidney. 1999. *The Second Part of the Countess of Montgomery's Urania*. Ed. Josephine A. Roberts, completed by Suzanne Gossett and Janel Mueller. Tempe, AZ: Renaissance English Text Society/ Arizona Center for Medieval and Renaissance Studies.
Wroth, Mary Sidney. 2011. *The Countess of Montgomery's Urania* (1621) (Abridged). Ed. Mary Ellen Lamb. Tempe, AZ: Arizona Center for Medieval and Renaissance Studies.

Secondary sources

Allen, Gemma. 2013. *Cooke Sisters: Education, Piety and Politics in Early Modern England*. Manchester: Manchester University Press.
Andrea, Bernadette. 2001. 'Pamphilia's Cabinet: Gender Authorship and Empire in Lady Mary Wroth's *Urania*'. *English Literary History* 68.2 (2001): 335–58.

Annals of English Drama 975–1700 (1964). 1989. Ed. S. Schoenbaum and Alfred Harbage, revised by Sylvia Stoler Wagonheim. London and New York: Routledge.

Axton, Marie. 1977. *The Queen's Two Bodies: Drama and the Elizabeth Succession*. London: Royal Historical Society.

Baines, Barbara J. ed. 1978. *Three Pamphlets on the Jacobean Antifeminist Controversy*. New York: Scholars' Facsimiles.

Barroll, Leeds. 2001. *Anna of Denmark Queen of England: A Cultural Biography*. Philadelphia: University of Pennsylvania Press.

Barton, Anne. 2006. 'Nature's Piece 'gainst Fancy: The Divided Catastrophe in *Antony and Cleopatra*' (1974/1992)'. In *Essays, Mainly Shakespearean*. Cambridge: Cambridge University Press. 113–35.

Bayman, Anna. 2010. 'Female Voices in Early Seventeenth Century Pamphlet Literature.' In *Women and Writing c.1340–c.1650: The Domestication of Print Culture*. Ed. Anne Lawrence-Mathers and Phillipa Hardman. Woodbridge: York Medieval Press. 196–210.

Beilin, Elaine V. 1987. *Redeeming Eve: Women Writers of the English Renaissance*. Princeton, NJ: Princeton University Press.

Bell, Ilona. 1998. *Elizabethan Women and the Poetry of Courtship*. Cambridge: Cambridge University Press.

Bell, Ilona. 2013. '"Joy's Sports": The Unexpurgated Text of Mary Wroth's *Pamphilia to Amphilanthus*'. *Modern Philology* 3.2 (November 2013): 231–52.

Bell, Ilona. 2015. 'Sugared Sonnets among Their Private Friends: Mary Wroth and William Shakespeare'. In *Mary Wroth and William Shakespeare*. Ed. Paul Salzman and Marion Wynne-Davies. New York and London: Routledge. 9–24.

Bell, Ilona. 2015. 'The Autograph Manuscript of Mary Wroth's *Pamphilia to Amphilanthus*'. In *Re-Reading Mary Wroth*. Ed. Katherine R. Larson, Naomi J. Miller and Andrew Strycharski. New York: Palgrave Macmillan. 69–81.

Belsey, Catherine. 1985. *The Subject of Tragedy: The Identity and Difference in Renaissance Drama*. London: Methuen.

Bentley, Gerald Eades. 1941–68. *The Jacobean and Caroline Stage*. 8 vols. Oxford: Clarendon Press.

Berg, Christine and Philippa Berry. 1981. '"Spiritual Whoredom": An Essay on Female Prophets in the Seventeenth Century'. In *1642: Literature and Power in the Seventeenth Century*. Ed. Francis Barker *et al.* Colchester: University of Essex.

Bevington, David and Jay L. Halio ed. 1979. *Shakespeare of Excelling Nature*. Newark: University of Delaware Press.

Bogard, Travis. 1955. *The Tragic Satire of John Webster*. Berkeley and Los Angeles: University of California Press.

Boklund, Gunnar. 1957. *The Sources of the White Devil*. Upsala: A. B. Lundequistska Bokhandeln.

Boklund, Gunnar. 1962. *The Duchess of Malfi: Sources, Themes and Characters*. Cambridge, MA: Harvard University Press.

Bolam, Robyn. 2000. 'The Heart of the Labyrinth: Mary Wroth's *Pamphilia to Amphilanthus*'. In *The Cambridge Companion to English Renaissance Literature and Culture*, ed. Michael Hattaway. Cambridge: Cambridge University Press. 257–66.

Bradbrook, M.C. 1980. *John Webster: Citizen and Dramatist*. London: Weidenfeld and Nicolson.

Bradbrook, M.C. 1980. *Themes and Conventions of Elizabethan Tragedy*. 2nd Edition. London: Cambridge University Press.
Brennan, Michael G. 2002. 'Creating Female Authorship in Early Seventeenth Century: Jonson and Lady Mary Wroth'. In *Women's Writing and the Circulation of Ideas: Manuscript Publication in England, 1550–1800*. Ed. George L. Justice and Nathan Tinker. Cambridge: Cambridge University Press, 73–93.
Brown, John Russell. 1952. 'The Dating of Webster's *The White Devil* and *The Duchess of Malfi*'. *Philological Quarterly* 31 (1952): 353–8.
Callaghan, Dympna. 1994. 'Re-Reading Elizabeth Cary's *The Tragedie of Mariam, the Faire Queene of Jewry*'. In *Women, 'Race', & Writing in the Early Modern Period*. Ed. Margo Hendricks and Patricia Parker. London: Routledge. 163–77.
Callaghan, Dympna, Lorvaine Helms and Jyotsna Singh ed. 1994. *The Weyward Sisters: Shakespeare and Feminist Politics*. Oxford: Blackwell.
Camden, Carroll. 1975. *The Elizabethan Woman* (1952). Mamaroneck: Paul P. Appel.
Capp, Bernard. 1999. 'The Double Standard Revisited: Plebeian Women and Male Sexual Reputation in Early Modern England'. *Past and Present* 162 (1999): 70–100.
Carlton, Katharine and Tim Thornton. 2011. 'Illegitimacy and Authority in the North of England, c.1450–1640'. *Northern History* 48 (2011): 23–40.
Carrell, Jennifer Lee. 1994. 'A Pack of Lies in a Looking Glass: Lady Mary Wroth's *Urania* and the Magic Mirror of Romance'. *Studies in English Literature* 34 (1994): 79–101.
Cavanagh, Sheila T. 2001. *Cherished Torment: The Emotional Geography of Lady Mary Wroth's Urania*. Pittsburgh, PA: Duquesne University Press.
Cavanagh, Sheila T. 2009. '"The Great Cham": East Meets West in Lady Mary Wroth's *Urania*'. In *Mary Wroth, Ashgate Critical Essays on Women Writers in England, 1550–1700*, Ed. Clare R. Kinney. 7 vols. Farnham: Ashgate. Vol. 4. 136–51.
Chamberlain, John. 1939. *The Letters of John Chamberlain*. Ed. Norman Egbert McClure. 2 vols. Philadelphia: American Historian Society.
Chambers, E.K. 1968. *Elizabethan Stage*, 4 vols. Oxford: Clarendon Press.
Charney, Maurice. 1961. *Shakespeare's Roman Plays: The Function of Imagery in the Drama*. Cambridge, MA: Harvard University Press.
Chedgzoy, Kate, Melanie Harsen and Susanne Trill ed. 1998. *Voicing Women: Gender and Sexuality in Early Modern England*. Edinburgh: Edinburgh University Press.
Clark, Sandra. 2010. 'Shrews, Marriage and Murder'. In *Gender and Power in Shrew-Taming Narratives, 1500–1700*. Ed. David Wootton and Graham Holderness. Basingstoke: Palgrave Macmillan. 29–47.
Clarke, Danielle. 2001. *The Politics of Early Modern Women's Writing*. Edinburgh: Pearson Education.
Clarke, Danielle and Elizabeth Clarke ed. 2000. *'his Double Voice': Gendered Writing in Early Modern England*. London: Macmillan.
Collinson, Patrick. 1967. *The Elizabethan Puritan Movement*. London: Methuen.
Crawford, Julie. 2014. *Mediatrix: Women, Politics, & Literary Production in Early Modern England*. Oxford: Oxford University Press.
Crawford, Patricia. 1993. *Women and Religion in England, 1500–1720*. London and New York: Routledge.

Croft, Pauline. 2003. *King James*. Basingstoke: Palgrave Macmillan.
Croft, Pauline. 2015. 'Howard, Thomas, First Earl of Suffolk (1561–1626)' *DNB*, online edn. [http://0-www.oxforddnb.com.catalogue.ulrls.lon.ac.uk/view/article/13942, accessed 22 Feb 2015]
Cross, Gustav. 1960. 'Marston, Montaigne, and Morality: *The Dutch Courtesan* Reconsidered'. *English Literary History* 27 (1960): 30–43.
Curtis, Mark H. 1962. 'The Alienated Intellectuals of Early Stuart England'. *Past and Present* 23 (1962): 25–43.
Danby, John F. 1952. *Elizabethan and Jacobean Poets: Studies in Sidney, Shakespeare and Beaumont and Fletcher*. London: Faber and Faber.
Das, Nandini. 2011. *Renaissance Romance: The Transformation of English Prose Fiction, 1570–1620*. Farnham: Ashgate.
Davies, Kathleen M. 1977. 'The Sacred Condition of Equality: How Original Were Puritan Doctrine of Marriage?' *Social History* 5 (1977): 563–80.
Daybell, James. 2006. *Women Letter-Writers in Tudor England*. Oxford: Oxford University Press.
Dent, R.W. 1960. *John Webster's Borrowing*. Berkeley: University of California Press.
Dent, R.W. 1966. 'The White Devil, or Vittoria Corombona?' *Renaissance Drama* IX (1966): 179–203.
Dickey, Franklin M. 1966. *Not Wisely But Too Well: Shakespeare's Love Tragedies*. San Marino, CA: Huntington Library.
Donaldson, Ian. 2011. *Ben Jonson: A Life*. Oxford: Oxford University Press.
Dragstra, Henk, Sheila Ottway and Helen Wilcox ed. 2000. *Betraying Ourselves: Forms of Self-Representation in Early Modern English Texts*. New York: St. Martins.
Duffin, Ross W. 2004. *Shakespeare's Songbook*. New York and London: W. W. Norton & Company.
Durant, David N. 1978. *Arabella Stuart: A Rival to the Queen*. London: Weldenfeld and Nicolson.
Dusinberre, Juliet. 2003. *Shakespeare and the Nature of Women* (1975). 3rd edition. Basingstoke: Palgrave Macmillan.
Edwards, Philip ed. 1980. *Shakespeare's Styles: Essays in Honour of Kenneth Muir*. ed. Inga-Stina Ewbank and G.K. Hunter. Cambridge: Cambridge University Press.
Edwards, Philip. 2008. 'Massinger's Men and Women'. In *Philip Massinger: A Critical Reassessment*. Ed. Douglas Howard (1985). Cambridge: Cambridge University Press. 39–49.
Ekeblad, Inga-Stina. 1968. 'The "Impure Art" of John Webster'. In *Twentieth Century Interpretations of 'The Duchess of Malfi'*. Ed. Norman Rabkin. Englewood Cliffs, Englewood Cliffs, N.J.: Prentice Hall. 49–65.
Ewbank, Inga-Stina. 1980. '"My Name Is Marina": The Language of Recognition'. In *Shakespeare's Styles*. Ed. Philip Edwards, Inga-Stina Ewbank and G.K. Hunter. Cambridge: Cambridge University Press. 111–30.
Falls, C.B. 1954. *Mountioy: Elizabethan General*. London: Obhama Press.
Ferguson, Margaret W. 1986. *Rewriting the Renaissance: The Discourse of Sexual Difference in Early Modern Europe*. Ed. Margaret W. Ferguson, Maureen Quilligan and Nancy J. Vickers. Chicago: University of Chicago Press.
Fincham, W.X. 1921. 'Notes from the Ecclesiastical Court Records at Somerset House'. *Transactions of the Royal Historical Society*, 4th series, IV (1921). 111–13.

Findlay, Allison. 1994. *Illegitimate Power: Bastards in Renaissance Drama.* Manchester & New York: Manchester University Press.

Findlay, Allison. 2006. *Playing Spaces in Early Women's Drama.* Cambridge: Cambridge University Press.

Finkelpearl, Philip J. 1969. *John Marston of the Middle Temple: An Elizabethan Dramatist in His Social Setting.* Cambridge, MA: Harvard University Press.

Fischer, Sandra K. 1985. 'Elizabeth Cary and Tyranny, Domestic and Religious'. In *Silent But for the Word: Tudor Women as Patrons, Translations, and Writers of Religious Works.* Ed. Margaret Patterson Hannay. Ohio: The Kent University Press. 235–7.

Fletcher, Anthony. 1994. 'The Protestant Idea of Marriage in Early Modern England'. In *Religion, Culture and Society in Early Modern England: Essays in Honour of Patrick Colins.* Ed. Anthony Fletcher and Peter Roberts. Cambridge: Cambridge University Press. 161–81.

Foucault, Michel. 1971. *The Order of Things.* Tr. Alan Sheridan-Smith. New York: Pantheon.

Fox, Eleanor and Martin Ingram. 2014. 'Bridewell, Bawdy Courts and Bastardy in Early Seventeenth-Century London'. In *Cohabitation and Non-Marital Births in England and Wales, 1600–2012.* Ed. Rebecca Probert. Basingstoke: Palgrave Macmillan. 10–32.

Franklin, H. Bruce. 1961. 'The Trial Scene of Webster's *The White Devil* Examined in Terms of Renaissance Rhetoric'. *Studies in English Literature 1500–1900*, 1 (1961): 35–51.

Freedman, Sylvia. 1983. *Poor Penelope: Lady Penelope Rich, an Elizabethan Woman.* Windsor: Kensal Press.

Frye, Susan. 1993. *Elizabeth I: The Competition for Representation.* New York and Oxford: Oxford University Press.

Fullerton, Georgiana. 1883. *The Life of Elizabeth Lady Falkland 1585–1639.* London: Burns and Oates.

Geckle, George L. 1980. *John Marston's Drama: Themes, Images Sources.* New Jersey: Rutherford University Press. 153.

Goldberg, Jonathan. 1983. *James 1 and the Politics of Literature: The Politics of Literature: Jonson, Shakespeare, Donne, and Their Contemporaries.* Baltimore and London: The Johns Hopkins University Press.

Gowing, Laura. 1996. *Domestic Dangers: Women, Words, and Sex in Early Modern London.* Oxford: Clarendon Press.

Green, M. Everett. 1909. *Elizabeth, Electress Palatine and Queen of Bohemia.* London: Methuen.

Greenblatt, Stephen. 1980. *Renaissance Self-Fashioning: From More to Shakespeare.* Chicago and London: University of Chicago Press.

Greenblatt, Stephen. 1988. *Shakespearean Negotiations: The Circulation of Social Energy in Renaissance England.* Oxford: Clarendon Press.

Griffith, Eva. 2013. *A Jacobean Company and its Playhouse: The Queen's Servants at the Red Bull Theatre (c.1605–1619).* New York: Cambridge University Press.

Griffiths, Paul. 1993. 'The Structure of Prostitution in Elizabethan London'. *Continuity and Change* 8 (1993): 39–63.

Griffiths, Paul. 2003. 'Contesting London Bridewell, 1576–1580'. *Journal of British Studies* 42 (2003): 283–315.

Griffiths, Paul. 2008. *Lost Londons: Change, Crime, and Control in the Capital City, 1550–1660*. Cambridge: Cambridge University Press.

Gristwood, Sarah. 2003. *Arbella: England's Lost Queen*. London: Bantam.

Grosart, Alexander B. 1880. '*Swetnam the Woman-Hater*'. *Manchester Occasional Issues* XIV. Manchester. xxiv.

Gunby, D.C. 1970. 'The *Duchess of Malfi*: A Theological Approach'. In *John Webster*. Mermaid Critical Commentaries. Ed. Brian Morris. London: Ernest Benn, 179–204

Hackett, Helen. 1992. '"Yet Tell Me Some Such Fiction": Lady Mary Wroth's *Urania* and the Femininity of Romance'. In *Women, Texts and Histories, 1570–1760*. Ed. Clare Brant and Diana Purkiss. London and New York: Routledge, 39–68

Hackett, Helen. 1998. 'The Torture of Limena: Sex and Violence in Lady Mary Wroth's *Urania*'. In *Voicing Women: Gender and Sexuality in Early Modern Writing*. Ed. Kate Chedgzoy, Melanie Harsen and Susanne Trill. Edinburgh: Edinburgh University Press, 93–110.

Hacket, Helen. 2000. *Women and Romance Fiction in the English Renaissance*. Cambridge: Cambridge University Press.

Hageman, Elizabeth H. and Katherine Conway ed. 2007. *Resurrecting Elizabeth I in Seventeenth-Century England*. Madison and Teaneck: Fairleigh Dickinson University Press.

Hall, Kim F. 1995. *Things of Darkness: Economies of Race and Gender in Early Modern England*. Ithaca and London: Cornell University Press.

Haller, William and Malleville. 1942. 'The Puritan Art of Love'. *Huntington Library Quarterly* 5 (1942): 244–5.

Hamlin, William M. 2005. 'What Did Montaigne's Scepticism Mean to Shakespeare and His Contemporaries?' *Montaigne Studies* 17 (2005): 195–210.

Hamlin, William M. 2005. *Tragedy and Scepticism in Shakespeare's England*. Early Modern Literature in History. Basingstoke: Palgrave Macmillan.

Hamlin, William M. 2013. *Montaigne's English Journey: Reading the Essays in Shakespeare's Days*. Oxford: Oxford University Press.

Hannay, Margaret P. ed. 1985. *Silent but for the World*. Kent, OH: Kent State University Press.

Hannay, Margaret P. 2010. *Mary Sidney, Lady Wroth*. Farnham: Ashgate.

Hannay, Margaret P., Noel J. Kinnamon and Michael G. Brennan ed. 2005. *Domestic Politics and Family Absence: The Correspondence (1588–1621) of Robert Sidney, First Earl of Leicester, and Barbara Gamage Sidney, Countess of Leicester*. Aldershot: Ashgate.

Hanson, Elizabeth. 2000. *Discovering the Subject in Renaissance England*. Oxford: Oxford University Press.

Haselkorn, Anne M. and Betty S. Travistky ed. 1990. *The Renaissance English Woman in Print: CounterBalancing the Canon*. Amherst: The University of Massachusetts Press.

Heinemann, Margot. 1980. *Puritan and Theatre: Thomas Middleton and Opposition Drama under the Early Stuarts*. Cambridge: Cambridge University Press.

Hibbard, G.R. 1980. '*Feliciter audax: Antony and Cleopatra*, I, I, 1–24'. In *Shakespeare's Styles: Essays in Honour of Kenneth Muir*. Ed. Philip Edwards, Inga-Stina Ewbank, G.K. Hunter. Cambridge: Cambridge University Press. 96–7.

Higgins, Patricia. 1973. 'The Reactions of Women, with Special Reference to Women Petitioners'. In *Politics, Religion and the English Civil War*. Ed. Brian Manning. London: Edward Arnold. 177–222.

Hill, Christopher. 1978. *The World Upside Down: Radical Ideas during the English Revolution*. Harmondsworth: Penguin.
Hill, Christopher. 1986. *Society and Puritanism in Pre-Revolutionary England*. Harmondsworth: Penguin.
Hinds, Hilary. 1996. *God's Englishwomen: Seventeenth-Century Radical Secretarian Writing and Feminist Criticism*. Manchester: Manchester University Press.
Hinds, Hilary. 2011. *George Fox and Early Quaker Culture*. Manchester: Manchester University Press.
Hodgson-Wright, Stephanie. 2015. 'Cary, Elizabeth, Viscountess Falkland (1585–1639)', *DNB*, online edn., May 2014 [http://0-www.oxforddnb.com.catalogue.ulrls.lon.ac.uk/view/article/4835, accessed 22 Feb 2015]
Howard, Jean E. and Phylis Rackin ed. 1997. *Engendering a Nation: A Feminist Account of Shakespeare's English Histories*. London and New York: Routledge.
Hubbard, Eleanor. 2012. *City Women: Money, Sex, and the Social Order in Early Modern London*. Oxford: Oxford University Press.
Ingram, Martin. 1985. 'Ridings, Rough Music and Mocking Rhymes in Early Modern England'. In *Popular Culture in Seventeenth-Century England*. Ed. Barry Reay. London: Routledge. 166–97.
Ingram, Martin. 1987. *Church Courts, Sex and Marriage in England, 1570–1640*. Cambridge: Cambridge University Press.
Ingram, Martin. 1994. '"Scolding Women Cucked or Washed": A Crisis in Gender Relations in Early Modern England?'. In *Women, Crime and the Courts in Early Modern England*. Ed. Jenny Kermode and Garthine Walker. Chapel Hill: The University of North Carolina Press, 48–80.
Ingram, Martin. 2014. 'Cohabitation in context in early seventeenth-century London'. In *Cohabilitation and Non-Marital Births in England and Wales, 1600–2012*. Ed. Rebecca Probert. Basingstoke: Palgrave Macmillan. 33–50.
Jackson, J. 1952. 'Sources of the Subplot of Marston's *The Dutch Courtesan*'. *Philological Quarterly* 31 (1952): 223–4.
Jones, Ann Rosalind. 1990. 'Counter Attacks on "the Bayter of Women": Three Pamphleteers of the Early Seventeenth Century'. In *The Renaissance English Women in Print*. Ed. Anne M. Haselkorn and Betty S. Travistky. Amherst: The University of Massachusetts Press. 45–62.
Jones, Ann Rosalind. 1990. *The Currency of Eros: Women's Love Lyric in Europe, 1540–1620*. Bloomington and Indiana Poles: Indiana University Press.
Jones, Ann Rosalind and Peter Stallybrass. 1984. 'The Politics of *Astrophil and Stella*', *Studies of English Literature* 24 (1984): 53–68.
Jones, Emrys. 1971. *Scenic Form in Shakespeare*. Oxford: Oxford University Press.
Jordan, Jennifer. 2007. 'Her-Story Untold: The Absence of Women's Agency in Constructing Concepts of Early Modern Manhood'. *Cultural and Social History* 4 (2007): 575–83.
Kelly, Philippa and L.E. Semler ed. 2010. *Word and Self Estranged in English Texts, 1550–1600*. Farnham: Ashgate.
Kelso, Ruth. 1956. *Doctrine for the Lady of the Renaissance*. Urbana, Illinois: Illinois University Press.
King, Sigrid ed. 1999. *Pilgrimage of Love: Essays in Early Modern Literature in Honour of Josephine A. Roberts*. Tempe, AZ: Arizona Center for Medieval and Renaissance Studies.

Kinney, Clare R. ed. 2009. *Mary Wroth. Ashgate Critical Essays on Women Writers in England, 1550–1700*, 7 vols. Vol. 4. Farnham: Ashgate.

Kinney, Clare R. 2015. 'Escaping the Void: Isolation, Mutuality and Community in the Sonnets of Wroth and Shakespeare'. In *Mary Wroth and Shakespeare*. Ed. Paul Salzman and Marion Wynne-Davies. New York and London: Routledge. 25–36.

Kinney, Clare R. 2015. 'Turn and Counterturn: Reappraising Mary Wroth's Poetic Labyrinths'. In *Re-Reading Mary Wroth*. Ed. Katherine R. Larson, Naomi Miller and Andrew Strycharski. New York: Palgrave Macmillan. 85–102.

Knight, G. Wilson. 1965. *The Imperial Theme: Further Interpretations of Shakespeare's Tragedies Including the Roman plays* (1931). 3rd edition. London: Methuen.

Knights, L.C. 1960. *Some Shakespearean Themes: An Approach to 'Hamlet'*. London: Penguin Books.

Kusunoki, Akiko. 1992. '"Their Testament at Their Apron-springs": The Representation of Puritan Women in Early Seventeenth-Century England'. In *Gloriana's Face: Women, Public and Private, in the English Renaissance*. Ed. S.P. Cerasano and Marion Wynne-Davies. New York and London: Harvester, 185–204.

Kusunoki, Akiko. 2003. 'Female Selfhood and Male Violence in English Renaissance Drama: A View from Mary Wroth's *Urania*'. In *Women, Violence, and English Renaissance Literature: Essays Honoring Paul Jorgensen*. Ed. Linda Woodbridge and Sharon Beehler. Tempe, AZ: Arizona Center for Medieval and Renaissance Studies, 125–48.

Kusunoki, Akiko. 2013. '"To Sorrow I'll Wed": Resolution of Women's Sadness in Mary Wroth's *Urania* and Shakespeare's *Twelfth Night*'. *Sidney Journal* 31 (2013): 117–30.

Kusunoki, Akiko. 2015. 'Wroth's *Love's Victory* as a Response to Shakespeare's Representations of Gender Distinctions: With Special Reference to *Romeo and Juliet*'. In *Mary Wroth and Shakespeare*. New York and London: Routledge. 73–83.

Lamb, Mary Ellen. 1990. *Gender and Authority in the Sidney Circle*. Madison: The University of Wisconsin Press.

Lamb, Mary Ellen. 1991. 'Women Readers in Mary Wroth's *Urania*'. In *Reading Mary Wroth*. Ed. Miller and Waller. Knoxville: The University of Tennessee Press. 210–27.

Lamb, Mary Ellen. 2015. '"Can You Suspect a Change in Me?": Poems by Mary Wroth and William Herbert, Third Earl of Pembroke'. In *Re-Reading Mary Wroth*. New York: Palgrave Macmillan. 53–68.

Larson, Katherine R. 2011. 'Conversational Games and the Articulation of Desire in Shakespeare's *Love's Labour's Lost* and Mary Wroth's *Love's Victory*'. In *Early Modern Women in Conversation*. Basingstoke: Palgrave Macmillan, 89–109.

Larson, Katherine R. 2014. 'Recent Studies in Mary Wroth'. *English Literary Renaissance* 44, no.2 (spring 2014): 328–59.

Larson, Katherine R. 2015. 'Voicing Lyric: The Songs of Mary Wroth'. In *Re-Reading Mary Wroth*. New York: Palgrave Macmillan. 119–36.

Larson, Katherine R., Naomi Miller and Andrew Strycharski ed. 2015. *Re-Reading Mary Wroth*. New York: Palgrave Macmillan.

Lawrence, Anne and Phillipa Hardman ed. 2010. *Women and Writing, c.1340–c.1650: Domestication of Print Culture*. Woodbridge: York Medieval Press/Boydell and Brewer.

Leech, Clifford. 1970. *John Webster*. New York: Haskell House.
Lewalski, Barbara Kiefer. 1993. *Writing Women in Jacobean England*. Cambridge, MA: Harvard University Press.
Lindley, David. 1993. *The Trial of Frances Howard: Fact and Fiction at the Court of King James*. New York: Routledge.
Lindley, David. 2006. *Shakespeare and Music*. London: Thomson Learning.
Lloyd, Michael. 1959. 'Cleopatra as Isis'. *Shakespeare Survey* 12 (1959): 88–94.
Lockyer, Roger. 2015. 'Lake, Sir Thomas (bap. 1561, d. 1630)' *DNB*, online edn. [http://0-www.oxforddnb.com.catalogue.ulrls.lon.ac.uk/view/article/15903, accessed 22 Feb 2015]
Lucas, R. Valerie. 1990. 'Puritan Preaching and the Politics of Family'. In *The Renaissance English Woman in Print: Counterbalancing the Canon*. Ed. Anne M. Haselkorn and Betty S. Travitsky. Amherst: University of Massachusetts Press. 224–40.
MacCaffrey, Wallace T. ed. 1970. *The History of the Most Renowned and Victorious Princess Elizabeth, Late Queen of England*. Chicago, London: University of Chicago Press.
Mack, Phyllis. 1988. 'The Prophet and Her Audience: Gender and Knowledge in the World Turned Upside Down'. In *Reviving the English Revolution: Reflections & Elaborations on the Work of Christopher Hill*. Ed. Geoff Eley and William Hunt. London and New York: Verso. 139–52.
Maginn, Christopher. 2015. 'Blount, Charles, eighth Baron Mountjoy and earl of Devonshire (1563–1606)', *DNB*, online edn, Jan 2008 [http://0-www.oxforddnb.com.catalogue.ulrls.lon.ac.uk/view/article/2683, accessed 15 Feb 2015].
Mann, David. 2008. *Shakespeare's Women: Performance and Conception*. Cambridge: Cambridge University Press.
Marshall, Rosalind K. 2004. 'Stuart, Lady Arabella (1575–1615)'. *DNB*. Oxford: Oxford University Press. [http://0-www.oxforddnb.com.catalogue.ulrls.lon.ac.uk/view/article/601]
Martin, Randall, ed. 1997. *Women Writers in Renaissance England*. London and New York: Longman.
Mascuch, Michael 1997. *Origins of the Individualist Self: Autobiography and Self-Identity in England, 1591–1791*. Cambridge: Polity Press.
Matchinske, Megan. 1994. 'Legislating Middle-Class Morality in Marriage Market: Ester Sowernam's *Ester hath hang'd Haman*'. *English Literary History* 24 (1994): 154–83.
Matulka, Barbara. 1931. *The Novels of Juan De Flores and Their European Diffusion: A Study in Comparative Literature*. New York: Publications of the Institute of French Studies.
McElwee, William. 1952. *The Murder of Sir Thomas Overbury*. London: Faber.
McInnes, Ian. 1968. *Arabella: The Life and Times of Lady Arabella Seymour, 1575–1615*. London: W. H. Allen.
McMullan, Gordon ed. 1998. *Renaissance Configurations: Voices, Bodies, Spaces 1580–1690*. Basingstoke: Macmillan.
Miller, Naomi J. 1991. 'Engendering Discourse: Women's Voices in Wroth's *Urania* and Shakespeare's Plays'. In *Reading Mary Wroth*. Knoxville: The University of Tennessee Press. 154–72.
Miller, Naomi J. 1996. *Changing the Subject: Mary Wroth and Figurations of Gender in Early Modern England*. Lexington, Kentucky: The University Press of Kentucky.

Miller, Naomi J. 2015. 'Re-Imaging the Subject: Traveling from Scholarship to Fiction with Mary Wroth'. In *Re-Reading Mary Wroth*. New York: Palgrave Macmillan. 269–79.

Miller, Naomi J. and Gary Waller. 1991. *Reading Mary Wroth: Representing Alternatives in Early Modern England*. Knoxville: The University of Tennessee.

Molekamp, Femke. 2013. *Women and the Bible in Early Modern England: Religious Reading and Writing*. Oxford: Oxford University Press.

Montrose, Louis Adrian. 1980. '"Eliza, Queene of Shepheardes," and the Pastoral of Power'. *English Literary Renaissance* 10 (1980): 153–82.

Montrose, Louis Adrian. 1983. 'Of Gentlemen and Shepherds: The Politics of Elizabethan Pastoral Form'. *English Literary History* 50 (1983): 415–59.

Morris, Helen. 1968–9. 'Queen Elizabeth I "Shadowed" in Cleopatra'. *Huntington Library Quarterly* 32 (1968–9): 271–8.

Muir, Kenneth. 1967. 'Elizabeth I, Jodelle, and Cleopatra'. *Renaissance Drama*, New Series, 2 (1967): 197–206.

Murray, Peter. 1969. *A Study of John Webster*. The Hague: Mouton.

Neale, J.E. 1990. *Queen Elizabeth I* (1934). London: Penguin Books.

Neely, Carol Thomas. 1998. 'Constructing the Subject: Feminist Practice and the New Renaissance Discourses', *English Literary Renaissance* 18 (1998): 5–18.

Neill, Michael. 2000. *Putting History to the Question: Power, Politics, and Society in English Renaissance Drama*. New York: Columbia University Press.

Nelson, Karen L. 2015. '"Change Partners and Dance": Pastoral Virtuosity in Wroth's *Love's Victory*'. In *Re-Reading Mary Wroth*. New York: Palgrave Macmillan. 137–56.

Norsworthy, Laura. 1935. *The Lady of Bleeding Heart: Lady Elizabeth Hatton 1579–1646*. London: John Murray.

Note, Beverly M. Van. 2015. 'Performing "fitter means": Marriage and Authorship in *Love's Victory*'. In *Re-Reading Mary Wroth*. New York: Palgrave Macmillan. 69–81.

O'Connor, John J. 1957. 'The Chief Source of Marston's *Dutch Courtesan*'. *Studies of Philology* 54 (1957): 509–15.

Oman, Carola. 1938. *The Winter Queen: Elizabeth of Bohemia*. London: Phoenix Press.

Orgel, Stephen. 1996. *Impersonations: The Performance of Gender in Shakespeare's England*. Cambridge: Cambridge University Press.

Ornstein, Robert. 1960. *The Moral Vision of Jacobean Tragedy*. Madison: University of Wisconsin Press.

Ornstein, Robert. 1966. 'The Ethic of the Imagination: Love and Art in *Antony and Cleopatra*'. In *Later Shakespeare*. Ed. John Russell Brown and Bernard Harris. Stratford-upon-Avon Studies 8. London: Edward Arnold. 31–46.

Outhwaite, R.B. 1995. *Clandestine Marriage in England, 1500–1850*. London and Rio Grande: Hambledon Press.

The Oxford Dictionary of National Biography (DNB), online edn., http://www.oxforddnb.com.

The Oxford English Dictionary (OED). 2009. 2nd edition on CD-ROM. Oxford: Oxford University Press.

Parry, Graham. 1985. *The Golden Age Restored: The Culture of the Stuart Court, 1603–42* (1981). Manchester: Manchester University Press.

Pascoe, David. 2000. 'The Dutch Courtesan and Profits of Translation'. In *The Drama of John Marston*. Ed. T.F. Wharton. Cambridge: Cambridge University Press. 162–80.
Pearson, Jacqueline. 1980. *Tragedy and Tragicomedy in the Plays of John Webster*. Manchester: Manchester University Press.
Pearson, Lu Emily. 1941. 'Elizabethan Widows'. In *Stanford Studies in Language and Literature*. Stanford: Stanford University Press.
Perry, Curtis. 1997. *The Making of Jacobean Culture*. Cambridge: Cambridge University Press.
Porter, Roy ed. 1997. *Rewriting the Self: Histories from the Renaissance to the Present*. London and New York: Routledge.
Quilligan, Maureen. 1990. 'The Constant Subject: Instability and Authority in Wroth's *Urania* Poems'. In *Soliciting Interpretation: Literary Theory and Seventeenth-Century English Poetry*. Ed. Elizabeth D. Harvey and Katherine Eisaman Maus. Chicago: University of Chicago Press.
Rawson, Maud Stephany. 1911. *Penelope Rich and Her Circle*. London: Hutchinson.
Raymond, Joad. 2003. *Pamphlets and Pamphleteering in Early Modern Britain*. Cambridge: Cambridge University Press.
Rickman, Johanna. 2008. *Love, Lust, and License in Early Modern England: Illicit Sex and the Nobility*. Aldershot: Ashgate.
Ritchie, Fiona. 2014. *Women and Shakespeare in the Eighteenth Century*. Cambridge: Cambridge University Press.
Roberts, Josephine A. 1977. 'An Unpublished Literary Quarrel Concerning the Suppression of Mary Wroth's *Urania* (1621)'. *Notes & Queries* 222 (1977): 532–5.
Roberts, Josephine A. 1990. 'Radigund Revisited: Perspectives on Women Rulers in Lady Mary Wroth's *Urania*'. In *The Renaissance Englishwomen in Print: Counterbalancing the Canon*. Ed. Anne M. Haselkorn and Betty S. Travitsky, Amherst: The University of Massachusetts Press, 187–207.
Roberts, Josephine A. 1991. 'Labyrinths of Desire: Lady Mary Wroth's Reconstruction of Romance'. *Women's Studies* 19 (1991): 183–92.
Rogers, Katherine. 1966. *The Troublesome Helpmate: A History of Misogyny in Literature*. Seattle: University of Washington Press.
Salingar, L.G. 1961. '*The Revenger's Tragedy* and the Morality Tradition'. In *Elizabethan Drama: Modern Essays in Criticism*. Ed. R.J. Kaufmann. New York: Oxford University Press. 212.
Salkeld, Duncan. 2012. *Shakespeare among the Courtesans: Prostitution, Literature, and Drama, 1500–1650*. Farnham: Ashgate.
Salzman, Paul. 1978. 'Contemporary References in Mary Wroth's *Urania*'. *Renaissance English Studies* n.s. 29 (1978): 178–81.
Salzman, Paul. 1986. *English Prose Fiction 1588–1700: A Critical History*. Oxford: Clarendon Press.
Salzman, Paul. 1997. '"The Strang(e)" Constructions of Mary Wroth's *Urania*: Arcadian Romance and the Public Realm'. In *English Renaissance Prose: History and Politics*. Ed. Rhodes Neil. Tempe, AZ: Arizona State University Press. 109–24.
Salzman, Paul. 2002. *Literary Culture in Jacobean England: Reading 1621*. Basingstoke: Palgrave Macmillan.
Salzman, Paul. 2006. *Reading Early Modern Women's Writing*. Oxford: Oxford University Press.

Salzman, Paul and Marion Wynne-Davies ed. 2015. *Mary Wroth and Shakespeare*. New York and London: Routledge.
Sawday, Jonathan. 1997. 'Self and Selfhood in the Seventeenth Century'. In *Rewriting the Self: Histories from the Renaissance to the Present*. Ed. Roy Porter. London and New York: Routledge. 29–48.
Scarr, Richard. 2000. 'Isatiate Punning in Marston's Courtesan Plays'. In *The Drama of John Marston*. Ed. T.F. Wharton. Cambridge: Cambridge University Press.
Schanzer, Ernest. 1960. 'The Marriage-Contracts in *Measure for Measure*'. *Shakespeare Survey* 13 (1960): 81–9.
Seigel, Jerrold. 2005. *The Idea of the Self: Thought and Experience in Western Europe since the Seventeenth Century*. Cambridge: Cambridge University Press.
Shapiro, Michael. 1994. *Gender in Play on the Shakespearean Stage: Boy Heroines and Female Pages*. Ann Arbor: University of Michigan Press.
Shepherd, Simon. 1981. *Amazons and Warrior Women: Varieties of Feminism in Seventeenth Century Drama*. Brighton: Harvester.
Smethurst, Mae. 2000. 'The Japanese Presence in Ninagawa's *Medea*'. In *Medea in Performance 1500–2000*. Ed. Edith Hall et al. Oxford: European Humanities Research Centre. 191–216.
Snook, Edith. 2006. *Women, Reading and the Cultural Politics of Early Modern England*. Aldershot: Ashgate.
Snook, Edith. 2011. *Women, Beauty and Power in Early Modern England: A Feminist Literary History*. Basingstoke: Palgrave Macmillan.
Sokol, B.J. and Mary Sokol. 2003. *Shakespeare, Law and Marriage*. Cambridge: Cambridge University Press.
Somerset, Anne. 1997. *Unnatural Murder: Poison at the Court of James I*. London: Weidenfeld & Nicolson.
Stanton, Kay. 2014. *Shakespeare's 'Whores': Erotics, Politics, and Poetics*. Houndsmills: Palgrave Macmillan.
Stone, Lawrence. 1977. *The Family, Sex, and Marriage in England, 1500–1800*. London: Weidenfeld and Nicolson.
Stone, Lawrence. 1979. *The Crisis of the Aristocracy 1558–1642*. Oxford: Oxford University Press (1965).
Stone, Lawrence. 1990. *Road to Divorce: England, 1530–1987*. Oxford: Clarendon Press.
Swift, Carolyn Ruth. 1984. 'Feminine Identity in Lady Mary Wroth's Romance *Urania*'. *English Literary Renaissance* 14 (1984): 328–46.
Taylor, G.L. 1925. *Shakespeare's Debt to Montaigne*. Cambridge, MA: Harvard University Press.
Tennenhouse, Leonard. 1986. *Power on Display: Politics of Shakespeare's Genre*. New York and London: Methuen.
Tilley, Morris P. ed. 1950. *A Dictionary of the Proverbs in England in the Sixteenth and Seventeenth Centuries*. Ann Arbor: Michigan.
Todd, Margo. 1987. *Christian Humanism and the Puritan Social Order*. Cambridge: Cambridge University Press.
Travisky, Betty ed. 1989. *The Paradise of Women: Writing by Englishwomen of the Renaissance*. New York: Columbia University Press.
Ure, Peter. 1974. 'John Marston's *Sophonisba*: A Reconsideration'. In *Elizabethan and Jacobean Drama: Critical Essays by Peter Ure*. Ed. J. C. Maxwell. Liverpool: Liverpool University Press.

Utley, Francis Lee. 1944. *The Crooked Rib: An Analytical Index to the Argument about Women in English and Scots Literature to the End of the Year 1568*. Columbus: Ohio State University.

Varlow, Sally. 2007. *The Lady Penelope: The Lost Tale of Love and Politics in the Elizabeth I*. London: Andre Deutsh.

Vaughan, Virginia Mason. 2003. '*King John*'. In *A Companion to Shakespeare's Works*. Volume II: The Histories. Ed. Richard Dutton and Jean E. Howard. Blackwell: Malden and Oxford. 379–94.

Waddington, Raymond B. 1966. 'What Venus Did to Mars'. *Shakespeare Studies* 2 (1966): 210–27.

Wadsworth, Frank W. 1956. 'Webster's *Duchess of Malfi* in the Light of Some Contemporary Ideas on Marriage and Remarriage'. *Philological Quarterly* 35 (1956): 394–407.

Wahrman, Dror. 2004. *The Making of the Modern Self: Identity and Culture in Eighteenth-Century England*. New Haven and London: Yale University Press.

Wall, Alison D. 1995. 'For Love, Money, or Politics? A Clandestine Marriage and the Elizabethan Court of Arches'. *Historical Journal* 38 (1995): 511–33.

Wall, Alison D. 2000. *Power and Protest in England 1525–1640*. London: Arnold.

Wall, Wendy. 1993. *The Imprint of Gender: Authorship and Publication in the English Renaissance*. Ithaca: Cornell University Press.

Waller, Gary F. 1985. 'Struggling into Discourse: The Emergence of Renaissance Women's Writing'. In *Silent but for the World*. Ed. Margaret P. Hannay. Kent, OH: Kent State University Press, 238–56.

Waller, Gary F. 1993. *The Sidney Family Romance: Mary Wroth, William Herbert and the Early Modern Construction of Gender*. Detroit: Wayne State University Press.

Ward, Haruko Nawata. 2009. *Women Religious Leaders in Japan's Christian Century, 1549–1650*. Fahnham: Ashgate.

Watkins, John. 2002. *Representing Elizabeth in Stuart England: Literature, History, Sovereignty*. Cambridge: Cambridge University Press.

Wedgewood, C.V. 2005. *The Thirty Years War* (1938). Foreword by Anthony Grafton. New York: New York Review Book.

Weidemann, Heather L. 1991. 'Theatricality and Female Identity in Mary Wroth's *Urania*'. In *Reading Mary Wroth*. Ed. Naomi J. Miller and Gary Waller. Knoxville: The University of Tennessee Press. 191–209.

Wharton, T.F. ed. 2000. *The Drama of John Marston*. Cambridge: Cambridge University Press.

White, Beatrice. 1965. *Cast of Ravens: The Strange Case of Sir Thomas Overbury*. London: Murray.

Wilson, Christopher R. and Michela Calore ed. 2007. *Music in Shakespeare: A Dictionary* (2005). London: Continuum.

Wilson, John Dover. 1949. *Life in Shakespeare's England*. Harmondsworth: Penguin.

Wilson, Violet. 1922. *Queen Elizabeth's Maids of Honour and Ladies of Privy Chambers*. London: John Lane.

Wiseman, Susan. 2007. *The Conspiracy & Virtue: Writing, Women, and Politics in Seventeenth England*. Oxford: Oxford University Press.

Woodbridge, Linda. 1984. *Women and the English Renaissance: Literature and the Nature of Womankind, 1540–1620*. Urbana and Chicago: University of Illinois Press.

Woodbridge, Linda and Sharon Beehler ed. 2003. *Women, Violence, and English Renaissance Literature: Essays Honoring Paul Jorgensen*. Tempe, AZ: Arizona Center for Medieval and Renaissance Studies.

Wooton, David and Graham Holderness ed. 2011. *Gender and Power in Shrew-Taming Narratives, 1500–1700*. Basingstoke: Palgrave Macmillan.

Wright, Louis B. 1964. *Middle-Class Culture in Elizabethan England* (1958). Ithaca: Cornell University Press.

Wynne-Davies, Marion. 2000. '"For *Worth*, Not Weakness, Makes in Use but One": Literary Dialogues in an English Renaissance Family'. In *'This Double Voice': Gendered Writing in Early Modern England*. Ed. Danielle Clarke and Elizabeth Clarke. London: Macmillan. 164–84.

Wynne-Davies, Marion. 2000. '"So Much Worth": Autobiographical Narratives in the Work of Lady Mary Wroth.' In *Betraying Ourselves: Forms of Self-representation in Early Modern English Texts*. Ed. Henk Dragstra, Sheila Ottway, and Helen Wilcox. New York: St. Martins. 76–93.

Wynne-Davies, Marion. 2007. *Women Writers and Familial Discourses in the English Renaissance: Relative Values*. Basingstoke: Palgrave Macmillan.

Wynne-Davies, Marion. 2015. 'Absent Fathers: Mary Wroth's *Love's Victory* and William Shakespeare's *King Lear*'. In *Shakespeare and Mary Wroth*. Ed. Marion Wynne-Davies and Paul Saltzman. New York and Abingdon: Routledge. 61–72.

Yates, Frances A. 1972. *The Rosicrucian Enlightenment*. London: Routledge and Kegan Paul.

Ziegler, Georgianna. 2007. 'A Second Phoenix: The Rebirth of Elizabeth I in Elizabeth Stuart'. In *Resurrecting Elizabeth I in Seventeenth-Century England*. Ed. Elizabeth H. Hageman and Katherine Conway, Madison and Teaneck: Fairleigh Dickinson University Press. 111–31.

Zurcher, Amelia A. 2007. *Seventeenth-Century English Romance: Allegory, Ethics, and Politics*. New York: Palgrave Macmillan.

Index

Note: Page numbers followed by '*f*' and '*n*' denote figures and notes, respectively.

absoluteness, 62
Adams, Thomas, 45–6, 156, 187*n*27
Admirable and Memorable Histories, 55
Aletheia, Countess of Arundel, 7
All's Well That Ends Well, 10, 90
Amends for Ladies, 46
Anne, Queen, 94, 150, 153, 154
anti-rationalism, 16
anti-women pamphlet controversy, Swetnam's, 152–5
Antony and Cleopatra (Shakespeare), 15, 26–32, 42, 98
Anything for a Quiet Life, 150, 152
An Apology for Women, 158
appearance, selfhood and, 51
The Araignment of Lewd, Idle, Froward, and unconstant women, 13, 37–9, 152
Arcadia, 89, 91, 125, 154
Arden of Faversham, 5, 97
Argenis, 125, 141, 146
Astrophel and Stella, 34, 89, 129
Asylum Veneris, Or A Sanctuary for Ladies, 152–3
As You Like It, 92
autonomy, 3
sexual, 91–2

The Bachelor's Banquet, 38
Bacon, Lady Ann, 7
bad woman, Vittoria's image as, 37–40
see also Vittoria *(The White Devil)*
Barclay, John, 125, 141, 146
Barkstead, William, 25
bashfulness, 9
the Bastard, in *King John*, 112–16, 118–19
Beard, Thomas, 55, 56, 59

Becon, Thomas, 187*n*28
Belsey, Catherine, 2, 51, 69–70, 75
blackness, 79, 102–3, 108–9
Blount, Charles, 33
Blount, Henry, 102
Boklund, Gunnar, 48, 58, 67
Bradbrook, M. C., 26–7, 62, 174*n*40
Brown, John Russell, 32, 43
Buddhism, 155

cabinets, Pamphilia's (in *Urania*), 119–26, 120*f*
Callaghan, Dympna, 79
Calvert, Sir George, 151
Camden, William, 137
The Carde of Fancie, 55, 58
Carlton, Dudley, 141
Carr, Robert, 4, 36
Cary, Elizabeth, 13, 50, 51, 93, 96–7, 100, 147, 164–5, 179*n*40, 185*n*6
The Tragedie of Mariam, see The Tragedie of Mariam
Cary, Lady Katherine, 74
Cary, Sir Henry, 74–5
Chamberlain, John, 141, 149–50, 151–2, 173*n*35, 177*n*15
The Changeling, 26
Characters, 4, 41, 61, 64
chastity, 4–5, 6, 92
children, illegitimate
in *Urania* Part II, 112–19
class *vs.* race, 79–80
Cleaver, Robert, 157
Clifford, Lady Anne, 7, 15–16, 36, 145, 153, 154
Coeffeteau, M. N., 125
Coke, Edward, 49, 54, 148, 150
The Comedy of Errors, 5
constancy, concept of, 142–4

Cornwallis, Lady, 145
The Countess of Montgomery's Urania
  (Mary Wroth), 3, 13, 48, 50, 87,
  152, 163, 165
  Mary Wroth *vs.* Murasaki Shikibu,
    126–31
  Pamphilia's cabinets, 119–26, 120f
  public and private, interconnection
    between, 117
  representations of two queens in
    Urania, 133–5
    concept of constancy, 140–2
    Pamphilia and, 135–40
  Urania Part I, 12–13, 21, 93–101
    publishing, 146–7
  Urania Part II, 12–13
    gender and representations of
      mixed-race relationships in,
      101–12
    illegitimate children in, 112–19
The Countess of Pembroke's Arcadia,
  129, 146
Court scandals
  in early Jacobean England, 33–7,
    178n19
  in late Jacobean years, publishing
    and, 147–50
Crawford, Julie, 166, 167
Cymbeline, 166

Danby, John F., 29
Daniel, Samuel, 28, 143, 147
Davies, Sir John, 147
democracy, in Japan, 1
Denny, Edward, 146
Description of England, 45
desire, concept of, 92
de Vere, Susan, 14
Devereux, Robert, 36
discretion, in women, 8–11
divorce, 79
Dod, John, 157
Donne, John, 7, 55
Drue, Thomas, 159
The Duchess of Malfi (Webster), 13, 15,
  26, 86, 98
  contemporary attitudes towards,
    55–8
  Duchess and men surrounding her,
    60–9

female selfhood and male violence,
  52–71
  vs. Kabuki *(Musume Dojoji)*, 71–3
  popular images of widows and
    Webster's portrayal of Duchess,
    58–60
  self-assertion, 62
  social significance of Duchess's
    assertion of self-actualisation,
    69–71
The Duchess of Suffolk, 159
The Duke of Milan, 84
duplicity, female, 97
Dusinberre, Juliet, 4
The Dutch Courtesan, 22

early Jacobean drama
  female selfhood and marriage
    ideologies, 49–86
  Elizabeth Cary's *The Tragedy of
    Mariam*, 73–86
  female desire in Kabuki *(Musume
    Dojoji)*, 71–3
  and male violence *(The Duchess
    of Malfi)*, 52–71
early Jacobean England, women in,
  15–48
  Court scandals, 33–7
  Florio's Montaigne, 19–26
  Marston's plays, 19–26
  Montaigne's idea of woman's
    nature, 16–19
  overview, 15–16
  Shakespeare's *Antony and Cleopatra*,
    26–32
  Vittoria as popular image of bad
    woman, 37–40
  Webster's *The White Devil*,
    'masculine vertue' as female
    virtue in, 32–48
education, of women, 145
  associated with moral failings, 7–8
  increase of, 7–8
Edwards, Philip, 84
egotism, male, Montaigne and, 16–18
Eliot, T. S., 26
Elizabeth, Countess of Rutland, 15
Elizabeth, Queen, of Bohemia, 132–3,
  166
  constancy and persistence, 142–4

Mary Wroth's representations in
   Urania, 132–40, 134*f*
Elizabeth I, Queen, 6, 13, 32, 55
   in Jacobean England
   constancy, concept of, 142–4
   Mary Wroth's representations in
      Urania, 132–40, 134*f*
   'The Queen's Two Bodies,' 140–2
   marriage with Frederick, 135
The English Civil War, 1
English Renaissance drama, 2, 51, 52,
   83, 85, 101, 107
the Enlightenment, 3
Epicoene, 7
*An Epitome of Fair Argenis and
   Polyarches*, 125
Essays, 12, 15, 28–9, 181*n*5
   Florio's translation, 19–26, 34, 74,
   76, 79–80, 94, 147, 170*n*1
Ewbank, Inga-Stina, 170*n*16, 177*n*14,
   179*n*33

Faire Designe, in *Urania* Part II,
   116–19
The Family of Love, 159
*The Famovs and Memorable Works of
   Josephus*, 83, 84
The Fawne, 24–5
female agency, representations
   (*Love's Victory*), 87–93
female desire
   in Kabuki (*Musume Dojoji*), 71–3
   see also self-assertion; selfhood
female duplicity, 97
female inferiority, concept of, 155
female selfhood, *see* selfhood
Field, Nathan, 46
Findlay, Alison, 115
*The First Blast of the Trumpet against
   the Monstrous Regiment of
   Women*, 139, 140
fitnesse, women, 11–12, 23, 24,
   29, 83
Florio, John, 12, 15, 34
   translation of Montaigne's *Essays*,
   19–26, 34, 74, 76, 79–80, 94,
   147, 170*n*1
Ford, John, 34
The Forest of Fancy, 55, 58
Foucault, Michel, 76

Frederick, Palatine, 132, 133, 135, 142
The French Revolution, 1

gender and mixed-race relationships
   (*Urania* Part II), 101–12
gender equality, concept of, 1, 159
globalisation, influence on Japan, 1–2
*A Godlie Forme of Householde
   Government*, 157
'Golden Age of Courtly Culture,' in
   Japan, 5
goodness, of women, 4–6
Gouge, William, 157
Goulart, Simon, 55
Greenblatt, Stephen, 3
Greene, Robert, 55
Grey, Lady Catherine, 55
Grey, Lady Elizabeth, 15
Grey, Lady Jane, 6, 32
Grey, Lady Mary, 54
Griffith, Eva, 153, 154, 160, 187*n*25
Grimeston, Edward, 55
grotesque elements, male violence,
   98–100, 176*n*8
grotesqueness, 98–100, 176*n*8
   see also male violence

Hackett, Helen, 117
Haec Vir: Or The Womanish-Man, 71,
   152, 154, 155
Hall, Kim, 108, 109
Hamlet, 10, 170*n*15
Hamlin, William M., 22
Hannay, Margaret P., 115
Hanson, Elizabeth, 94
Harington, Lucy, 133, 135
Harrison, William, 45
Hatton, Frances, 49
Hatton, Lady Elizabeth, 7, 54, 150
Heale, William, 157–8
Henry, Prince, 133
Henry VI, Part I, 112
An Heptameron of Ciuill Discourses, 55,
   57–8
Herbert, Mary Sidney, 145
Herbert, Philip, 36
Herbert, William, 50, 92, 116, 117,
   133, 166
Hic Mulier: Or, the Man-Woman,
   published, 152, 154, 155

The History of the Life, Reign, and Death of Edward II, 50
Hoby, Lady Margaret, 145
Honour's Academy, 42
Hosokawa, Lady Tama Gracia, 168
household, concept of, 11
Howard, Frances, 36–7, 80
Howard, Robert, 49
Howard, Thomas, 148
human emotions, changing, 76
human integrity, Montaigne's concept of, 18

illegitimate children, in *Urania* Part II, 112–19
The Imperial Theme, 29
innocence, 81–2
The Insatiate Countess, 25, 90
intellectual independence, 74
intelligence, in women, 6–8
Itinerary, 34

Jacobean England
  Elizabeth I in, 132–44
    constancy, concept of, 142–4
    Mary Wroth's representations in *Urania*, 132–5, 134f
    Pamphilia and two Queen Elizabeths (in *Urania*), 135–40
    'The Queen's Two Bodies,' 140–2
  Overbury's *A Wife* in, 4–12
    see also *A Wife*
  Vittoria's 'masculine vertue' and, 45–8
    see also Vittoria *(The White Devil)*
  see also early Jacobean England; late Jacobean England
James, King, 7, 12, 13, 32–3, 36, 45, 54, 80–1, 132, 133–5, 143, 150, 151, 166
  see also Elizabeth I, Queen
Japan
  after World War II, 1–2
  democracy in, 1
  'Golden Age of Courtly Culture,' 5
  influence of globalisation, 1–2
Japanese women
  development after World War II, 1–2
  see also women
jealousy, 43, 51, 89, 103, 105–7

John, Prester, 109
Jones, Ann Rosalind, 89, 161
Jonson, Ben, 7, 12, 34, 142, 147, 170*n*12, 185*n*7
  Cythia's Revels, 180*n*1
Josephus, Flavius, 83

Kabuki, 168, 177*n*10
  Musume Dojoji, 71–3, 85–6
    vs. *The Duchess of Malfi*, 71–3
    (see also *The Duchess of Malfi* (Webster))
  Tokaido Yotsuya Kaidan (The Ghost Story of Yotsuya), 98–100
Katherine of Aragon, 6
Keeper, Lord, 55
King John, 112–16
  the Bastard in, 112–16
King Lear, 10, 112, 114
knowledge, in women, 6–8
Knox, John, 139, 140

Lacan, Jacques, 76
Lake, Sir Thomas, 148, 149, 151
Lake–Roos case, 148–50, 186*n*11
Lamb, Mary Ellen, 117
Lanyer, Emilia, 132
late Jacobean England
  ideologies of marriage in (Wroth), 87–131
  gender and mixed-race relationships in *Urania* Part II, 101–12
  illegitimate children in *Urania* Part II, 112–19
  Love's Victory (c.1619), 87–93, 88f
  Murasaki Shikibu and, 126–31
  Pamphilia's cabinets in *Urania*, 119–26, 120f
  Urania Part I and Part II, 93–101
  women and publishing their works in, 145–63
  Court scandals, 147–50
  Mary Wroth (*Urania* I), 146–7
  overview, 145
  Puritan women's religious activities, 155–63
  social climate against women's self-assertion, 150–2

Swetnam's anti-women pamphlet controversy, 152–5
Laud, William, 33
Leech, Clifford, 60
Le Grys, Sir Robert, 141
Lodge, Thomas, 83, 84
Long, Kingesmill, 141
Love's Victory, 3, 13, 50, 87–93, 88f, 94, 130, 165, 166–7, 180n2
 female agency representations, 87–93
 love vs. marriage, 18
 see also marriage
Lucas, F. L., 61, 152, 178n25
Lucas, R. Valerie, 157
Lucy, Countess of Bedford, 7, 15, 153, 166
lusty Widowe, concept of, 58–9

The Maid's Tragedy, 47
The Malcontent, 19–20, 21, 22, 26
male authority, 8
 modesty in women and, 11
 Puritan perspective, 155–63
male egotism, Montaigne and, 16–18
male superiority, concept of, 155
male violence, 85
 female selfhood and
  The Duchess of Malfi, 52–71
  in marriage (*Urania* Part I and Part II), 93–101
  grotesque elements, 17n8, 98–100
Man, Judith, 125, 126
marriage
 detached attitudes toward, 18
 in early modern England, 169n5
 ideologies, in early Jacobean drama, 49–86
  The Duchess of Malfi, 52–71
  Elizabeth Cary's *The Tragedy of Mariam*, 73–86
  female desire in Kabuki *(Musume Dojoji)*, 71–3
 ideologies, in late Jacobean England (Wroth), 87–131
  gender and representations of mixed-race relationships in *Urania* Part II, 101–12

illegitimate children in *Urania* Part II, 112–19
Love's Victory (c.1619), 87–93, 88f
Murasaki Shikibu and, 126–31
Pamphilia's cabinets in *Urania*, 119–26, 120f
Urania Part I and Part II, 93–101
Puritan perspective, 155–63
vs. love, 18
Marston, John, 4, 15, 16, 27, 90, 170n13
 Florio's translation of *Essays* and, 19–26
 Montaigne's influence on palys of, 19
 women in early Jacobean England, 19–26
Mary, Countess of Pembroke, 7, 35
'masculine vertue,' as female virtue in *The White Devil*, 32–48
 arraignment scene in Act III Scene ii, 40–3
 Court scandals in early Jacobean England, 33–7
 of Vittoria, 43–4
 of Vittoria, and Jacobean England, 45–8
 Vittoria as popular image of bad woman, 37–40
masculinity, of women, 41, 52, 80–1, 152
The Mask of Blackness, 34, 94
Massinger, Philip, 84
Middleton, Thomas, 4, 5, 97, 159
A Midsummer Night's Dream, 87–8, 102
Miller, Naomi J., 106
The Mirrour of Princely Deeds and Knighthood, 102
mixed-race relationships, and gender representations in *Urania* Part II, 101–12
modesty, in women, 9–11, 126
Montaigne, Michael, 12, 15, 66, 171n4, 181n5
 Florio's translation of *Essays*, 19–26, 34, 74, 76, 79–80, 94, 147, 170n1
 on human integrity, 18
 influence on Marston's plays, 19

Montaigne, Michael – *continued*
  on male egotism, 16–18
  on marriage *vs.* love, 18
  scepticism, 16, 18, 22–3
  on sexuality, 92
  on uncontrollable female
    sexuality, 26
  on woman's nature (early Jacobean
    drama), 16–19
Montrose, Louis Adrian, 89
moral failings, women's learning
  associated with, 7–8
More, Anne, 55
Mortalities Memorandum, 161
Moryson, Fynes, 34
motherhood, 28
Mountjoy, Lord, 33
A Movzell for Melastomvs, 160
Much Ado About Nothing, 9, 23,
  108, 112
Munda, Constantia, 153
Musume Dojoji, 52, 71–3
  vs. The Duchess of Malfi, 71–3
  see also *The Duchess of Malfi*
    (Webster)

Nanboku, Tsuruya, 99
naturalism, 18, 22, 25
  of women contradicts, 24
naturalness, of sexuality, 25
Nevill, Lady Marie, 15

obedience, 92
Ornstein, Robert, 29, 66
Othello, 10, 101–2, 106
Overbury, Sir Thomas
  Characters, 4, 41, 61, 64
  murder of, 148, 174*n*37
  A Wife, 3, 4–12, 19, 32, 37, 49,
    53, 83
  see also *A Wife*

Painter, William, 55
The Palace of Pleasure, 25–6, 55, 56
Pamphilia's cabinets, in *Urania*,
  119–26, 120*f*
Parr, Catherine, 6
Pearson, Jacqueline, 40
Pericles, 10

Perron, Cardinal, 165
persistence, concept of, 142
physicality, 24, 25
Polyhymnia, 173*n*26
publishing, in late Jacobean years,
  women and, 145–63
  Court scandals, 147–50
  Mary Wroth (*Urania* I), 146–7
  overview, 145
  Puritan women's religious activities,
    155–63
  social climate against women's
    self-assertion, 150–2
  Swetnam's anti-women pamphlet
    controversy, 152–5
The Puritan, 159
Puritan women's religious activities,
  in late Jacobean England,
  155–63

'The Queen's Two Bodies,' 139,
  140–2

race
  and class, difference in, 79–80
  mixed-race relationships and
    gender representations in
    Urania Part II, 101–12
Raleigh, Sir Walter, 55
Raymond, Joad, 153
*A Relation of a Journey begun: An: Dom:
  1610*, 147
religious activities, of Puritan women,
  in late Jacobean England,
  155–63
Renaissance England, goodness of
  women defined in, 5
Renaissance idealism, 60
Renaissance Self-Fashioning, 3
The Revenger's Tragedy, 22
Rich, Barnaby, 9
Rich, Lady Penelope, 7, 15, 33–4, 49,
  71, 129, 173*n*28
Rickman, Johanah, 176*n*1
The Roaring Girl, 23, 46–7
Roberts, Josephine A., 108, 116, 135,
  140
Romeo and Juliet, 92
Roper, Margaret, 32

Sackville, Richard, 36
Salingar, L. G., 22
Salzman, Paul, 117, 142, 143–4
Sandy, George, 147
Satires, 19
Sawday, Jonathan, 3
scepticism, Montaigne on, 16, 18, 22–3
The Schole House of Women, 38
The Second Part of The Countess Montgomery's Urania, 163
see also *The Countess of Montgomery's Urania* (Mary Wroth)
self, 3, 62, 169n2
  Puritanism and, 159
self-actualisation, 2, 147, 164, 167
  social significance of Duchess's assertion of *(The Duchess of Malfi)*, 69–71
self-assertion, 2, 12, 29, 36, 38, 47, 93, 167
  The Duchess of Malfi, 62–5, 69–71
  Kabuki *(Musume Dojoji)*, 71–3
  male violence and, 93–101
  see also male violence
  reactions against, 80
  social climate against, publishing and, 150–2
  Swetnam's anti-women pamphlet controversy and, 152–5
  see also *The Countess of Montgomery's Urania*
self-awareness, 43, 81
self-composure, 59
self-confidence, 161
self-consciousness, 77
self-expression, 119, 144, 164, 167
self-fashioning, 3
selfhood, 1, 14, 29, 169n2
  appearance, 51
  construction of, 144
  defined, 3
  early Jacobean drama, 49–86
    Elizabeth Cary's *The Tragedy of Mariam*, 50, 73–86
    female desire in Kabuki *(Musume Dojoji)*, 71–3
    Lady Mary Wroth and, 50
    and male violence *(The Duchess of Malfi)*, 52–71

Lady Mary on, 2–3, 87
  see also *The Countess of Montgomery's Urania*
  in marriage, male violence and *(Urania* Part I and Part II), 93–101
  Puritan perspective, 155–63
  The Tragedie of Mariam, 73–86
self-identity, 91, 126
self-realisation, 66
self-satisfaction, 69
sexual autonomy, 91–2
sexuality
  Montaigne's views, 92
  naturalness of, 25
  society's attitude towards, Montaigne's criticism on, 17
  The Tragedy of Mariam, 93
  uncontrollable female, concept of, 25
sexual transgression, 49, 50, 97
sexual virtue, 4
Seymour, William, 35, 55, 173n33
Sforza, Lodovico, 84
Shakespeare, William, 2, 3, 4, 9, 10, 15, 16, 23, 39, 47, 62–3, 87, 90, 92, 98, 103, 109, 112, 168, 170n8
  All's Well That Ends Well, 10, 90
  Antony and Cleopatra, 15, 26–32, 42, 98
  As You Like It, 92
  King John, 112–16
  King Lear, 10, 112, 114
  Hamlet, 10, 170n15
  A Midsummer Night's Dream, 87–8, 102
  Much Ado About Nothing, 9, 23, 108, 112
  Othello, 10, 101–2, 106
  The Taming of the Shrew, 11, 47–8
  Titus and Andronicus, 10, 98, 99, 103
  Troilus and Cressida, 90
  Twelfth Night, 91, 182n19
  The Winter's Tale, 10
shamefastness, 9
Shepherd, Simon, 159
Shikibu, Lady Murasaki, 5, 8, 14, 135
  vs. Mary Wroth, 126–31

Shintoism, 155
Sidney, Lady Barbara
  portrait of, 127f
Sidney, Philip, 87, 89, 91, 101, 125, 129, 143, 146, 154, 166
Sidney, Robert, 101, 133, 166
Sidney, William, 133
silence, female, 92, 126, 157–8
social significance, of Duchess's assertion of self-actualisation, 69–71
Sokol, B. J., 114
Sokol, Mary, 114
Sophonisba, 25
Sowernam, Ester, 153, 154, 160
Speght, James, 160
Speght, Rachel, 132, 153, 155–6, 160–2, 163, 188n33
Spenser, Edmund, 89, 143
'Stigma of Print,' 145, 184n1
  see also publishing, in late Jacobean years, women and
stoicism, 18
Stone, Lawrence, 58
Stuart, Charles Louis, 133, 134f, 135
Stuart, Lady Arabella, 35, 58, 71
subjectivity, concepts of, 2
The Subject of Tragedy, 2, 51
Swetnam, Joseph, 37–9, 172n22, 175n53
  anti-women pamphlet controversy, 152–5
Swetnam the Woman-Hater Araigned by Women, 140–1, 154

The Tale of Genji, 5–6, 8, 10–11, 14, 126, 128–31, 135
The Tamer Tam'd, 47
The Taming of the Shrew, 11, 47–8
Tanfield, Sir Lawrence, 74
The Theatre of Gods Iudgement, 55, 56
Titus and Andronicus, 10, 98, 99, 103
Tokaido Yotsuya Kaidan (The Ghost Story of Yotsuya), 98–100
Tourneur, Cyril, 22
The Tragedie of Antonie, 28
Tragedie of Cleopatra, 28

The Tragedie of Mariam (Cary), 13, 50, 73–86, 93, 96, 164–5, 179n40
  publishing, 147
The Triumph of Death, 130
Troilus and Cressida, 90
Tuvil, Daniel, 152–3
Twelfth Night, 91, 182n19

uncontrollable female sexuality, concept of, 25
'the unified self,' 3
  see also self; selfhood
Urania Part I, 12–13, 21, 183n23
  female selfhood in marriage and male violence, 93–101
  Pamphilia and two Queen Elizabeths in, 135–40
  publishing, 146–7
  see also *The Countess of Montgomery's Urania*; Wroth, Lady Mary
Urania Part II, 12–13
  Faire Designe in, 116–19
  female selfhood in marriage and male violence, 93–101
  gender and representations of mixed-race relationships in, 101–12
  illegitimate children in, 112–19
  publishing, 147
  see also *The Countess of Montgomery's Urania*; Wroth, Lady Mary

Vaughan, Virginia Mason, 115
Villiers, John, 49
Villiers, Sir John, 150
violence, male, 8
  female selfhood and
  The Duchess of Malfi, 52–71
  in marriage (*Urania* Part I and Part II), 93–101
  grotesque elements, 17n8, 98–100
Vittoria *(The White Devil)*
  masculine vertue of, 43–4
  masculine vertue of, and Jacobean England, 45–8
  as popular image of bad woman, 37–40
  see also *The White Devil* (Webster)
Volpone, 7

Waller, Gary, 87
Webster, John, 3, 4, 13, 15, 16, 18, 26, 29, 52, 85, 94, 97, 98, 150, 174n45
  The Duchess of Malfi, 13, 15, 26
    contemporary attitudes towards, 55–8
    Duchess and men surrounding her, 60–9
    female selfhood and male violence, 52–71
    popular images of widows and Webster's portrayal of Duchess, 58–60
    self-assertion, 62
    social significance of Duchess's assertion of self-actualisation, 69–71
    vs. Kabuki *(Musume Dojoji)*, 71–3
  'masculine vertue' as female virtue in *The White Devil*, 32–48
    arraignment scene in Act III Scene ii, 40–3
    Court scandals in early Jacobean England, 33–7
    Vittoria as popular image of bad woman, 37–40
    Vittoria's 'masculine vertue,' 43–4
    Vittoria's 'masculine vertue' and Jacobean England, 45–8
    see also The White Devil (Webster)
weeping, 94
Weidemann, Heather, 100–1
Weldon, Anthony, 149
Wentworth, Lady Anne, 125
Wentworth, William, 125
Whetstone, George, 55, 57
The White Devil (Webster), 9, 15, 18, 52, 55, 65, 68
  arraignment scene in Act III Scene ii, 40–3
  Court scandals in early Jacobean England, 33–7
  'masculine vertue' as female virtue in, 32–48
  Vittoria as popular image of bad woman, 37–40
  Vittoria's 'masculine vertue,' 43–4
  Vittoria's 'masculine vertue' and Jacobean England, 45–8
The Widow of Watling Street, 159
widows, popular images of
  and Webster's portrayal of Duchess (early Jacobean drama), 58–60
The Widow's Tears, 53, 59
A Wife (Overbury's), 3, 19, 32, 37, 49, 53, 83
  Discretion, 8–11
  Fitnesse, 11–12, 23, 24, 29, 83
  Goodnesse, 4–6
  in Jacobean England, 4–12
  Knowledge, 6–8
  overview, 4
wifehood, 50, 165
  ideologies of, 83
  traditional concept, 82–3
  see also A Wife
William, Leigh, 135
The Winter's Tale, 10
Wiseman, Susan, 117
womanhood, 90, 164
  concepts, in early modern England, 1–14
  ideal image of, 24
  Mary Wroth *vs*. Murasaki Shikibu, 126–31
  self-assertion, *see* self-assertion
  society's image, 3
The Tragedie of Mariam, 73–86
The Woman's Prize, 47
women
  chastity in, 4–5, 6, 92
  discretion in, 8–11
  duplicity, 97
  fitnesse, 11–12, 23, 24, 29, 83
  goodness of, 4–6
  intelligence in, 6–8
  knowledge in, 6–8
  'masculine vertue' as female virtue in *The White Devil*, 32–48
    arraignment scene in Act III Scene ii, 40–3
    Court scandals in early Jacobean England, 33–7
    of Vittoria, 43–4
    of Vittoria, and Jacobean England, 45–8

women – *continued*
   Vittoria as popular image of bad woman, 37–40
   modesty in, 9–11, 126
   Montaigne on nature of, early Jacobean drama and, 16–19
   and publishing their works in late Jacobean Years, 145–63
      Court scandals, 147–50
      Mary Wroth (*Urania* I), 146–7
      overview, 145
      Puritan women's religious activities, 155–63
      social climate against women's self-assertion, 150–2
      Swetnam's anti-women pamphlet controversy, 152–5
   Puritan, religious activities in late Jacobean England, 155–63
   self-assertion, *see* self-assertion
   selfhood, *see* selfhood
   sexual autonomy, 91–2
Women Beware Women, 26, 97
women's masculinity, 41, 52, 80–1, 152
World War II, 1
   Japan after, 1–2
Wright, Louis B., 155
Wright, Robert, 49

Wroth, Lady Mary, 2–3, 7, 12, 13, 29, 34, 48, 50, 51, 153, 163, 165, 169n1, 171n5, 180n2
   on female selfhood, 2–3
   and ideologies of marriage in late Jacobean England, 87–131
   gender and representations of mixed-race relationships in *Urania* Part II, 101–12
   illegitimate children in *Urania* Part II, 112–19
   Love's Victory (c.1619), 87–93, 88f
   Murasaki Shikibu and, 126–31
   Pamphilia's cabinets in *Urania*, 119–26, 120f
   Urania Part I and Part II, 93–101
   vs. Murasaki Shikibu, 126–31
   portrait of, 127f
   and publishing *Urania* I, 146–7
   representations of two queens in *Urania*, 133–40
      concept of constancy, 140–2
      Pamphilia and, 135–40
   see also The Countess of Montgomery's Urania
Wynne-Davies, Marion, 117, 118, 129, 136, 169n1, 176n5, 181n7, 182n12, 183n25, 185n4, 188n31

CPSIA information can be obtained
at www.ICGtesting.com
Printed in the USA
LVOW04*0727090216
474323LV00008B/424/P